ARUNACHAL PRADESH AND THE TRIBES
SELECT BIBLIOGRAPHY

ARUNACHAL PRADESH AND THE TRIBES

SELECT BIBLIOGRAPHY

By

Sipra Sen

GYAN

ARUNACHAL PRADESH AND THE TRIBES

SELECT BIBLIOGRAPHY

ISBN : 9788121202022

Published in 2015 in India by
Gyan Publishing House
5, Ansari Road, Daryaganj,
New Delhi - 110002
Phones : 011-47034999, 9811692060
e-mail : books@gyanbooks.com
website : gyanbooks.com

1. Monpa girls of Tawang District

2. Muji woman of West Kameng District

DEDICATED

WITH LOVE AND TEARS

TO

THE MEMORY OF MY FATHER

LATE SHRI SATYA RANJAN SEN

SPECIAL SUPDT. OF POLICE, SHILLONG

WHO

LEFT FOR HEAVENLY ABODE WHILE IN SERVICE

WHOSE

HONESTY, SENSE OF JUSTICE, HUMANITY AND IDEALISM INSPIRED ME

CONTENTS

LIST OF ILLUSTRRTIONS

3. Khowa oldman of Kameng District

4. An Aka couple of Kameng District

5. An Apatani girl of Lower Subansiri District

6. Nishi girls of Lower Subansiri District

7. Hill Miri couple of Upper Subansiri District

8. A Tagin of Upper Subansiri District

9. A Gallong Couple of West Siang District

10. Membas of West Siang District

No.1 MAP OF INDIA (Position of Arunachal Pradesh)

CHAPTER I

INTRODUCTION

There is continuous increase of research publications in different periodicals, books, proceedings, etc. about Arunachal Pradesh. The researchers and the general public have been feeling much want of comprehensive bibliographies on Arunachal Pradesh. This bibliographical book is second in the series[1] to facilitate micro and macro level researches on the tribes of Arunachal Pradesh. This will fill up an important gap to select future new research projects which are not covered so far.

Arunachal Pradesh, the Union Territory, presents a most fertile field for the study of Anthropology and Sociology. This is the land of the rising sun, situated in the extreme corner of North East boundary of India and is bounded by the Himalayas on the North and by the Patkoi Hill ranges on the South. This is lying between 26°28'N to 29°30'N latitudes and 91°31'E to 97°30'E longitudes. The average elevation ranges between 4,900 metres to 7,000 metres above sea level. It is bordered by Bhutan on the West, Tibet and China on the North, Burma on the East and Assam on the South.

The total population is 628,050 (1981 Census, of which 335,941 males and 292,109 females (Table-I). The density of

1 *Tribes of Meghalaya* (1985), Delhi, Mittal Publication, was first in this series

population is 7 per sq. km. It is a thinly populated area due to some difficulties. It is, almost, a mountainous region except for thin strips of flat land (most of which are adjoined to Assam); bad climate of heavy average rainfall; frequent landslides; fluctuating temperature; hum dity; dense forests; lack of proper road communication and bridges on the rivers; inner line permit; wild animals like leopards, elephants, pythons, cobras; tribal people's hostility, etc. kept this region almost unexplored until the beginning of the present century. The physical environment is so much hostile that it obstructed the unification of some tribes of this region. For that, some tribals know only their immediate neighbours as their mobility is very much restricted due to unfavourable rigorous climate. There is hardly any east west communication among them. During the time of British rule, the Christian Missionaries could not succeed here much and it seems, they worked here half-heartedly due to crude enmity of some sensitive tribals of this region.

Arunachal Pradesh is intersected by rivers and streams. Dihang (Siang) river divided this territory completely into two halves, the east and the west, by flowing from north to south (Map No. 4). The other rivers are Bharuli, Subansiri, Siyom, Shimong, Dibong, Dri, Lohit, Sessei, Yamne, Dikrang, Noa Dihing, Delei, Du, Namkiu, etc. All these drain into the mighty Brahmaputra river in the south.

The monsoon starts here from April to May and continues upto August and some times the middle of September. Heavy rain is found in June-July. The average rainfall is 260 cm. Snowfall is almost a regular matter in the northern part of Arunachal Pradesh specially during the winter season.

There is no railway line within the territory except for a stretch of one and half miles near Banderdewa in the Subansiri District. From Dibrugarh (Assam) there is air route upto Tezu (*Vayudoot* service) in the Lohit District of Arunachal Pradesh. Construction of roads and bridges over the rivers is very much costly. Thus, there is less surface communication. In 1873, a traffic regulation was made by the British (*Bengal East Regulation - I*) for hill areas and the plains by introducing an *Inner Line* permit to protect the interests of both the tribals of

Arunachol Pradesh and the plain-people of the other parts of of India. Beyond this line no visitor can go inside the territory without a license from the Government.

Almost all varieties of flora is available here such as rhododendron, bamboo, climbers, cane, cactus, etc. Rice, maize, millets, wheats, mustard are growing in large quantity Pine-apples, apples, etc. are grows much and well marketed in the plains. Some species of flora and fauna of this region are used largely in tribal medicines. Arunachal Pradesh is the habitat for numerous medicinal plants and herbs, these are Musk Dana, Dipo Talom, Lemon Grass, Java Citronella, Pippermint Palmarosa, Saffron, Acours Calamus, etc. The Regional Research Laboratory has undertaken experimental work in Senua area of Tirap District. It has raised with Solanum Khasyanum berries, Citronella and Lemongrass primarily for perfumed oil. One of Arunachal's economic crop "*Mishmi Teeta*" is considered to be vital antidebillity tonic. The fauna are mithun (*Bos frontalis*) which is a semi-domesticated animal and is available all over the territory. Tiger, black panther, wild elephant, barking deer, different varities of snakes (python, king cobra, cobra), rhinoceros, snow leopard, wild bear, monkey and langur, wild buffalo, wild goat, etc. are very common in Arunachal Pradesh. The forest area now covers 61,000 sq. km. of this territory which was 51,438 sq. km. in 1972-75 (Table-IV). Thus, the forest area has gone up in Arunachal Pradesh.

In 1914, Arunachal Pradesh was known as *North East Frontier Tract*. There was a discussion between China and the Government. of Tibet and Britain about mutual relations. In Simla, the conference was held in 1913-14. Tibet and Great Britain decided a correct frontier between these two countries. A line was marked for 1" : 8 miles on a map which was signed by Sir Henry McMahon on behalf of Great Britain, which is now popularly known as the *McMahon Line*.

Table—I

POPULATION

State/Union Territory	Population (1981)*	Percentage of total population	Male	Female	Percentage of literates to total population
Assam	19,902,826**	—	10,472,712	9,430,114	—
Manipur	1,433,691	0·21	727,108	706,583	41·99
Maghalaya	1,327,874	0·19	678,883	648,991	33·22
Nagaland	773,281	0·11	414,231	359,050	41·99
Tripura	2,060,189	0·30	1,057,714	1,002,475	41·58
Arunachal Pradesh	628,050	0·09	335,941	292,109	20·09
Mizoram	487,774	0·07	251,988	235,786	59·50

* Census of India 1981,

** Projected figures

Table—II
LITERACY

India/State/Union Territory	Population 1981	Percentage to total population	Total Literate	Percentage of literates to total population
1	2	3	4	5
India	683,810,051	100·00	237,991,932	34·80
1. Uttar Pradesh	110,858,019	16·21	30,358,013	27·38
2. Bihar	69,823,154	10·21	18,163,410	26·01
3. Maharashtra	62,693,898	9·17	29,695,721	47·37
4. West Bengal	54,485,560	7·97	22,271,867	40·88
5. Andhra Pradesh	53,403,619	7·81	15,989,266	29·94
6. Madhya Pradesh	52,131,717	7·62	14,502,063	27·82
7. Tami Nadu	48,297,456	7·06	22,111,593	45·78
8. Karnataka	37,043,451	5·42	14,228,947	38·41
9. Rajasthan	34,102,912	4·99	8,201,615	24·05
10. Gujarat	33,960,905	4·97	14,858,075	43·75
11. Orissa	26,272,054	3·84	8,964,625	34·12
12. Kerala	25,403,217	3·71	17,571,819	69·17
13. Assam*	19,902,826	2·91	—	—
14. Punjab	16,669,755	2·44	6,791,547	40·74

*Projected figure.

Table II (*contd.*)

1	2	3	4	5
15. Haryana	12,850,902	1·88	4,605 649	35·84
16. Delhi	6,196,414	0·91	3,733.611	61·06
17. Jammu & Kashmir*	5,981.600	0·87	—	—
18. Himachal Pradesh	4,237,569	0·62	1,777,201	41·94
19. Tripura	2,060,189	0·30	856.688	41·58
20. Manipur	1,433,691	0·21	601,943	41·99
21. Meghalaya	1,327,874	0·19	441,077	33·22
22. Goa, Daman & Diu	1,082,117	0·16	604,489	55·86
23. Nagaland	773,281	0·11	324,700	41·99
24. Arunachal Pradesh	628,050	0·09	126,185	20·09
25. Pondichery	604,136	0·09	327,600	54·23
26. Mizoram	487,774	0·07	290.241	59·50
27. Chandigarh	450,061	0·07	291,091	64·68
28. Sikkim	315.682	0·05	106.780	33·83
29. Andaman & Nicobar Islands	188,254	0·03	96.520	51·27
30. Dadra & Nagar Haveli	103,677	0·01	27,578	26·60
31. Lakshadweep	40.237	0·01	22.018	54·72

* Projected figures

Table—III
MAIN TRIBES

District	H. Qs.	Population (1981)*	Main Tribes	Percentage of literates to total population
Tawang	Tawang	—	Monpas	—
West Kameng	Bomdila	62,946	Monpas, Sherdukpen	21·45%
East Kameng	Seppa	42,722	Sulungs, Bangnis, Nishang	6·94%
Upper Subansiri	Daporijo	36,40[illegible]	Adi, Hill Miri	12·43%
Lower Subansiri	Ziro	113,300	Apatani, Nishi, Nishang, etc.	18·93%
West Siang	Along	74,151	Adi (Gallogs, Minyong	22·25%
East Siang	Pasighat	70,274	Adi	25·15%
Lohit	Tezu	69,400	Mishmi, Khamptis.	27·35%
Dibang Valley	Anini	27,716	Mishmi	25·00%
Tirap	Khonsa	128,135	Tangsa, Wancho, Nocte, Singpho	18·17%
	TOTAL	628,050	TOTAL	20·09%

* Census of India, 1981

Table—IV*

FOREST AREAS

State/Union Territory	Forest Area in Sq. Km. 1972-75	1980-82	Change of forest area in Sq. Km. (+) Increased (—) Decreased
Assam	21,055	19,796	(—) 1,259
Manipur	15,090	13,572	(—) 1,518
Meghalaya	14,390	12,458	(—) 1,932
Nagaland	8,154	8,095	(—) 59
Tripura	6,330	5,138	(—) 1,192
Arunachal Pradesh	51,438	58,104	(+) 666
Mizoram	13,860	11,971	(—) 1,889

*Himalaya : Man and Nature, VIII (11), April, 1985.

In 1919, the North East Frontier Tract was divided into three divisions on the recommendation of Sir Beaston Beli,. Chief Commissioner of Assam. These are : *Balipara Frontier Tract*, *Sadiya Frontier Tract* and *Lakhimpur Frontier Tract*. In 1943, a post of *Adviser* was created to administer these divisions. From 1948, it was placed under direct administration of the Union Govt. and was redivided into *Sadiya Frontier Tract*, *Lakhimpur Frontier Tract*, *Tirap Frontier Tract*, *Se La Sub-Agency*, *Subansiri Frontier Tract* and *Tuensang Frontier Tract*. Each of these region was administered by a *Political Officer*. In 1950, this territory was included in the 6th Schedule. Constitutionally it was a part of Assam, and specially administered by the Governor of Assam, who acted as an Agent of the President of India. The Governor had an *Adviser*. The Secretariat of the Adviser was situated in Shillong (Meghalaya).

In 1954, it was renamed as *North East Frontier Agency* (popularly *NEFA*) with six Frontier Divisions : *Kameng Frontier Division*, *Subansiri Frontier Division*, *Siang Fron-*

tier Division (Daporijo Sub-Division, Along Sub-Division, Pasighat Sub-Division), *Lohit Frontier Division* (Roing Sub-Division), (Tezu Sub-Division), *Tirap Frontier Division* and *Tuensang Froniter Division*. In 1957. the Tuensang Frontier Division was excluded from NEFA to join Nagaland. The remaining five frontier divisions were converted, in 1964, into a District. In 1965, Central Home Ministry took over NEFA Administration. The *Panchayati Raj* formed a traditional *Council*, in 1967, with five Ministers and twentysix MLAs. There were thirtytwo *Anchal Samitis* with thirty nine members. This was set up for each village. The members were all elected bodies. For each district, a *Zila Parishad* was formed with a Govt. personal called *Political Officer*. All these Political Officers were the advisory body for their districts. And, an *Agency Council* was formed for NEFA as a whole. This Agency Council was the highest body and can discuss any matter relating to administration.

From 1st January, 1972, NEFA became a Union Territory under a Chief Commissioner and was renamed as *Arunachal Pradesh*. Five *Counsellors* were appointed on 6th October, 1972, for each of the districts. On 20th April, 1974, the capital of this territory was shifted from Shillong (Meghalaya) to Itanagar in Lower Subansiri District of Arunachal Pradesh. Till May 1980 Arunachal Pradesh consisted of five districts. After that, under Arunachal Pradesh Reorganisation of Districts Act, 1980, four new districts were formed by dividing the areas of Kameng District, Subansiri District, Siang District and Lohit District. These are : West Kameng District, East Kameng District, Lower Subansiri District, Upper Subansiri District, West Siang District, East Siang District, Dibang Valley District, Lohit District and Tirap District. On October 6, 1984, the Tawang District was formed by bifurcating from West Kameng District. At present, Arunachal Pradesh has got total ten districts mentioned above and each of this is under a Deputy Commissioner who was formerly called Political Officer. By abolishing the post of the Chief Commissioner, a post of Lt. Governor was created on 15th August, 1975 and the Pradesh Council converted into a

Legislative Assembly under the Constitution (Thirty Seven Amendment Act, 1975). A Council of Ministers was also constituted which is responsible to the Union Cabinet. Prior to 1912-13, this Union Territory was a part of the districts of Lakhimpur and Darrang of Assam State, and its administration was looked after by the Deputy Commissioners of the two districts. At present the strength of Arunachal Pradesh Legislative Assembly has increased to 33 with the Centre's nomination of 3 persons as members.

The number of Agency Council, Zila Parishads and Anchal Samitis as on 3rd December, 1969 are given below :

Table-V

Arunachal Pradesh Council

Kameng Zila Parishad	Subansiri Zila Parishad	Siang Zila Parishad	Lohit Zila Parishad	Tirap Zila Parishad
5 Anchal Samitis	12 Anchal Samitis	11 Anchal Samitis	8 Anchal Samitis	3 Anchal Samit s

and, 838 total number of Gram Panchayats were there in this territory.

The total literate persons of Arunachal Pradesh is 126,185 (Census 1981). The percentage of literates to total population is 20·09 which is considerd very low and is due to late starting of education in comparison to other parts of India (Table-II). Attention has been given to education in this territory only after the Independence of India and it is showing a good progress in education. Female literacy is also now improving very much. The overall literacy of Arunachal Pradesh was 7·13% in 1961 which has increased to 11·29% in 1971. Literacy is now, however, progressing at a faster rate.

The scheduled tribes of this region are 79% (Census 1981). Most of them are Indo-Mongoloid. Out of 110 tribes and sub-tribes the following are considerd as major. They are : Monpas, Hrussos, Khowas, Bangnis, Sherdukpens, Mijis, Nishis, Apatanis, Miris, Sulungs, Gallongs, Minyongs, Adis,

Membas, Tagins, Khamptis, Mishmis, Singphos, Tangsas, Noctes, Wanchoos and Lisus (Yobin). The colourful tribes of this region are speaking in their own 80 plus different tribal dialects but, '*Nefamese*' which is, as much as similar to Assamese language, is their common Lingo. They have their own developed special qualities of culture myths and legends, etc. which usually differ from tribe to tribe of this territory.

About 46% of the total population of Arunachal Pradesh is engaged in cultivating work like agricultural labourer, plantation, forestry, fishing, hunting, etc. The available irrigated area is 17% of the total cultivated area of about 14.000 hectares. Jhuming, a kind of shifting cultivation, is their traditional method of agriculture. The forests are cleared and crops are raised for one to three years depending upon the fertility of the soil. After that, the cultivators move to some other site to agriculture under jhuming. Here, generally, the soil is very much fertile. The wet terraced rice cultivation is found here in few areas in Tawang, West Kameng, Lower Subansiri and Lohit districts.

A number of minerals (coal, limestone, iron ore, mica, etc.) are reported to occur in Arunachal Pradesh and need to be investigated in detail. A number of mineral investigation programmes is, however, sponsored by the North Eastern Council in Arunachal Pradesh. A good deposit of high alluvial clay was discovered at Tezu in Lohit District by Geological Survey of India. Mini cement plant (30 ton per day), has been set up by NEC at Tezu. Namchik-Namphuk coalfield in Arunachal Pradesh proved 18 metre coal.

The Monpas of Tawang district have developed their cottage industries much better than the other tribes. They do beautiful wood carving and prepare Buddha images out of clay. They have a tradition of carpet weaving with wool etc. Tawang's Buddhist Monastery, built by Mira Lama in 1640 is the oldest in Asia, stands at about 10,000 feet above the sea level and offers a picturesque view of the Tawang valley. Most of the tribes of Arunachal Pradesh weaves their own clothes, prepare baskets, bows and arrows, etc. for their own use. The Adis are very much skilled at bridge building which are astonishing others and they have built as long as 240 metres tubular cane loop suspension bridges. Their principal industries are forest based. At present, some industrial units have been started in some suitable sites of this territory. Saw Mills, Ply Wood Plant etc. are seen at Pasighat (East Siang District), Namsai (Lohit District), and Deomali (Tirap District).

The archaeological ruins of this territory are : *Ita, Bhalukpung, Malinithan, Tamresvari, Bhismak Nagar, Brahmakund, Roing*, and *Parashuram Kund*. All these are rich in myths of the *Mahabharata* and the *Puranas*. These reflects the history of this region.

Tribal women of this region hold a high position in work. They work with their menfolk in the jhum and play important role in agricultural activities. But, they have almost no right to their property. Unmarried girls, however, have their right on their own earnings. In some tribes, there is taboo to their female members to eat certain animals' meat and fish while their menfolk can eat all types of meat and fish to get much protein for their health. They are patrilineal, patrilocal and patriarchal.

The religious communities are mainly Hindus, Muslims, Christians, Sikhs, Buddhists, Jains, etc. The tribal people of Arunachal Pradesh believe in the evil spirits for calamities, disease, death, etc. They have several rituals for birth and death. Payment of bride-price, in most of the tribes, is essential among them. They are generally endogamous. Clan exogamy is the fundamental rule of their marriage. Monogamy is their normal practice though polygamy is not treated as a crime. Polygamy is, however, practised by some rich people of them. Polyandry is never allowed. Parallel cousin marriage is strictly prohibited among them.

The Arunachal Pradesh Administration is trying to get electrification to more and more villages of this territory. (see table VII on the next page). Child mortality rate among them is almost high. The common diseases are skin disease, stomach disease, goitre, malaria, respiratory diseases, tuberculosis, syphilis and leprosy. These are, perhaps, due to bad climate, uncleanliness, unhygenic activities and lack of drinking water, etc. They usually like to get treatment from their indigenous medicine men. If not cured, they go to the dispensaries etc.

The table regarding the electric Power scheme in 1971 is furnished below :

Table—VII

District	Power Plants
TAWANG	Micro-hydel 3010 KW
WEST KAMENG	
EAST KAMENG	Micro-hydel 1500 KW
UPPER SUBANSIRI	Micro-hydel 10 KW
LOWER SUBANSIRI	Micro-hydel 2000 KW
WEST SIANG	Micro-hydel 600 KW
EAST SIANG	Micro-hydel 200 KW
LOHIT	Micro-hydel 400 KW
DIBANG VALLEY	Micro-hydel 850 KW
TIRAP	Micro-hydel 850 KW

At the initial stage, the tribal studies in Arunachal Pradesh were undertaken mainly by the British Administrators, Surveyors, Defence Employees, Christian Missionaries and Travellers. British Administrators like Wilcox (1832), Griffth (1836-1847), Dalton (1845-1872), Hannay (1847), Vetch (1848-1873), Hudson (1850), Fr. Krick (1853), Jenkins (1870), Peal (1872-1896), Cooper (1873), Badgley (1876), Woodthorpe (1878), Hunter (1879), Needham (1884-1894), Growe (1890), Dun (1897), Ward (1901), Brown (1913-1916), Kennedy (1914), Dunbar (1915) and others published their reports on the tribes of Arunachal Pradesh in various Handbooks, Census Reports, Proceedings, Journals, etc.

Several excellent works done by good number of Scholars after independence specially Verrier Elwin (1956-70), C. von Fueer-Haimendorf (1955, 1962, 1980, 1982), J P. Mills (1952), Sachin Roy (1953-67), Gemini Paul (1958), B. K. Roy Burman (1965, 1970, 1975), Parul Dutta (1959, 1978, 1983). There was no comprehensive monograph on any tribe of Arunachal Pradesh in preindependence period except *Desriptive Ethnology of Bengal* by E. T. Delton (1872). There is, however, an edited book entitled, *India's North East Frontier in the Nineteenth Century* by Late Dr. Verrier Elwin (1959) where almost all the preindependence publications are inserted; all these original documents are rather rare to come by now. One can use this book as a dependable source book to know the past-work on Arunachal Pradesh.

There is now several monographs, published by Arunachal Pradesh Research Department, on Dafla (Shukla 1959); Tangsa (Dutta 1959); Padam Minyong (Roy 1960); Sherdukpen (Sharma 1961) ; Gallong (Srivastava 196) ; Idu Mishmi (Baruah 1960); Aka (Sinha 1962); Wanchoo (Srivastava 1973, Dutta 1983); Tangam (Bhattacharjee 1975); Hill Miri (Chowdhury 1970, Pandey 1978); Nocte (Dutta 1978); Beris (Kumar 1978); Pailibos (Kumar 1979); Singpho (Barua 1977, Dutta 1985); Monpa & Sherdukpen (Sarkar 1980); Sulung (Deuri 1982). Only Prof. C. von Fiirer-Haimendorf, an eminent foreign anthropologist, restudied a tribe Apatani (1962 and 1980) over a time period to give a more definite account of changes on them. A monograph on Lower Siang People (Lal and Das Gupta 1979) of Arunachal Pradesh has been published by Anthropological Survey of India.

This is a multi-disciplinary bibliography which covers the important writings on the tribes of Arunachal Pradesh in the pre-and post independence period. A detailed study of this bibliography will reveal the important gaps in our Knowledge on them. A large number of publications listed here are papers published in journals and presented to various seminars and conferences. Monograph type of books are less published than articles. Further, this bibliographical work indicates that a large number of studies have been done on the Akas (Hrussos).

Sherdukpens, Nishis, Apatanis, Hill Miris. Gallongs. Minyongs, Adis, Khamptis, Monpas, Singphos. Tangsas, Sulungs, Tagins, Noctes and Wanchoos. But, less work has been done on the Bangnis. Miju-Mishmis, Membas, Khowas, Mijis, Lisus (Yobin), Lishpas, Chugpas, Raus, Rishi-Mashis, Nidu-Moras, Chikum-Duis, Ngas, Khambas and many other tribes and sub-tribes of this territory. It is also observed that, social and cultural ethnographic works on them are much more than Demographic and physical anthropological work.

The main purpose of compiling this bibliography is, however, to assist the scholars and researchers so that, the anthropologists, sociologists, ethnologists, archaeologists, historians, geographers, psychologists, linguists, politicians, economists, botanists, zoologists, geologists as well as librarians may get quick ready references about their reference queries without wastage of their valuable time. Moreover, an individual researcher may select his own research theme from this.

For this bibliography several old and new records, periodicals, books, newspapers, etc. are consulted from 1832 ownards. All the photographs, which have been used here, are by the Directorate of Information and Public Relations, Arunachal Pradesh. I have not found it necessary to annotate this bibliography. A serious student must read the relevant material himself and cryptic annotations are rarely of much use. I have, also, access here to the unpublished research reports, seminar papers and symposiums and even dissertations. The preparation of bibliography is an ongoing process. I have been compelled to decide at some point of time to stop adding entries. As a result of this, there may be some ommission of publications which have been brought out after March, 1985. In spite of my best efforts few references are not complete as those collected from secondary sources and could not procured for vertification. The choice before me was either to reject them or to include. I chose the latter because some information are better than none. Now, if this bibliography helps the scholars that will be the real satisfaction for my hard work's pain. I shall welcome suggestions, additional informations and comments from the users to improve this in near future.

My grateful thanks are due to S/Shri G.R. Taye, Inspector of Statistics, Anini and Daporiji, B.K. Borthakur, District Statistieal Officer, Khonsa and J. Biswas, Inspector of Statistics, Pasighat for their kind cooperation and help rendered to me.

In the end, I must express my sense of grateful ness to the National Library, Calcutta; Gauhati University Library, Guwahati; Departmental Reference Library, Directorate of Research, Arunachal Pradesh, Shillong and Library, Anthropological Survey of India, Shillong. I like to record my debt to my brother Dr. Salil Ranjan Sen who helped me to get the entire manuscript typed. Finally, I must express my deep respectful gratitude to my mother Mrs. Malati Sen for her kind help rendered to me and constant encouragement. Had it not been for the active help of my mother, the work would not have accelerated as at its present tempo.

Rehabari, Guwahati.
June, 1985.

SIPRA SEN.

11. Padam Miniyong couple of East Siang District

12 A Mishmi youth of Dibang Valley District

13. A Digaru Mishmi couple of Lohit District

14. A Khampti group of Lohit District

15. A Singhpho man of Tirap District

16. A Nocte youth of Tirap District

17. A Tangsa girl of Tirap District

18. A Wancho couple of Tirap District

No.2. MAP OF NORTH EASTERN INDIA (Position of Arunachal Pradesh)

CHAPTER II

KEY TO BIBLIOGRAPHY

All the references have been alphabetically arranged in a chronological order with reference to each author. For books the author's name is followed by year, title of reference, place of publication and publishsr's name.

For journals the author's name is followed by year, title of article, name of the journal, volume, number, month and pages. In case of newspapers, etc., the author's name is followed by year, title of article, name of the newspaper and date of publication.

Most of the references are in English but French, German, Hindi, Assamese and Bengali publications are also included in this Bibliography.

CHAPTER III

BRIEF DESCRIPTION OF THE DISTRICTS

1. Tawang District

It was formed by bifurcating from West Kameng District of Arunachal Pradesh on October 6, 1984. This district is situated to a remote corner between Bhutan and Tibet in the west on a plateau at ten thousand feet above the sea level among the snow-bound high mountains of north western corner of Arunachal Pradesh. This region is well-known due to the Chinese aggression of 1962.

The great lamasery of Tawang, founded some 350 years ago stands here. It is the home of the Monpas. The total population of Tawang district is 9,218. Out of which 4,904 are males and 4,314 are females. The approximate area of this district is 4,740 sq. km. It's earlier three circles Tawang, Mukto and Thingbu has been upgraded to Sub-divisions soon after the formation of this district. Tawang is the district headquarters.

2. West Kameng District

It was formed from earlier Kameng District of Arunachal Pradesh in 1980. This district is situated in the south western corner of Arunachal Pradesh. It is the home of the Monpas, and Sherdukpens. Bomdila, the headquarters of the district is situated at nine thousand feet above the sea level.

The available minerals of this district are dolemite and limestone. The approximate area of West Kameng District is 4.855 sq. km. Buddhist temple, museaum, library and handicraft centre attract the visitors of Bomdila town. This district has three Sub-divisions. These are Bomdila, Nafra-Buragaon and Lumla. Bomdila Sub-division has four Circles: Nafra-Buragaon and Lumla Sub-division has two Circles each.

3. East Kameng District

It was formed from earlier Kameng District in 1980. Nishang, Sulung and Bagnis are the main tribes of this district. Limestone and basemetal are the main minerals of this district. The total population of East Kameng District is 42,722. Total scheduled Tribe population is 37,286, out of which 18,410 are males and 18,876 are females. The approximate area of this district is 4,134 sq. km. It has two Sub-divisions These are Seppa and Chayengtajo. There are total eight Circles. The headquarters of East Kameng District is Seppa.

4. Lower Subansiri District

It was formed from earlier Subansiri District. Apatani and Nishang are the main tribes of this district. The total scheduled tribe population is 87,605. Out of these 43,539 are males and 44,066 are females. Graphite and basemetal are the minerals of this area. Here forest based industries are found. The headquarters is at Ziro. The approximate area of this district is 13,010 sq. km.

Itanagar, the capital of Arunachal Pradesh, is situated in the southern part of this district. Itanagar and New Itanagar Complex are situated at about two hundred to seven hundred metres above from the sea level. The area of Itanagar Capital is approximately 2,500 acres. The climate is moderate and pleasant.

Lower Subansiri District has four Sub-divisions. These are Ziro, Sagalee, Capital Complex and Koloriang. There are total fifteen Circles.

5. Upper Subansiri District

It was formed from earlier Subansiri District. Tagin, Hill Miri, Adi (Gallong) are the main tribes of this area. The headquarters is situated at Daporijo. The approximate area of this district is 5,353 sq. km. Dolemite and limestone are the minerals of this district.

The total population of this area is 39,410. The density of population is 7 per sq. km. This district has two Sub-divisions. These are Nacho and Daporijo. There are total eight Circles under these Sub-divisions.

6. West Siang District

It was formed from earlier Siang District of Arunachal Pradesh. The district headquarters is at Along. Adi is the main tribe of this district. The approximate area of this district is 12,006 sq. km. Limestone and Graphite are the minerals of this district. Total Scheduled tribe population is 6 ,323, out of which 30,922 are males and 3. ,401 are females.

It has four Sub-divisions. These are Along, Basar, Mechuka and Tuting There are total sixteen Circles under these Sub-divisions.

7. East Siang District

It was formed from earlier Siang District. The headquarters is situated at Pasighat. The approximate area of this district is 6, 12 sq. km A College is situated at Pasighat. The total population of this district is 70,451. Density of population is 11 per sq. km. Literate persons are 25·15% of the total population of this district. Minyong, Padam, Pangi, Simong, Gallong, Karko and Milang are the main tribes of this district.

East Siang District has two Sub-divisions. These are Pasighat and Mariyang. There are total eight Circles under these two Sub-divisions.

8. Dibang Valley District :

It was formed from Lohit District of Arunachal Pradesh. The headquarters is situated at Anini. The Dibang Valley district has the largest area of 13,029 sq. km. with total population of 30,988 persons inhabiting at the rate of 2 persons per sq. km. The Idus and the Padams are the main tribes in this district. The Idu-Mishmis are the main dominant tribes and inhabit in the foothill areas of Roing and Dambuk Circle, the Padams (Adis) are pre-dominant. They originally came from the Damroh area of the East Siang district but now constitute more than half of the population of the Roing and Dambuk Circles.

This district has two Sub-divisions. These are Anini and Roing. There are total six Circles under these two Sub-divisions.

9. Lohit District

The approximate area of this district is 11,402 sq. km. The headquarters is situated at Tezu. The Khamptis and Mishmis are the main tribes of this district. Limestone, Graphite are the minerals of this area. The total population of the district is 69,498. The density of population per sq. km. is 6. The total scheduled tribe population is 30,130. This district has three Sub-divisions. There are total eleven Circles under these three Sub-divisions.

10. Tirap District

The approximate area is 7,024 sq. km. The population of this district is 1,28,135, out of which 68,442 are males and 59,693 are females. The literacy rate is 18·17%. The density of popualtion is 18 per sq. km. This district is the thickest population area of Arunachal Pradesh.

Table—VI

DISTRICTS, SUB-DIVISIONS, CIRCLES AND TOWNS

DISTRICT Name of the District and Headquarters	SUB-DIVISION Name of the Sub-Division	CIRCLE Name of the Circle	TOWN Name of the Town
1	2	3	4
1. TAWANG Tawang Hqs.	Tawang Mukto Thingbu		
2. WEST KAMENG Bomdila Hqs.	Bomdila	Bomdila Kalaktang Dirang Bhalukpong	Bomdila
	Nafra Buragaon	Nafra Thrizino	
	Lumla	Lumla Zemithang	
3. EAST KAMENG Seppa Hqs.	Seppa	Seppa Pakkekeshang Pipu-Dipu Lada Seuosa	
	Chayengtajo	Chayengtajo Bameng Khenewa	
4. LOWER SUBANSIRI Ziro Hqs.	Ziro	Ziro Palin Raga Tali Kimin	
	Sagalee	Sagalee Doimukh Balijan Mengio	

1	2	3	4
	Capital Complex	Itanagar (Old) New Itanagar	Old Itanagar New Itanagar
	Koloriang	Koloriang Sarli Damin Nyapin	
5. UPPER SUBANSIRI Daporijo Hqs.	Nacho	Taksing Limeking Nacho Siyum	
	Daporijo	Daporijo Dumporijo Taliha Giba	
6. WEST SIANG Along Hqs.	Along	Along Liromoba Payum Rumgong Kaying Darak	Along
	Basar	Tirbin Basar Gensi Likabali	
	Mechuka	Mechuka Tato Monigong	
	Tuting	Tuting Gelling Singa	

1	2	3	4
7. EAST SIANG Pasighat Hqs.	Pasighat	Pasighat Pangin Mebo Dosing (Boleng) Nari	Pasighat
	Mariyang	Mariyang Yingkiong Karko	
8. DIBANG VALLEY Anini Hqs.	Anini	Anini Etalin Alelih	
	Roing	Roing Dambuk Desali	
9. LOHIT Tezu Hqs.	Tezu	Tezu	Tezu
	Namsai	Namsai Wakro Chowkham Lekang	
	Hayuliang	Hayuliang Chaglongam Hawai Walong Kibithoo Goiliang	
10. TIRAP Khonsa Hqs.	Khonsa	Khonsa Namsang Laju	
	Miao	Miao Vijoynagar Bordumsa Diyun	

1	2	3	4
	Longding	Niausa Wakka Pongchou Kanubari	
	Changlang	Changlang Nampong Manmao	

The district derives its name from its principal river, the Tirap which flows through the mainland starting from the south to the north until it falls into the Noa Dehing river. The highest hilly area is the *Diphi Bum* in north east with an attitude of 4506 mtrs., the nearest place being Vijaynagar on the banks of Noa Dihing river.

The headquarters is situated at Khonsa. Wancho, Nocte, Tangsa, Singpho and Lisu (Yobin) are the main tribes of this district. Total 192 schools are there. Ninety million tonnes of coal deposits are there at Namchik Namphuk hills. Oil and Gas have been discovered at Kharsang.

This district is situated in a unique geographical setting bounded in the east and south by Burma. The land has a picturesque beauty of it's own, the Noa Dihing river rising from the snow heights in the northeast and flows through a fertile region.

The climatic condition ranges from humid and hot in the plains portion and cold in the interior places of the hilly areas. The climatic condition of Khonsa, the district head-quarters, is moderate and pleasant. The average annual rain fall of this district is being 310 cm.

Road communication of Tirap district is better than other districts of Arunachal Pradesh. At present 141 places in the district are electrified. There are craft centres, weaving units and sericulture demonstration centres. Tirap district has divided into four Sub-divisions. There are total fourteen Circles under these four Sub-divisions.

CHAPTER IV

BRIEF DESCRIPTION OF THE TRIBES

1. Monpa

They inhabited in Tawng and West Kameng Districts of Arunachal Pradesh. They are divided into three geographical units : Tawang inhabitants of the North Monpas, Dirang (West Kameng) inhabitants of the Central Monpas and Kolaktang (West Kameng) inhabitants of the Southern Monpas. They are distinguished from each other on the basis of their dialectal variations. Their dialect belongs to Tibeto-Burmese group. Perhaps they migrated through Bhutan. They are Buddhist by religion. They are quiet, gentle, friendly, courteous, industrious, good to animals, good to children and artistic people. Their decorated hat and silver sword are excellent work.

Their houses are Alpine style, double-storied, strongly constructed on stone or wood with plank-floors and having doors and windows. They dress well in Tibetan fashion. Men wear woolen undercoats, overcoats and trousers. Men cut their hair short and wear a dome shaped hat with edges of fur. Women wear sleeveless chemises which reach down to the calves, tying them round the waist with a long and narrow piece of cloth and a jacket made of woollen stuff. Women use a round cap on their head.

They love music and dance. Their musk-dances are very much famous. They are exceptional in drinking milk and making ghee which is taboo to most of other tribes of this territory. The Monpa women weave beautiful designed carpets, mats, etc. The influence of Tibet and Bhutan is strongly marked in the Monpa textiles and ornaments. Monpa men are expert in wood-carving, prepare Buddha images out of clay and even manufacture paper.

They practise terrace cultivation. Besides rice the other cereals like maize, wheat, burley are also grown. They keep bees in most villages and collect wild honey. Monogamy appears to be the form of marriage. Tatooing is absent among them. Now-a-days they bury their deads. But, they have three other methods of disposal of deads. These are by keeping the dead body in open place for vultures to eat, by burning, by cutting into 108 pieces and then throwing into nearest river, perhaps, for fishes to eat.

2. Sherdukpens

They inhabit six villages in the southern part of West Kameng District in the valleys of Tengapani river. They belong to the Tibeto-Mongoloid group and are strongly influenced by Tibetan and Bhutanese culture, traditions and customs. They are Buddhist by religion. They are keen traders and migrates to the low places for several months every year to trade with the plains and to avoid the cold of their hilly areas during winter. Thus, their agriculture is neglected due to their migratory habits. They are expert weavers and fine silver craftsmen and blacksmiths.

They are fair complexioned and midium statured. Tatooing is absent among them. Their houses are constructed on stone and 5' to 7' high from the ground. Men cuts their hair short and wear a cap made from yak's hair. Monogamy is found among them. They have their village-council headed by the '*gaonbura*'. They practised both shifting and permanent cultivation. Paddy, wheat, barley, maize are cultivated by them. Beef, pork, chiken, and mutton are taboo among them.

Their houses are constracted on stone foundations of

five to seven feet high. The basement serves to keep goats and other domestic animals. The house-owner with his family lives on the upper floor made up with wooden planks.

3. Mijis Dhammais)

They inhabit the valley of the Bichom river in West Kameng District. They are a small group of people having much similarities with the Akas (Hrussos). They call themselves *Dhammai*.

They are scattered over 25 villages. They are surrounded on the north and the east by the Daflas, on the south by the Akas (Hrussos) and on the west by the Monpas. Their houses are 30′ to 70′ feet long, 12′ to 20′ feet broad and built on platform. They are fond of ornaments. Miji women wear necklaces of multi-coloured beads, brass made ornaments, etc. Both men and women keep their hair long. Men ties their hair and makes a '*bun*' on the top of the head like the Akas. A Miji strong man carries a small knife, a midium size knife suspended from the neck and one big size sword on right side of their waist, hanging from the neck.

Slavery is found among the lowest classes of the Mijis. Polygamy is almost common. Burial is the common method for disposal of dead bodies.

4. Khowas (Buguns)

They inhabitthe West Kameng District. They are small group of people living among the Akas (Hrussos) but in separate villages of their own under their headmen. They call themselves '*Buguns*' in their own language.

They are very much similar with the Akas in their appearance but they are little-bit darker in complexion. They work for the Akas (Hrussos) whom they believe as their overlords. They are hard workers. Maize, millet, wheat, potato, and sweet potato are their main agricultural products.

A man can marry more than one wife if he can pay the bride-price. Sons are get the property equally which is left behind by their father and unmarried girls get ornaments only. They bury their deads.

5. Akas (Hrussos)

The Aka called themselves '*Hrussos*' which means "man". The name Aka has been given by the plain peoples of Assam as they paint their faces very much. They inhabit the south of the West Kameng District of Arunachal Pradesh. They have animist religious ideas.

They are fierce looking people, well built, fair complexioned, flat-nosed, prominent cheek boned. The stature of men is about 5′ 4″ and women about 5′. Men tie their long hair in the middle of their head and women tie their long hair at the back of their head.

Their language belongs to the Tibeto-Burmad group. They are of Mongoloid stock. They have adopted various elements of Tibetan dress and ornaments. They put a long piece of cotton cloth wrapped round the body and pinned over the shoulders. Sometimes they wear a jacket. Ladies jackets are big in length. Women put a piece of cloth to cover their head. Sometimes, they wear bamboo-made ring cap. In front of their hats,plumes of cock's feather or bamboo leaves are fixed for decoration. Aka men have their ear-lobes pierced and bamboo tubes are inserted into the holes and sometimes they wear ear-rings. Men always carry a *dao* or a sword which they keep either in their belt or hang from one side of their shoulder. Men also carry a bow in their hand or hang across their back and a quiver

Women are fond of wearing several bead-necklaces of different colours. They wear a number of silver ornaments. Women wear large silver made ear-rings. Aka women put silver-chain round their head. Tatooing is common among them. They are not much advanced economically or culturally but they are influenced by the ideas of their Buddhist neighbours. They are, however, keen traders. They are famous for their trade in swords, cloth and blankets as well as bamboo and cane materials.

Their large houses are raised on platforms of about 6 feet above the ground and are divided into three compartments. Aka houses are scattered here and there in their viliage. Each village belong to a particular clan. They have their village council under their '*Gaon-Bura*' (Chief of the village) who usually decides the cases of offences according to their customary laws. Slavery, at one time in the past, was found much among them.

Rice, maize and potato are their main agricultural products. Shifting cultivation (*jhuming*) is practised by them. They eat pork and beef. Cross-cousin marriage is popular among them. Their family generally consists of wife, husband, unmarried children and slave, if any. Their deads are buried with the materials which were used by the deceased such as, dress, utensils, weapons, etc.

6. Bangnis

They are living in East Kameng District and are akin to Deflas (Nishis) of Arunachal Pradesh. They have taken to a little cultivation. Agriculture is almost difficult here because of steep slopes. They are skilled in cane work.

Men keep their hair long after their 12 to 13 years of age and women let their hair grow from the age of 5 to 6 years. Men make a '*bun*' on the forehead which is called '*podum*'. But, now-a-days, the school going boys cut their hair short at some intervals. Tatooing is common among the women. This is to be done before the attainment of their puberty. They are fond of ornaments.

7. Sulungs

They are small group of tribals who inhabit East Kameng District of Arunachal Pradesh. Their physical stature is slightly lower than other neighbouring tribes. Their dress and appearance is almost similar with the Daflas (Nishis). There is no compulsion that one is to have tatoo.

Their houses are constructed on a slope and resemble those of the Nishis. Many of them are little better than slaves to the Nishis. Long back, they did not know agriculture and lived in a semi-nomadic manner of hunting and food gathering like Bangnis. They are now following *jhum* cultivation. They use bows and arrows as their weapons. Some of them are good blacksmiths of iron and brass. They bury their dead body near their houses.

8. Daflas (Nishis)

The Daflas inhabit Lower Subansiri and East Kameng Districts of Arunachal Pradesh. The name *Dafla* was given by the plain's people to a unrully warrior like tribe. They are now known as *Nishis* which means *man* in their language. They are very much skilled in war.

They are strong and stout and muscular, having round and flat face with a broad nose, prominent cheek bones, high stature, deep-set eyes. Dafla men make their hair as crown over their forehead with yellow strings and long brass pin. They wear cane-made helmet which looks very beautiful as it is surmounted by the red-dyed beak of hornbill and sometimes with hornbill's feathers. They are fond of bamboo and cane ornaments to decorate their body.

Their weapons are bow and arrow, a long spear, *dao* or sword. They are polygamous but not polyandrous. Their clan is exogamous. Their houses are long. Each wife has her own separate establishment in that house. The senior wife is the mistress of that house. Their long houses resemble the houses of the Borneo people of South East Asia.

Shifting cultivation is practised by them. They believe in dreams very much. They also believe in the survival of the soul after death which according to them travels to meet its dead ancestors in the heavenly abode. They bury theif dead near their houses. They are used to cry very loudly for their deceased person.

9. Apatanis

The Apatanis are a small tribe and most advanced as well as developed people amongst the tribal groups of Lower Subansiri District. They are peace loving tribe. It is observed in their custom that those who can spoil or dedicate their own property are rich and they occupy the highest place in their society. They are almost like the Red-Indians of America.

They are tall, and good looking. They have prominent nose and elongated face. Their complexion is fair. Their dress is very much similar to that of their neighbour Daflas (Nishis). Men tie up their hair in a knot just on the top of the forehead with a twelve inches brass-made thin rod and keep it there horizontally through the knot. Tatoo marks are seen over their chin. The women are tatooed with broad blue lines from the top of their forehead to the tip of the nose and from the lower lip to the base of the chin. The men have totoos only below their mouth which is a horizontal line drawn across the under-lip and a straight line downward from it to the point of their chin. The women coil their hair on the top of their head. It is an ambition of every woman to wear the largest possible nose-plungs, made of wood. Men used cane-made caps which is almost pointed in it's back and front side. The women wear skirt of the same gray cloth as men, with broad bluish borders, reaching below the knees and a jacket of their own.

Marriage among them is a simple matter. There is no wedding ceremony. If a boy and a girl want to live together as husband and wife, the girl moves to the parental house of the man. A youth, generally, after marriage will set up a separate household.

Their village is built on high ground. The houses are built on wooden planks, bamboo walls and thatched with rice-straw. Most of their houses are standing wall to wall in streets and narrow lanes. Space is limited in Apatani village. They are very good farmers who have developed an extensive system of irrigation. Rice is their staple food. They practise terrace cultivation from time immemorial. Ploughing done by manual labour with the help of hoes. Rice, maize, potato, cucumber, chillie, tobacco, etc. are raised by them.

10. Hill Miris

They are inhabit the hilly areas of Upper Subansiri District. They were hardly known before 1911. The name *Miri* is purely an Assamese word to denote this people who inhabited between the Daflas (Nishis) and the Abors (Adis). They are considered to be members of the Tibeto-Burman family and resemble the Bangnis and Nishis with an exceptional character that they have a milder and more cooperative temperament. Their villages are small and scattered.

Polygyny is found among them but polyandry is seen in rare cases. They have no generic name but are called after their villages. They have their own coloured dress with attractive designs woven by them. They do a lot of cane work and men as well as women adorn their bodies with as many as a hundred woven bands of cane. They believe in magical-cures from their illness. The disposal of dead is by burial.

11. Tagins

They inhabit on the slope of a hillock of the Upper Subansiri District on the left bank of the river Subansiri. They live in barrack—like long houses built on bamboo and wooden platforms. More than one house-holds are accommodated in it. There is no window and only one main entrance in the front. When all the ovens are in use, the entire house remains filled with smoke.

Rice, maize, millet are their staple food. They eat mithun, cow, pig. goat, dog, deer, monkey, birds, fish, snakes, rats and insects. Generally, all the members of the house-hold take their food from a common plate. They are not fond of dress Men wear sleeveless black coats and cotton blanket. Women wear woollen blanket. The unmarried girls put Tibetan type of woollen round caps. They are fond of beads and use metal bangles.

The Tagins are fierce by nature and are expert hunters for food. They seem to be undernourished and relatively less hygienic in their appearance and habits which is, perhaps, the cause for huge incidence of skin diseases among them. Monogamous marriage are found among them but, polygamy is however practised by a few rich people of them. The disposal of dead is by burial.

12. Adis (Abors)

The word *Adi* is now used instead of the word *Abor* which means unruly, independent. The Assamese in the plains of Brahmaputra Valley gave the name Abor to this Tibeto-Burman speaking people who inhabit the hilly areas of East and West Siang Districts and also Upper Subansiri District.

The Adis are divided into two broad divisions : they are the Padam, Minyongs, Pasi, Pangi, Shimong, Bori, Ashing and Tangams in one division and the other division by Gallong with Ramos, Bokars and Pailibos. They are all of Mongoloid origin. All these divisions are on regional basis. The Gallong division occupies the Upper Subansiri District. The Adis are scattered over a large area and they are bound together by a common language. Adis are less conservative than any other tribes of Arunachal Pradesh. Their village organisations are democratic.

The Adis are short statured and healthy built except the Padams who are slightly taller than the rest. The complexion is dark brown to light brown, straight eyes with a trace of the Mongoloid fold. They have dark brown eyes and straight black hair. The face is flat oval shape and the forehead is broad. The nose is upward with wide nostrils. They are dolichocephalic Mongoloid group. The Minyongs, Padams and Shimongs crop their hair. The Gallongs cut their hair about two inches round the head. The Gallong ladies do not cut their hair.

Their chief weapons are bow and arrow, the *dao* and a long sword. The men wear cane-made hat. The Gallong hat is very much oval in shape and looks like a bowl. The Adis a e good in weaving. Their artistic designs are excellent. The men use a loin cloth and a jacket of their own. The women put two cloths: one round the loins, to form a petticoat and the other round their bosom. The women wear heavy necklaces. The *beyop* plates girdle round their waist. Tatooing is common among them.

They are practising shifting cultivation. The main crops are rice, maize, tobacco, suger-cane, opium, etc. They consumes the flesh of elephant. buffalo, cow, squirrel. deer, duck, fowl, etc. *Sulung* is their main festival. They domesticate dogs and they cut dogs. sometimes, during their worship to God. *Puime* or serpent worship, Ettor, Tapu. Darung and Chalang are their main religious festivals.

The Adi villages are generally situated in a highland along the river sides by avoiding the low lands. Their skill at bridge buildings is astonishing the people which they have built long (240 metres) tubular cane loop suspension bridges with rigid bamoo footways. Adi houses are constructed on piles raised from the ground 4' to 6' feet high. Their houses are about 40' x 20' feet each in size without any inner partitions. Each of their villages has a Council called *Kebang*. It is largely an informal body and any male person (Adi) can be its member. It settles administrative matters, such as, when and where to clear the forests, when to go hunting or fishing, when and in what manner a festival will be performed, etc. They have judicial powers and offenders are brought before them for sentence of punishment. The head of this council is a chosen member.

Bachelor's dormitory *Moshup* is used as a sleeping house for young boys over the age of ten and *Resheng* is for unmarried girls. Moshup is known by different names among different sections of them. When a man marries, he sets up his own house. The eldest son gets two-thirds of the whole property and the rest by the youngest son after the death of their father. Daughters gets nothing. Adi women are fine weavers and carpet makers. The dead are buried. The Gallongs dig their graves a little deeper than the other groups of the Adis.

13. Gallongs

They inhabit West Siang District of Arunachal Pradesh. They are medium statured with broad nose. They construct their houses on wooden or bamboo pillars at a height of 4' to 12' feet from the ground level and are square size. The male and female have got separate ladders to enter their houses.

All the brothers have their sex-rights over a woman whom a brother brought home as a bride because fraternal polyandry is practised by them. Cross-cousin marriage is allowed among them. The Gallongs differ from the Minyongs and Padams in keeping their hair long and they are looking fine physique.

14. Minyongs

They inhabit West Siang District. They are closely allied to the Padams. They live in about 70 villages. They have dormitories for boys and young men and separate dormitories for unmarried girls. They are good weaver and dancer. Like the Padams and the Idus, both men and women cut their hair short. They have *Kebang* or Council of elders. Women hold a high position in their society.

Rice is the staple food. Pork is frequently eaten by them. They consumes rice-beer of black Apong and white Apong. According to their old custom, the marriage is settled by the parents without consulting the boy or the girl. In some cases the marriages are fixed even before the birth of a child. Divorce and widow remarriage are allowed. The disposal of dead is by burial.

15. Membas

They inhabit the northern borders of West Siang District of Arunachal Pradesh. They are very much like the Monpas of Tawang District. They are Buddhists by religion. They are fond of dances. They are, however, economically and culturally much poorer than the Monpas.

16. Khamptis

They inhabit the low lands of the south-east part of the Lohit District. They speak an Indo-Chinese language of the Tai group and are the only tribe in Arunachal Pradesh with a script of their own which has close affinities with the Shams of Burma, China, Thailand, Cambodia, Vietnam, Laos, etc. The word *Khampti* means *'land of gold'*. They are alike Ahoms of Assam and they originally belong to the *'Tai'* race of China (before they migrated to this region). They are Hinayana Buddhists by religion. But, they eat fowl's meat and fish, if those killed by others. Rice is their stapple food. They are settled agriculturists. They are very much advanced tribe.

Dao is their main weapon. Their houses are constructed on the ground. A house is about 80' to 100' feet in length and 18' to 20' feet in breadth. The interior is divided into chambers, private and for reception separately and there is an open balcony in the front side which is an extension beyond the roof of the house.

The Khamptis are good settled-agriculturists. They use plough. Rice is their main product. Women are known for their beautiful embroidery and weaving. Khampti men and boys generally use their own traditional Khampti *lungi* (*Fa-Noy*) and jacket (*Fa-Chyu*) and a turban of white cloth and women use *mekhala* (*Chi-Enu*),*riha* (*Langeet*) and a jacket. The rich people of them can have many wives and their society accepts them. Marriage is generally settled by the parents. Widow remarriage is allowed by them. Divorce is very rare. The dead bodies are generally disposed of by burning but in special cases, they bury their dead

17. Mishmis

They inhabit the Dibang Valley and Lohit Districts of Arunachal Pradesh. They are divided into Idu, Taraon(Digaru) and Kaman (Miju) groups. Their languages are different but not the customs. The Idu-Mishmis were popularly known as *Chulikatas*. They cut their hair round the head in Padam-Minyong fashion. The Idu-Mishmi villages are usually named after the stream of the river near which those are. Their houses are scattered. Houses are long (sometimes running to 50 metres) and narrow and having several rooms. Their socio-cultural life is rich for their traditional songs and dances.

The Mishmis are well built, short statured, broad shouldered; the head is broad (square looking), nose is flat with wide nostrils, eyes small and oblique. The Mishmis are distinguished by their dress. The Mishmi women are expert weavers. All kinds of meat are forbidden to the women except small birds and wild rats. Their weapon is cross-bow and arrow, Men wear cane helmet. After death, the body is generally kept by them in the house for a day. Then, it is buried for 5 days and therefter is taken up and burnt.

18. Singphos

They inhabit Bordumsa Circle of Tirap District and some adjoining parts of the Lohit District. They are said to be a branch of the Kachins of Upper Burma. Many words of their language are common with Adis (Abors). Burmese and Manipuri dialects. They are Buddhists by religion. Once they were a very powerful and warlike tribe. They have colourful folk festivals. The main festival is *Fra-Poi*.

They are divided into a number of clans or groups, each under a chief. Their clan organisation is based on lineage or sub-lineage groups. Their house type is more or less similar to that of the Khamptis. A house i 80' to 100' long and 20' broad with several apartments.

Physically they represent most of the mongolian traits. They have oblique eyes. their cheek bones are high. The complexion is tawny yellow to dark brown. The Singpho men tie their long hair in a large knot on the crown of the haed. The married women tie their long hair in a large knot on the crown of the head and it is secured by silver-chains and tussels. They wear ornaments of enamelled beads, etc. Married women are tatooed on both legs from the ankle to the knee The men atoo their limbs slightly.

Their dress is made up of a coloured jacket of cotton and undergarment of cotton or silk. Men wear *lungi* made of yarn of various colour combination, a jacket and a turban. Women dress consists of a skirt with design on lower border, a jacket. a designed scart, a piece of coloured cotton cloth fastened round the waist, and a scarf.

They practise permanent rice cultivation and a variety of rice they grow is fine and tastᵉful. Some of them are good blacksmiths of iron to make *dao*, spear etc. The women are expert weavers at their looms.

19. Noctes,

They inhabit the central part of the Tiran District of Arunachal Pradesh. They follow Vaishnavism. Nocte society is under their powerful chiefs who controll a number of villages. Till 1945, they were very skilful head hunters. Boys and girls dormitories are found among them. The social life of the Noctes is divided into two distinct classes: the Chief and his kinsmen form one class while the rest form the other. They have colourful folk festivals. The main festival is *Chahlo Loku.*

Polygamy is almost common but polyandry is not practised. Nocte villages are situated on hill tops, generally thickly populated with a cluster of houses huddled together. The houses are constructed on stilts high above the ground, forming a *chang* pattern. They use wooden pillars and *toko* leaves for thatching. The roofless portion of that *chang* forms a varandah. They are skilled crafts-men of bamboo and cane made materials which reveal their fine and artistic workmanship.

They are well built and of medium stature, Mongoloid appearance, light to medium brown complexion. Dress of men consists of a loin cloth. The women wear round the waist a piece of cloth, reaching down to their knee. They now-a-days prefer short blouses for the upper part of their body. The men consists of numerous cane belts round their waist. They shave off the front part of their heads keeping hair at the back and gathered into a knot over the neck like few South-Indian Brahmins. The women use coloured beads. Tatooing is found among them

They have their own councils of elders which is presided over by the Chiefs. They are doing wet rice cultivation as well as *jhum* cultivation. They dispose the dead by exposure on open platforms.

20. Tangsas

Tangsas live in the central part of the Tirap District along the Indo-Burmese border. They are medium statured and well built. Their facial features are of mongoloid type with a fair complexion. They are divided into a number of sub-groups and each group has a number of exogamous clan divisions.

They generally live in steep hills where there are availability of water sources and suitable land for cultivation. They are pile-dweller. A house has three main parts. They have separate bachelors' dormitories for boys and girls. The villages are sparsely populated. They practise *jhum* cultivation. They have colourful folk festivals. The main festival is *Moh*.

Men's clothes consist of a loin cloth or almost chequer pattern of *lungi* (like the Burmese style), sleeveless shirt and a turban. The dress of women consist of a skirt (generally black colour) reaching below the knee and sometimes coming down to the ankles, a blouse and a piece of white cloth thrown over the body and wrapped round the head. They have close similarities with the people of Burma.

Like Noctes and Wanchos, the Tangsas are good craftsmen. Tangsa women are good weavers. Their textile designs are mostly of geometrical patterns; they have a special fascination for scarlet, red, black and dark green colours. They are experts in cane and bamboo basketry works.

The method of disposal of the dead body is different among different sub-groups. Some of them bury their dead while the others cremate.

21. Wanchs

They inhabit the south-western part of the Tirap District. Their society is organised under their chiefs. According to their status, society is divided into four classes. Once they were very much skilled in head-hunting like the Noctes. Physically they are well built, tall and sturdy. They are mongoloid in appearance. Men are used to have fillets made of carved wooden human heads or hand.

Their houses are usually built on slopes of hills. Like the Noctes, their social life is governed by the traditional chieftainship system assisted by a Council of elders. The Wanchos wear less clothes. Men wear loin cloth *lenghutis* and women have their small skirts. *Shawls* are common to both men and women. They wear ivory ornaments, and bone-made beads. Tatooing is very important feature in their lives, both men and womem. Men tatoo when they reach manhood and girls when they reach maidenhood. The women generally cut their hair short.

They are famous for their wood-carving, hand-wove bags of various designs, beads and busketry worketry works. They have colourful folk festivals. The main festival is *Oziale.* The Wanchos do not dispose their dead body before twenty four hours and they dispose the dead by exposure.

22. Lisus (Yobins)

They inhabit mostly in the place Vijaynagar on t banks of the river Noa Dihing of Tirap District. They have rich heritage of culture which is different from other neighbouring tribal cultures. They have very small number of population.

They have close similarities with some people of Burma. Apart from jhuming there is no worthwhile economic activity. Due to geographical reason they have very little contact with the outside world. This tribe has its own trend of religious beliefs and practices.

CHAPTER V

FULL BIBLIOGRAPHY OF THE TRIBES

1. ABROL. Mridula (1974) British relations with frontier states (1863-1875). New Delhi, S. Chand & Co, 157 p.
2. AHMAD, S. H. and CHAKRAVARTY, S. K. 1977) Physical Anthropology of viliage Ragi Doke in Siang District of Arunachal Pradesh. *Report* submitted to Anth. Survey of India (*Unpublished*).
3. ———— (1978) Body dimensions, fertility and selection in a section of Gallong with endemic hypothyroidism and congenital defects of the central nervous system. Proceedings of a Seminar on '*Genetical Demography*", Anth. Sur. of India, Calcutta.
4. AITCHISON. C. U. (198) A collection of treaties, engagements and sanads, Vol. XII. Delhi, Mittal Publications (Reprinted).
5. ALI, S. and Dillon, S. (1948) The birds of the Mishmi Hills. *Jour. Natural History Society* (Bombay), 48 1), Dec., p. 1-37.
6. AGARWAL, A. K. (1984) Transformation from community owned land system to individual ownership in Arunachal Pradesh. Proceedings of a Seminar on "*Land Reforms*" organised by NEICSSR. Shillong.

7. ———— (1984) Changing picture of population in Arunachal.
Proceedings of a Seminar on "*Pattern and problems of population in North East India: a multidimensional Study*". Shillong, NE CSSR, 7-8 Dec, 1984.

8. ALLAN, I. M. and WOOTON, Anthony (1960) A note on the origin of a form of Primitive Currency from the Abors of the Assam Tibet Frontier.
Numismatic Circular. London, Spink & Sons.

9. ALLEN, B. C. (1902) Census of India 1901, Vol. IV, Assam, pt. I. Report. Shillong, Govt. Press (Abor. 121, Aka: 122, Defla: 126-27, Khamti. 134).

10. ———— (1905) Assam District Gazetteers. Vol. VIII, Lakhimpur. Calcutta, Printed at the City Press; 48-71, 75-9.

11. ———— (1905) Archaeological remains among the foot-hills of Arunachal Pradesh.
Resarun (Itanagar), 5(1), Spring-Summer : 68-71, (1979, *Reproduced* from Assam Dist. Gazetteers, Vol. V, Barrang : 67-68, Allahabad.

12. ———— (1928) Diatrict Gazetteers : Assam, Vol. XI) Balipara Frontier Tract. (Pt. II). Shillong, Assma Secretariat Press.

13. ———— (1928) District Gazetteers : Assam, Sadiya Frontier Tract (Vol XI, Pt. I).
Shillong, Assam Secretariat Press. (Mishmi : 27-9, Khamptis : 29-30).

14. AMRITA Bazar Patrika : (1983) Save Singphos' scheme. *Amrita Bazar Patrika* (Calcutta), dt. 21.4.1983.

15. ANDERSON, J.D. (1896) Short vocabulary of the Aka language. Shillong, Assam Secretariat Press, 20p.

16. ANGU, Joken (1971) Solung festival and its significance. *NEFA Information* (Shillong), 6(3), Oct : 31-4

17. ANONYMOUS (1863) Our North East Frontier. *Calcutta Review*, 38 : 264-85.

18. ———— (1872) The Hill Tribes of the North East Frontier.
Indian Antiquary, 1 : 62-3.

19. ———— (1924) Handbook of Castes and Tribes employed on Tea Estates in North East India. Calcutta, Tea District Labour Association.

20. ———— (1957) Ten years progress in NEFA. Shillong.

21. ———— (1958) NEFA Highlanders.
Indian Folklore (Calcutta), 1 (1), Jan-March : 85-8.

22. ———— 195?) NEFA : The Frontier Land of India.
Social Welfare, 5(4), July : 16.

23. ———— (1963) NEFA Then and Now.
Indian and Foreign Review, 1(2), Nov : 11-2.

24. ———— (1963) The Sentinel of our frontier NEFA.
Social Welfare, 10(2), May : 15-8.

25. ———— (1963) People of our Himalayan Border : Mishmis of Dibang Valley.
March of India (Delhi), 15(7), July : 7-10.

26. ———— (1963) People of our Himalayan Border : Abors of Siang.
March of India, 15(6) : 26-7.

27. ———— 1964) Progress in NEFA.
Indian and Foreign Review, 2(4), Dec : 12-4.

28. AONCK, S. Wati (1956) Morung organization among the Nocte Nagas.
Vanyajati (Delhi), 4(1), April : 73-81, (1956)

29. ARUNACHAL Directorate (1976) Twenty Point Economic Programme and Arunachal. Shillong, Directorate of Information & Public Relations, Arunachal, 16p.

30. ———— (1977) Cultural cum development convention, Pasighat, 1976.
Shillong, *Report of the Directorate of Inf. and Pub. Relations, Arunachal*, 20p.

31. ARUNACHAL, Econimics & Statistics (1977) Statistical Handbook 1976-77 : Arunachal Pradesh (Economics and Statistics).

Shillong, Govt. of A.P, Directorate of Eco. & Sta., 109 p.

32. ARUNACHAL NEWS (1972) Mol festival at Changlang.
Aru. News (Shillong), 1(3), April : 12-5.

33. ——— (1972) Ali-Aye-Ligang festival.
Aru. News, 1(3), April : 19-21.

34. ——— (1972) Introducing members of the Pradesh Council.
Aru. News, 1(8), Oct. : 15-25.

35. ——— (1972) From NEFA to Arunachal.
Aru. News, 1(1), Feb. : 33-8.

36. ——— (1973) Dree festival.
Aru. News, 2(4), July : 7-8.

37. ——— (1973 Arunacal : A flash back on culture.
Aru. News, 2(8), Nov : 10-2.

38. ——— (1973) Role of Cottage Industry.
Aru, News. 2(4), July : 15-6,

39. ——— (1972) Cultural festival.
Aru. News, 1(2), March : 15-9.

40. ——— (1947) Festivals of Arunachal.
Aru. News, 3(1), Feb.-March : 23-4.

41. ——— (1975) Celebration of Mopin festival.
Aru. News. 4(3). April-May : 11-5.

42. ——— 1974) Crafts of Arunachal : Past and Present.
Aru. News. 3(5), July : 12-5.

43. ——— (1975) Festivals of Arunachal.
Aru. News, 4(1), Feb. : 1-3

44. ——— (1977) "Si Donyi" mythology.
Aru. News, 5(9), Jan-Feb : 28-30.

45. ——— (1977) Chronology for Khamti History.
Aru. News, 6(4). August : 30-1.

46. ——— (1977) Health care in Arunachal Pradesh.
Aru. News, 6(9) 31-3,

47. ——— (1978) New Horizon of Progress.
Aru. News, 7(4), August 29.

48. ———— (1978) Adult education programme in Arunachal.
Aru. News, 7(6) : 1-3.

49. ———— (1978) Arunachal on the wheels of progress.
Aru. News, 7(9) : 1-10.

50. ———— (1978) Parasuram Kunda.
Aru. News, 6(9), Jan, Republic Day Issue : 13-4.

51. ———— (1979) Problem of Assam-Arunachal boundary : A note in brief.
Aru. News, 8(1) : 28-31.

52. ———— (1979) Welfare activities in Arunachal Pradesh Police.
Aru. News, 8(:) : 39-42.

53. ———— (1979) Development News.
Aru. News, 8(4) : 16-20.

54. ———— (1979) Annual operating plan : 1979-80.
Aru. News, 8(5), August : 6-12.

55. ———— (1975) "Si Donyi" mythology.
Aru. News, 4(7), October : 8-9.

56. ———— (1979) Subansiri District : Some basic facts.
Aru. News, 8(6) : 19-22.

57, ARUNACHAL Research Dept. (1976) Resarun' 75
Shillong. Dir. of Research, Arunachal Pradesh, 133 p.

58. ———— (1977) Resarun' 76.
Shillong, Dir. of Research, Arunachal Pradesh.

59. ———— (1977) Research in Arunachal Pradesh.
Shillong. Research Dept., Arunachal Govt.

60. ———— (1978) Research in Arunachal Pradesh.
Shillong. Research Dept., Arunachal Govt.

61. ———— (1958) Bulletin of the Research Dept. NEFA (Shillong). 1(1), June (Mimeographed).

62. ASSAM Census Report (1881) Assam Census Report, 1881.
In India's North East Frontier...Edited by Verrier Elwin.
Bombay, Oxford University Press (1959) : 159, 183-84, 285-86.

63. ASSAM Quarterly (1962) Cultural Notes: Development in NEFA.

Assam Quarterly (Gauhati), 2(3), July : 52-3.

64. ASSAM Tribune (1957) Re-introduction of Assamese language in NEFA demanded.
The Outlook on NEFA. Compiled by Parag Chaliha. (1958).
Jorhat, Assam Sahitya Sabha : 48-51 *Assam Tribune* (Gauhati). March 29. 1957.

65. ———— (1976) Arunachal.
Assam Tribune, March 21, (1976)

66. ———— (1983) Socio Economic Change in Arunachal.
Assam Tribune, dt. 6.8.1983.

67. BADGLEY, W.F. (1876) Report on the Treacherous attack made by the Nagas.
General Report on the Topographical Surveys of India for the season 1874-5.
(It describes the messacre of a survey party by the Wanchos of Ninu).

68. ———— (1876) Extract from the Narrative report of Capt W.F. Badgley.
General Report on the Topographical Surveys of India for the season 1874-5. (Calcutta, 1876).
India's North East Frontier... by Verrier Elwin. Bombay, Oxford University Press (1959) : 50-3, 70-3.

69. BAGCHI, R.N. n. d. Malinithan : Heritage of Arunacal. Shillong. Research Dept., Govt. of A.P., 19 p.

70. ———— (1977) The deities and spirits of the Tagins.
Resarun (Shillong), 3(3), July : 36-40.

71 ———— (1977) The life cycle of a Tagin.
Aru. News. 5(10), March : 11-4.

72. ———— (1977) Marriage system of the Tagins.
Aru. News, 6(4), August : 17-21.

73. ———— (1979) Family system and inheritance of property among the tribes of Arunachal Pradesh.
Resarun, 5(1), Spring-Summer : 38-41.

74. BAGRA, Jumke (1981) A note on the indigenous food

habit of the four major tribes of Subansiri District in Arunachal Pradesh.
Resarun, 7(1-2) : 42-4.

75. BAILEY. F.M. (1912) Journey through a portion of South Eastern Tibet and the Mishmi Hills.
Geographical Journal (London), 39 : 334-471.

76. ———— (1945) China-Tibet-Assam : A Journey, 1911. London, Jonathan Cape : 175 p.

77. ———— (1957) No Passport to Tibet.
London. (It has a description of Mishmis and Monpas).

78. BALFOUR, H. (1925) Thorn-lined Traps and their distribution.
Man (London), March, no. 22.

79. BANERJI, G.S. (1971) Adi society and literature in transition.
Pines (Shillong), 1(1), March : 57-65.

80. BANERJEE. R.D. (1924-25) Neolithic impliments from the Abor country.
Bulletin, Archaeological Survey of India, Annual Report : 102.

81. BARDOLOI, G.C. (*Comp.*) (192.) Notes on certain frontier tribes.
Census of India 1921, Vol. III, Assam, pt. I : Report, Appendix-B. Shillong, Govt. Press : XV-XVI.

82. BARDOLOI, Muktinath (?) Aami Bharator Simanta Rakhi. (Gitavali, in Assamese).
Shillong, Research Dept., Govt. of A.P., 28 p.

83. ———— (1958) A peep into the costumes of the Tribal People of the NEFA.
The outlook on NEFA. Comp. by Parag Chaliha.
Jorhat, Assam Sahitya Sabha : 84-90.

84. BARDOLOI, M.N. (*Comp.*) (1964) Land of the Hornbill and Myna. Shillong, Research Deptt., Govt. of A.P., 57p.

85. ———— (*Comp,*) (1968) Our Festivals.
Shillong Research Dept., Director of Information & Public Relations, 59 p.

86. BARKATAKY, M. and DUTTA, P.C. (1972) Pakam, socio-economic survey of a Gallong village in Arunachal Pradesh Jorhat, Agro Economic Research Centre.

87. BARKATAKI, Padma (1958) Behind the inner line. *The Outlook on NEFA. Comp.* by Parag Chaliha. Jorhat, Assam Sahitya Sabha : 95-100.

88. BARMAN, S.G. 1963) NEFA, the land and its people. *Indian Quarterly*, 19(4).

89. BARPUJARI, H.K. (1970) Problems of the Hill Tribes : North East Frontier, 1822-42, Vol. I. Gauhati, Lawyer's Book Stall : 202-207.

90. ———— (1978) Problems of the Hill Tribes of North East Frontier, 1843-72. Gauhati, Modern Book Depot (2nd edition), 165 p.

91. ———— (1978) Problems of the Hill Tribes : North East Frontier, Vol. 3, Inner Line to McMahon Line (1873-1962). Gauhati, United Publishers.

92. BARTHAKUR, I. K. (1975) A study on literacy in Arunachal Pradesh.
Aru. News, 4(7), Oct : 17-29 & 32.

93. ———— (1976) Tribal welfare through integrated agricultural technology.
Aru. News, 5(7), Oct : 11-26.

94. ———— (1977) Jhooming and its consequences.
Yojana (Delhi), Jan. 26 : 120-23.

95. ———— (1978) Economic Review of Arunachal Pradesh, 1977.
Aru. News, 7(4) : 6-19 ; 7(6) : 19-29 ; 7(7) : 27-46 ; 7(8) : 12-19.

96. BARTHAKUR, J.K. (1971) Census of India 1971, NEFA series no. 28, paper I of 1971 : Supplement, Provisional population Tables. Shillong, Directorate of Census, NEFA 33 p.

97. ———— (1971) Census of India 1971, series 24, Arunachal Pradesh, pt. IV-A Housing Report and Housing Subsidiary Tables; part IV-B Housing Tables. Delhi, Controller of Publications, 180 p.

98. ———— (1971) Census of India 1971, NEFA, series 28, paper no. 1, Provisional Population Total. Shillong, Director of Census, NEFA, 46 p.

99. ———— (1972) Census of India 1971, series no. 24 : Arunachal Pradesh, pt. II-A, General Population Tables. Delhi, Manager of Publications, 296 p.

100. ———— (1972) Census of India 1971, series 24, Arunachal Pradesh, District Census Handbook, Subansiri District. Shillong, Directorate of Census Operations, Arunachal Pradesh, 313 p.

101. ———— (1972) Census of India 1971, series 24, Arunachal Pradesh, District Census Handbook, Siang District. Shillong, District Census Operations, A.P., 301p.

102. ———— (1972) Census of India 1971, series 24, Arunachal Pradesh, District Census Handbook, Lohit District. Shillong, Directorate of Census Operations, A.P., 268 p.

103 ———— (1972) Census of India 1971, series 24, Arunachal Pradesh, District Census Handbook, Tirap District. Shillong, Directorate of Census Operations, Arunachal Pradesh, 255 p.

104. ———— (1972) Census of India 1971, series 24, Arunachal Pradesh, District Census Handbook : Kameng District. Shillong, Directorate of Census Operations, A.P., 243 p.

105. ———— (1972) Census of India 1971, series no. 24, Arunachal Pradesh, pt. III-A : Establishment Reports, pt. III-B : Establishments Tables. Delhi, Controller of Publications, 216 p.

106. ———— (1972) Census of India 1971, series-24, Arunachal Pradesh, pt. II-C(i) : Social and Cultural Tables. Delhi, Controller of Publications, 496 p.

107. ———— (1972) Census of India 1971, series no. 24, Arunachal Pradesh, part I: General Report. Delhi, Manager of Publications, 359 p.

108. ———— (1973) Census of India 1971, series 24, Arunachal Pradesh, pt. II-B: Economic Tables. Shillong, Directorate of Census Operations, A.P., 125 p.

109. ———— (1973) Census of India 1971, series 24, Arunachal Pradesh, a portrait of Population. Delhi, Controller of Publications, 128 p.

110. BARUAH, D. (1962) Life in NEFA. *The Assam Quarterly* (Gauhati), 2(2) April : 63-7.

111. BARUA, Hem (1958) Re-introduction of Assamese in NEFA. *The Outlook on NEFA. Comp.* by Parag Chaliha. Jorhat, Assam Sahitya Sabha : 37-41.

112. ———— (1960) Tribes and Races : North East Frontier. *United Asia*, 12 : 323-27.

113. ———— (1962) The Red River and the blue hills. Gauhati, Lawyers' Book Stall, 205 p. (3rd Edition).

114. BARUA, S. (1983) Indigenous health practices among Tangsas of Tirap District of Arunachal. *Report* submitted to Anth. Survey of India. (Unpublished)

115. BARUA, Subir Kumar (1976) The Khamtis and their religian. *Resarun*, 2(1), Jan : 1-12,

116. ———— (1977) Role of dormitories in the social and political l'fe of the Wanchos of Arunachal Pradesh. Proceedings of a seminar on "*Social and Political Institution*" organised by NEICSSR, Shillong.

117. ———— 1978) Baskets of Arunachal Pradesh: A study based on Museum collection. *Research in Arunachal* (Shillong) : 62-5.

118. ———— (1979) Role of dormitories in the social and political life of the Wanchos of Arunachal Pradesh. *Resarun*, 5(2), Aut & Winter : 5-9 (1979).

119. BARUA, S.N. (1966) Wild life in Tirap. *The Hornbill* (Shillong) : 22-8.

120. ———— (1977) Khomong and the Khamtis. *Aru. News*, 6(6). Oct : 9-11.

121. ———— (1978) Colony of Slaves : Khomong and the Khamtis. *Aru. News*, 7(4), Aug : 55-8.

122. BARUA, S.P. (1980) Problem of tuberculosis and its influence on Socio-Economic factor.
Aru. News, 9(3), June-July : 11-4.

123. BARUAH, Tapan Kumar M. (1960) The Idu Mishmis. Shillong, P. C. Dutta on behalf of the NEFA Adviser's Secretariat, 110 p.

124. ———— (1966) The Goddess Tamreswari.
The Hornbill (Shillong) : 44-54.

125. ———— (1985) Nocte love-songs. Shillong, Directorate of Research, Govt. of A.P.

126. ———— (1976) The effect of bried price on a Mishmi.
Resarun '75, Cum. Vol : 110-13.

127. ———— (1977) The Singphos and their religion.
Shillong, Research Dept., Directorate of Inf. & Pub, Relations, Govt. of A.P., 177 p.

128. ———— (Tr.) (1977) Lik-Pu - Can - Lan. Shillong, Research Dept., Directorate of Inf. & Pub. Relations, Govt. of A.P., 28 p.

129. ———— (1982) Wanchos love-songs. Shillong, Dir. of Res., Govt. of A.P.

130. BASAK, R. G. (1967) History of North East India. Calcutta, Sambodhi Publications, 432 p.

131. BASU, Pravash Chandra (1929) Head dress of the hill tribes of Assam.
Jour. Royal Asiatic Society of Bengal 25 (new series) : 103-14 (It has illustrations of the cane work of the Nagas, Miris, Mishmis and Abors).

132. BATT, Hage 1972) Zero : Yesterday, today and tomorrow.
Aru. News, 1(5), July : 35-7.

133. BAVEJA, J.D. (1961) Across the golden heights of Assam and NEFA. Calcutta, Modern Book Depot, 144p.

134. ———— (1982) New Horizons of North East. Gauhati, Western Book Depot. 152p.

135. BEAMES, J. (1867) Outlines of Indian Philology.
Calcutta. (Appedix gives Abor, Miri and Dafla numerals).

136. ——— (1868) Outline of Indian Philology with a map showing the distribution of Indian Languages. London, Trubner.

137. BEDFORD, J. (1826) The Brahmakund. Government Gazettee, 21st Sept. *India's North East Frontier...Edited by Verrier Elwin.* Bombay, Oxford University Press, 1959 : 8.

138. BEDI, Freda (1958) Women are born pioneers. *Social Welfare*, 5(4), July : 18.

139. BEIERWALTES, W.H. and RAMAN, G. (1957) Endemic goitre and criticism in Michigan and in the North Eastern Frontier Agency Area *Current Medical Practice*, 1(11) : 613-18.

140. BENTINCK, A. (1915) The Adi expedition : Geographical results. *Geographical Journal* (London), 41(2)

141. BERESFORD, G.W. (1881) Notes on the North Eastern Frontier of Assam. Shillong, (Reprinted in 1906).

142. ——— (1881) Notes on the North Eastern Frontier of Assam. *India's North East Frontier...Ed. by Vertier Elwin* Bombay, Oxford University Press, 1959 : 281-85, 342-45 and 352-54.

143. BETTS, Ursula (BOWER, Ursula Graham) (1940) The founding of Chingjaroi. *Folklore*, 51 : 211-13.

144. ——— (1948) The village duel in Apatani society. *Man in India*, 28(3), Sept : 163-69.

145. ——— (1949) The Daflas of the Subansiri area. *R. Cent. Asian Journal*, 36 : 145-54.

146. BEVERLEY, H. (Comp) (1872) Census of India 1871, Bengal : Report. Calcutta, Govt. Press (Abor : 199, Khamtis : 201).

147. ——— (Comp) (1883) Census of India 1881. Assam : Report. Calcutta, Govt. Press (Miri, Dapla, Abor).

148. BEZBARUAH, Prafulla : (1958) History Yells : The Hills and the plains of Assam are but one.
The Outlook on NEFA. Comp. by Parag Chaliha. Jorhat, Assam Sahitya Sabha : 101-105.

149. BHADRA, R.K. (974) Indian Tribes and their modernization.
Vanyajati, 22(2). April : 40-9.

150. ———— (1975) Indian tribes and their modernization.
North Eastern Research Bulletin (Dibrugarh), 6 (Summer) : 41-50.

151. BHAGABATI, Annada (1972) Aspects of economic change in a hill village of Arunachal.
Vivekananda Kendra Patrika 1(2), Aug : 240-49.

152. BHAGABATI, A.C. and KAR, R.K. (Ed) (1978) Cultural and Biological Adaptability of Man with Special Reference to North East India.
Bull. Dibrugarh Uni., Dept. of Anth. 1977, Vol. 6.

153. BHAGAWATI, D.P (1983) Research Publications 1956-1981 : A Bibliography of Published Materials of the Research Department Govt. of A.P. Shillong, Directorate of Research, Govt. of A.P., 50 p

154. BHANDARI, J S. (1961) Miri dances.
Assam Quarterly (Gauhati), 1(4), Oct. : 38-40.

155. ———— (1962) Family organization of the Mishing (Miri) of Assam.
Bulletin of the Dept. of Tribal Culture and Folklore Research, Gauhati University, Assam : 46-56.

156. ———— (1968) Land and Social Structure : An economic study of a Mishing village.
Eastern Anthropologist (Lucknow), 21(1), Jan-April : 21-36.

157. ———— (1972) Land and Social Structure : An economic study of a Mishing village.
Tribe, Caste and Peasantry. Ed. by K.S. Mathur and B.S. Agarwal. Lucknow, Ethnographic Folk Culture Society : 8-20.

158. ———— (1973) Changing emphasis in the religious beliefs : Study in Ideological conflict among the Mishing. *Studies in Social Change*. Ed. by K.S. Mathur. Lucknow, Ethnographic & Folk Culture Society.

159. BHARGAV, G.S. (1964) The battle of NEFA : The undeclared war. Bombay, Allied Publishers, 187 p.

160. BHATT, Sudhakar (1975) The challenge of the North East. Bombay, Popular Prakashan, 146 p.

161. BHATTACHARYYA, A.K. (1977) Expanding Health care in Arunachal Pradesh. *Aru. News*, 6(4), Aug : 22-4.

162. ———— (1978) Health and family welfare : Basic tents. *Aru. News*, 7(4), Aug : 20-5.

163. BHATTACHARYYA, Birendra Kumar (1958) The Language of NEFA and national unity. *The Outlook on NEFA*. Comp. by Parag Chaliha. Jorhat, Assam Sahitya Sabha : 32-6.

164. BHATTACHARJEE, Jayanta Bhusan (*Ed*) (1981) Proceedings of the North East India History Association. Shillong, North East India History Association, Dept. of History, NEHU, 202 p.

165. BHATTACHARYA, Pramod Chandra (*Ed*) (1962) Asamar Janajati (in Assamese). Jorhat, Assam Sahitya Sabha, 334 p.

166. BHATTACHARJEE, Padma Nath (1958) Blood Group investigations in the Abor tribe. *Bulletin of the Dept. of Anth.* (Anth. Survey of India, Calcutta), 3(1), January (1954) : 51-4.

167. BHATTACHARJEE, P.N. (1955) Dermatoglyphics of the Abor people in Assam. *The Anthropologist*, 2(2), Aug : 22-35.

168. ———— (1957) A study on ABO, MN Blood Groups, and the ABH Secretion in the Nocte of NEFA. *Bull. Dept. of Anth.* (Anth. Survey of India), 6(1) : 77-80.

169. BHATTACHARJEE, Punyabrata (1979) Flora of Ziro. *Aru. News*, 8(4) : 6-7.

170. BHATTACHARJEE, Tarun (1977) The Adis origin and migration.
Aru. News, 5(9) : Jan-Feb : 34-5 & 45.

171. BHATTACHARYA, T.K. (1965) Myths of the Shimongs of Upper Siang.
Shillong, DIPR, NEFA, 82 p.

172. ——— (1966) Visit to Doni Lipik.
The Hornbill (Shillong) : 46-52.

173. ——— (c. 1971) The Adis : Origin and migration.
Pines, 1 (II), Arunachal number : 20-3.

174. ——— (1971) The folk of the Tangams.
Pines, 1(1), March : 27-33.

175. ——— (1975) The Adis, their origin and migration.
Resarun, 1(2), April : 1-6 and *Reasrun* 75, (Cum. Vol. 1976) : 39-42.

176 ——— (1975) The Tangams of Northern Siang.
Shillong, Res. Dept., DIPR, Govt. of A.P., 96 p.

177. ——— (1981) The Idus of Mathun and Dri Valley.
Shillong, Directorate of Research, Govt. of A P.

178. ——— (1982) Concept of Doni Polo, an assessment.
Resarun, 8(1), Spring-Summer : 14-5.

179. BHAUMIK, H. (1979) Arunachal is awaking.
Aru. News, 8(1) : 13.

180. BHOWMIK, D.C., SEN, Sipra and MUKHERJEE, S.K. (*Comp*) (1979) Silver Jubilee Celebration, North East India, Shillong, 1953-1978 : Anthropological Literature of North East India (Researches conducted by Anthropological Survey of India). Shillong, Anth. S.I. (Mimeographed).

181. BHOWMIK, D.C. and PAL, Anadi (1984) Indigenous health practices among the Nocte of Arunachal Pradesh. *Human Science* (Anth. Survey of India, Calcutta), 33(1), March : 35-53.

182. BHUYAN, S.K. (c. 1933) Tungkhungia Buranji (in Assamese).
Gauhati, Dept. of Historical & Antiquarian Studies in Assam, 294 p.

183. ————(1949) Early British Relations with Assam. Gauhati, Dept. of His. & Anti. Stu. in Assam, 57 p.
184. ————(1949) Anglo-Assamese Relations 1771-1826. Gauhati, Dept. of His. & Anti. Stu. in Assam, 636 p.
185. ————(1965) Studies in the history of Assam. Gauhati, Lakheswari Bhuyan, 270 p
186. ————(1983) A History of Assam 1681-1826 A.D. (Tungkhungia Buranji). New Delhi, D. K. F. Trust (Reprinted).
187. BILLOREY R.K. (1976) An interesting sculpture from Malinithan.
Resarun '75, Cum. Vol. : 123-25.
188. ————(1975) Archaeological ruins.
The Statesman, Sunday, Nov. 29.
189. ———— (1976) Iconographic study of some sculptures from Malinithan.
Resarun, 2(3), July : 23-6.
190. ————(1977) Iconographic study of some Malinithan sculptures.
Research in Arunachal Pradesh : 8-10.
191. ————(1981) Frontier trade, 1914-1962 : Case studies of two tribes of North East India.
Proceedings of the North East India Hisiory Association. Ed. by Jayanta Bhusan Bhattacharjee.
Shillong, N.E.I. History Association, Dept. of History, NEHU : 193-202.
192. ————(1984) The Memba of Arunachal : A brief note on their migration.
The Tribes of North East India. Ed. by S. Karotemprel. Calcutta, Firma KLM Pvt. Ltd : 58-61.
193. BISWAS, J. (1966) Jara, a draft village in NEFA. New Delhi, Social Study Unit, Registrar General of India, 57 p.
194. BISWAS, Saswati (1981) Land and economic development in Arunachal Pradesh.
(Proceedings of a seminar on "*Land Relations*" organised by NEICSSR, Shillong).

Land and Land Relations in the Hills of North East India. Ed by B. B. Dutta. Delhi, Peoples Pub. House (in Press)

195. BLISS, C. (1914) Report on the Debong Survey and Exploration Mission, 1912-13. Shillong.
196. BOMJEN, Ligin (1977) Traditional demogratic system of administration.
Aru. News, 6(1), April : 7-11.
197. BOR, E. (1955) Adventures of a Botanist's wife. London.
198. BOR, N.L. (1936) The Daflas and their oaths.
Jour. Royal Asiatic Society of Bengal (Letter), 2 (Third series) : 27-39.
199. ————(1938) Yano Dafla Grammar and vocabulary.
JRASB, 4 (Third series) : 217-81.
200. BORA, D.K. (1984) Itafort and the Chutias.
Aru. News, 12(5), Aug-Sept : 26-8.
201. BORA, D.P. (1967) Is there a wild man.
The Hornbill (Shillong) : 1-3.
202. BORAH, Hemalata (1858) A peep into the Religious songs and dances of the NEFA plople.
The Outlook on NEFA. Comp. by Parag Chaliha.
Jorhat, Assam Sahitya Sabha : 91-4.
203. ————(1962) Dafla (in Assamese).
Asamar Janajati. Ed. by Pramod Chandra Bhattacharya.
Jorhat, Assam Sahitya Sabha : 79-86.
204. BORANG, Katon (1981) Traditional and customary laws of Adis : How to preserve them.
Aru. News, 10(3), April-May : 25-8.
205. BORDOLOI, M.N. (1964) Land of the Hornbill and the Myna. Shillong, 58 p.
206. ————(1968) Our festivals.
Shillong, 59 p.
207. BORGOHAIN, B.K. (1975) Folk tales of Arunachal Pradesh and Meghalaya New Delhi, Sterling Publications.
208. BORGOHAIN, Hiren (1979) Technology and material culture of the Adis with special reference to their Bamboo and cane culture.
Resarun, 5(2), Aut-Winter : 15-21.

209. ———— (1980) A folk tale of Siang.
Aru. News, 9(6), Oct-Nov : 20-21.

210. ———— (1980) Spinning and weaving among the Gallongs.
Resarun, 6(1), Spring-Summer : 42-8.

211. ———— (1980) Land ownership and its inheritance among the Adis.
Resarun, 6(1), Aut-Win.

212. ———— 1981) Socio-religious prohibition among the Adis.
Resarun, 7(1-2) : 46-9.

213. ———— (1982) An investigation on the finger patterns of the Turungs.
Jour. NEICSSR (Shillong), 6(1), April : 29-34.

214. BORGOHAIN, H. (1982) Bari : An Abang of the Minyong.
Resarun, 8(1), Spring-Summer : 33-4.

215. ————(1982) Changes and development in the Socio-economic life of the Adis of West Siang District.
Resarun, 8(2), Aut-Win : 36-40.

216. ———— (1983) Development of Industries and handicrafts in Arunachal Pradesh with reference to the Adis of Siang District.
Resarun, 9(2), Aut-Win : 41-7.

217. ———— (1984) The story of a dog and pig : A Gallong folktale of Arunachal Pradesh.
Folklore Calcutta), 25(2), February : 41-41.

218. BORGOHAIN, Manik Chandra. The Nebula of the North East Frontier. (in Assamese).

219. BORO, A (1978) Miju Dictionary.
Shillong, Res. Dept., Directorate of Inf. & Pub. Relations, 210 p.

220. BORPARDIKAR, B.P. (1972) Prehistoric Investigation : Daphabum Scientific Survey Expedition (NEFA). Nagpur University, Archaeological Congress and Seminar Paper : 1-8.

221. BORTHAKUR, M (*Ed.*) (1968) Assam, an outline : Souvenir. Gauhati, Gauhati University, Dept. of Geography: 40-4.

222. BOSE, M.L. (1971) North east frontier of British India. *North Eastern Research Bulletin* (Dibrugarh), 2(Summer) 60-7.

223. ——— (1972) Impact of British administration on the North East Frontier.
North Eastern Research Bulletin, 1(Summer) 65-72.

224. ——— (1978) Some prospects of progress in Arunachal Pradesh.
Social and Economic Profile of North East India. Ed. by B. Datta Ray. Delhi, B.R. Pub : 303-307.

225. ——— (1979) British Policy in the North East Frontier Agency. New Delhi, Concept Pub. Company, 236 p.

226. ——— (1979) Historical and constitutional documents of North Eastern India 1824-1973.
Delhi, Concept Publishing Company, 378 p.

227. BOSE, N.K. (1962) Book Review : The Idu Mishmis by T.K.M Baruah, 1960, Cultural Research Officer, NEFA Secretariat, Shillong.
Man in India, 42(2),April-June : 170-71.

228. ——— (1963) Present NEFA policy short sighted, (Report of his talk at Congress Bhawan, Gauhati on Nov. 26, 1963).
The Assam Tribune (Gauhati), November 27 : 1 & 5.

229. ———(1967) National Seminar on Hill People, (It is a concluding address on "Hill People of Assam, Manipur, Tripura, Nagaland and NEFA", 4th Dec. 1966).
Man in India, 47(1) : 1-7.

230. ——— (1971) Tribal life in India. New Delhi, National Book Trust, 84 p.

231. ——— (1972) Some Indian Tribes. New Delhi, National Book Trust : 68-82.

232. BOSE, Saradendu, GHATAK, S. and BERA, R.K. (1982) Shifting cultivation in India.
Economics of the Tribes and their transformation. Ed. by K.S. Singh. New Delhi, Concept Pub. : 216-25.

233. BOWER, Ursula Graham (1953) The Hidden Land. London, John Murray, 244 p.

234. BRIGHT. J.S. (1983) Guide to North East : The unknown land of enchantment. New Delhi, Parichay Overseas : 56-8

235. BRONSON, M. (1839) Missionary Magazine of the Baptist, (General Convention for Foreign Mission, Boston).
India's North East Frontier. Ed. by Verrier Elwin. Bombay, O.U.P., 1959 : 31-2.

236. BROWN, J. Coggin (1913-16) The Abors and Galongs : Notes on certain tribes of the Indo-Tibetan Frontier.
Memoir of the Asiatic Society of Bengal (Calcutta), 5, Extra no. Pt. III : 93-113.

237. BROWN, N. (1837) Comparison of Indo-Chinese Languages.
JASB, 6 : 1023-36 (It has vocabularies of Aka, Abor, Mishmi and Singpho).

238. BURAGOHAIN, Satyendra Nath (1972) Mid digital hair among the two tribes of the Kameng District, Arunachal Pradesh.
Bulletin : Dept. of Anth. (Gauhati Uni.), 1, December : 38-44.

239. BURKILL, I.H. (1924) The Botany of the Abor expedition.
R.B.S.I., 10(1).

240. BURMAN, Shavitri G. (1963) NEFA : The Land and its People.
Indian Quarterly (New Delhi), 19(4), Oct-Dec : 344-69.

241. ———— (1963) NEFA : its land and its people.
India Cronicle, 19(4), Oct-Dec : 12.

242. ———— (1963) NEFA : The Land and its People.
Indian Quarterly, 19(4) : 26.

243. BURRARD, S.G. (1914) Records on the Survey of India exploration on the North East Frontier of India during 1911, 12, 13. Calcutta.

244. BURTT, B.L. (1965) Studies in the Gesneriaceae of the old world XXVI: A contribution to the styudy of Chirita. *Kew Bulletin*, 26 : 265-266.

245. BUTLER, John (1847) A sketch of Assam. *India's North East Froniier*...Ed. by Verrier Elwin. Bombay, O.U.P. (1959) : 224-26, 325-31, 362-63, 399-404.

246. ——— (1847) A sketch of Assam, with some account of the hill tribes, by an officer. London, Smith Elder & Co., 220 p.

247. ——— (1855) Travels and adventures in the province of Assam. London, Smith Elder & Co., 268 p.

248. CAMPBELL, George List of words and phrases showing languages of the hills surrounding Assam and Cachar. *Specimens of languages* by George Campbell. London : 220-35.

249. ———(1874) Specimens of the languages of India including those of the Aboriginal Tribes of Bengal, the Central Provinces and the Eastern Frontier. London : 238-51.

250. CENSUS (1954) Assam, Manipur, Tripura 1951, Part I-A, Vol. XII, Report.

251. CHAKMA, U. (1974) The religious beliefs of the Minyongs. *North Eastern Affairs* (Shillong), 3 (2-3), July-Dec : 11-5.

252. ——— (1975) The beliefs and rites of Galongs for curing the sick. *North Eastern Affairs*, 3(4), Jan-March : 15-6.

253. CHAKRAVORTY, B.C. (1983) Progress of education in North Eartern Region. *Social Research : Jour. of Institute of Social Research* (Shillong), 3(2), April-June : 14-23.

254. CHAKRAVARTY, Kanti (1978) Tonga festival of the Monpas. *Aru. News*, 7(1), Feb-March : 13-6.

255. CHAKRAVARTY, L.N. (n.d.) Prasuram Kundu. Shillong, Directorate of Research, Govt. of A.P.

256. ————(1958) Danegeld in NEFA.
Bulletin of the Research Dept., NEFA (Shillong), 1(1), June : 36-63.

257. ————(1967) Excavation in NEFA.
NEFA Information (Shillong), 2(4), Nov : 1-6.

258. ————(1968) Glimpses of early history of NEFA.
NEFA Information, Aug : 16-20; Sept : 19-23; Nov : 20-6; Dec : 8-13.

259. ————(1969) A short note on 'Posa'.
The Hornbill : 26-31.

260. ————(1970) Glimpses of Early History of NEFA.
NEFA Information, 4(8), March : 8-11.

261. ————(1971) Glory that was Malinithan.
NEFA Information, April.

262. ————(1972) Malinithan.
Aru. News, 1(4), May : 9-17.

263. ————(1973) Glimpses of the early history of Arunachal Pradesh. Shillong, A.P. Administration, 143 p.

264. ————(1975) Malinithan.
Resarun, 1, Jan : 1-11 and *Rerarun* 75 (Cum. Vol. 1976): 1-7.

265. ————(1976) Evolution of the administrative set up of Arunachal.
Aru. News, 5(5), Sept : 1-6.

266. ————(1976) Evolution of the administrative set up in Arunachal Pradesh.
Resarun, 2(3), July : 2-7 and *Resarun* 75 Cum. (Vol. : 91-9. and *Aru. News*, 5(5), Independence Day Number : 1-6.

267. ————(n.d.) Malinithan.
Shillong, Direc. of Res, Govt. of A.P.

268. ————(1976) Historical Evolution of Arunachal Pradesh.
Resarun, 2(2), April : 1-12 and *Resarun* 75, Cum. Vol. : 43-51.

269. ————(1977) A short note on Posa.
Resarun, 3(3), July 1-10.

270. ——— (1978) Early History of Lohit District.
Resarun, 4(1), Jan-March : 1-6.

271. ——— (1979) Glimpses of early history of Arunachal Pradesh. Shillong, Dir. of Res., Govt. of A.P.

272. CHAKRAVARTY, S.R. (1982) The changing food habit in Pasighat area : A brief note.
Resarun, 8(1), Spring-Summer : 28-30.

273. CHAKRAVORTY, B.C. (1964) British relations with the Hill Tribes of Assam since 1858.
Calcutta, Firma K.L. Mukhopadhyay : 38-46, 142-48, 157-60.

274. CHALIHA, Parag (*Comp.*) (1958) The Outlook on NEFA. Jorhat, Assam Sahitya Sabha, 134 p.

275. CHANA, S.S. (1969) Farm forestry in Apatani village.
NEFA Information, 3(9), April : 10-3.

276. CHANDA, Asok (1969) NEFA perspective : Need for an imaginative policy.
The Times of India (New Delhi), June 9 : 3.

277. CHANDA, Satish (1973) Problems of University Education in North East India.
North Eastern Research Bulletin (Dibrugarh), IV (Summer) 1-6.

278. CHANDOLA, Harish (1967) Troubled Frontier.
A Common Perspective for North East India Ed. by Rathin Mitra and B. Das Gupta. Calcutta, Pannalal Das Gupta : 153-59.

279. CHARI, M.V.,BARUA, B.D. and DAS, D.(1953) Report on the investigation of the 'Unknown Fever' in Kimin, Subansiri area. Shillong.

280. CHARI, R.B. (1975) Census of India 1971, series I, India, paper I of 1975 : Scheduled Castes and Scheduled Tribes (Table C-VIII Parts A & B).
Delhi, Manager of Publications, 169p.

281. CHATER, A.F. (1912) Abor suspension bridges.
Royal Engineers Journal, 16 : 217-18.

282. CHATTERJEE, D. (1947) A new genus of Cucurbitaceae.
Kew Bulletin, 1. 119.

283. ———— (1948) New plants from India and Burma. *Kew Bulletin*, 2 : 57-65.

284. CHATTERJEE, Subid (1976) Representation of Lakshmi among the females sculptures at Malinithan. *Resarun* '75, Cum. Vol : 95-8.

285. ———— (1977) Fragmentary epigraphs on brick tiles from Bhismoknagar. *Research in Arunachal* : 5-7.

286. ———— (1977) Private records at Mechukha. *Aru. News*, 8(5), Aug : 27-30.

287. CHATTERJEE, S. (1977) A new inscribed cannon of the time of Gadadharasimha. *Resarun*, 3 (2), April : 29-32.

288. ———— (1978) Inscription in Arunachal Pradesh. *Resarun*, 4 (1), Jan-March : 44-7.

289. ————(n.d.) Published References on Archaeological sites in Arunachal Pradesh. Shillong, Research Dept., Govt. of A.P.

290. CHATTERJEE, Suniti Kumar. (1950 Kirata-Jana-Krti, the Indo-Mongoloids : Their contribution to the History and Culture of India. *Jour., Royal Asiatic Society of Bengal* (Calcutta), 16 (2) : 1-94.

291. ———— (1953) The language of the Adivasis. *March of India* (Delhi), 6(2), Nov-Dec : 14-6.

292. CHATTERJEE, S.K. (1969) Wild life and its conservation in NEFA. *The Indian Forester* (Dehradun), 95(2), Nov : 771-75.

293. ———— (1973) Manpower and occupational pattern. *Aru. News*, 2(8), Nov : 6-9.

294. ———— (1975) Position of women in Subansiri. *Aru. News*, 4(8) Nov : 21-4.

295. ———— (1978) Arunachal Pradesh Forest Corporation limited. *Aru. News*, 7(4), Aug : 70-1.

296. ———— (1981) Economic development of Arunachal Pradesh. *Aru. News*, 10(5), July : 25-35.

297. CHOUDHURY, D.P. (1970) British Policy on the North East Frontier of India 1865-1914. London University Dissertation (unpublished).

298. CHIB, Sukhdev Singh (1977) *This Beautiful India : Union Territories.*

New Delhi, Light & Life Publications : 26-42.

299. ———— (1984) Caste, Tribes and Culture of India : North Eastern India, 8 Vols. Delhi.

300. CHOUBE, S.K. (1969) Origin and development of the Administration of NEFA.
Proceedings of a Seminar on Political Science, Shillong

301. ———— (1972) From a Frontier to a Territory.
North Estern Affairs (Shillong), April-June : 17-9 *and* 52.

302. ———— (1973) Hill Politics in North East India.
Bombay, Orient Longman, 258p.

303. ———— (1981) Administrative set up of NEFA.
Mainstream, July 6 : 25-6A.

304. ———— (1984) Electoral Politics in North East India.
Bombay, Orient Longman.

305. CHOUDHURY, Abhijit (1983) Planning and people's participation in rural development : Pangin Block of East Siang in retrospect (1978-80).
Planning in North East India : Retrospective and Perspective. Ed. by K. Alam. New Delhi, Omsons (in Press).

306. CHOUDHURY, A.S. (1972) Finger and palm prints of the Duania. Dissertation submitted for the Degree of M.Sc. in 1972, Gauhati University. Gau. Uni., Anth. Dept. (unpub. disser.)

307. CHOUDHURY, B. (1978) Colour Blindness among Three Tribes of Lohit District, Arunachal.
Cultural and Biological Adaptability of Man with Special Reference to North East India. Ed. by A C. Bhagabati *and* R.K. Kar.
(It is *Bull. Dibrugarh Uni., Dept., of Anth.*, 6, 1977 : 204-80).

308. CHOUDHURY, B.C. *and* BANERJEE, S.K. (1978) A note on the incident of middle Phalangeal hair (MPH) among the Wanchos and Noctes of Arunachal Pradesh.
Cultural and Biological Adoptability of Man with Special Reference to North East India. Ed. by A. C. Bhagabati *and* R.K. Kar.
(It is *Bull. Dibrugarh Uni. Dept. of Anth.* 6, 1977 : 209-14).

309. CHOUDHURY, J.N., CHOUDHURY, B. *and* DAS, P.B. (1976) Arunachal Panorama : Frequencies of colour blindness in some population of Arunachal Pradesh.
Jour. Uni. of Gauhati, 13-25(2), Science: 1-7.

310. CHOUDHURY, J.N. (1982) Basic Pattern in myth Making : Myths of Arunachal tribes.
Proceedings of a seminer on "Folklore in North East India" organised by NEICSSR, Shillong.
Folklore in North East India. Ed. by Soumen Sen. New Delhi, Omsons (In Press).

311. CHOUDHURY, R. (1970) Changing pattern of NEFA leadership. *Mainstream*, May 30 : 11 & 32.

312. ———— (1972) Arunachal in the setting of Indian culture.
Jour. Assam Research Society, 20 : 49-55.

313. CHOUDHURY, Rabjit C. (1971) A note on the Sadiya fair.
Pines, 1 (III), Arunachal Number : 76-81.

314. CHOUDHURY, Sibadas (*Comp*): 1954-55 : A Bibliography on the published material on the people of the North Eastern Frontier of India.
Quarterly Journal of Mythic Society, 45 : 171-86 *and* 258-59.

315. ———— (Comp) (1955-56) A Bibliography of the Published material of the people of the North Eastern Frontier of India.
Quarterly Journal of the Mythic Society, 46 : 32-42 *and* 119-26.

316. ———— (*Comp*) (1956-57) A Bibliography of the Published material of the People of the North Eastern Frontier of India.
Quarterly Journal of the Mythic Society, 47 : 47-51.

317. CHOUDHURY, A.K. (1960) A short note on Shorea Assamica (Mekai).
The Indian Forester (Dehradun), April : 86-94.

318. ———— (1972) Forests and Agriculture.
The Indian Forester (Dehradun), 98(3), March : 178-86.

319. CHOUDHURY, J.N. (1968) Indo-Mongoloid and Indo-Aryan Cultural Amalgam.
NEFA Information, 3(5), Dec : 2-7.

320. ———— (1969) Genesis of Tribal Administration and India's North Eastern Frontier. *The Hornbill* : 2-7.

321. ———— (1969) The Hill Miri. Shillong, Res. Dept., Govt. of A.P.

322. ————(1970) Tantric traditions in North East India.
NEFA Information, 5(3), Dec : 11-4.

323. ———— (1970) The Hill Miris of Subansiri. Shillong Res. Deptt., Dir. of Inf. & Pub. Relations, Govt. of NEFA, 66p.

324. ———— (1971) The conception of the super-natural among the Adis.
Pines, 1(I), March : 51-6.

325. ———— (1971) A comparative study of Adi religion. Shillong, T.P. Khound, Directorate of Inf. & Pub. Relations, A.P. 130p. (Reprinted in 1977).

326. ———— (1973) Arunachal Panorama. Shillong, Smt. J. Choudhury, Chapala Book Stall, 290 p. (Reprinted in 1982).

327. ———— (1974) 'Mon' in legend and history.
Aru. News, 3(5), July : 1-5.

328. ———— (1974) A pilgrimage to Tawang.
Aru News, 3(3), May : 6-10.

329. ———— (1975) The children of the Sun and Moon, another version.
Aru. News, 4(5), July : 64-5.

330. ——— (1975) Evidence of caste like features in some Arunachal tribes.
Resarun, 1(2), April : 1-25 *and Resarun '75*, (Cum. Vol. 1976) : 43-56.

331. ——— (1983) Arunachal Pradesh : From frontier tracts to Union Territory. Shillong, Chapala Book Stall.

332. CHOUDHURY, J. N. and CHOUDHURY, R. (1971) Subansiri upajati (in Bengali). Calcutta, 107p.

333. CHOUDHURY, P.C. (1959) The History of Civilization of the people of Assam to the Twelfth century A.D. Gauhati, Dept. of Historical & Antiquarian Studies in Assam : 36, 92-3, 103, 382.

334. CHOUDHURY, Uma (1953) The role of women among the Padam tribe.
March of India (Delhi), 6(2), Nov-Dec : 20-3.

335. CLARKSON, James D. (1963) India's North East Frontier Agency. Chicago, University of Chicago, (unpublished Dissertation).

336. COOPER, R.E. (1933) Bhutan : Thailed People "Daktas" People with a Tail in the East Bhutanese Himalaya. *Man* (London), 33(131). [It has a description on the Monpas round Tawang who carry a felt sitting-pad attached to their backs].

337. COOPER, T.T. (1873) New routes for Commerce : The Mishmee Hills, an account of a journey made in an attempt to penetrate Thibet from Assam to open new routes for commerce. London, Henry S. King & Co., 270p.

338. ——— (1873) Mishmi customs & house.
(New Routes for Commerce : The Mishmee Hills).
India's North East Frontier... Ed. by Verrier Elwin.
Bombay, O.U.P. (1959) : 339-41, 370-72.

339. CROOKE, W. (1908) Abor, Abor Miri.
Hasting's Encyclopaedia of Religion & Ethics, Vol. I,
Edinburg, T.T. Clark : 33.

340. CROWE, H.M. (1890) Mr. Crowe's account of a journey to Apa Tanang country. Shillong.

341. ———— (1890) Mr. Crowe's account of a journey to Apa Tanang country.
India's North East Frontier Ed. by Verrier Elwin. Bombay, O.U.P. (1959) : 192-98.

342. CULTURAL Section (n. d.) Arts and Crafts of NEFA. (Brochure). Shillong, Research Section (Cultural), Govt. of NEFA.

343. CUMMING, R.C.R. (Comp.) (1923) Notes on certain frontier tribes.
Census of India 1921, Assam, Vol. 3, pt. I, Report, Appendix-B. Shillong, Govt. Press : 13-14 (Abor, Miri).

344. CUST, R.N. (1879) A sketch of the Modern languages of the East Indies. London : 95-102.

345. DAI, Kado (1981) Solung festival.
Aru. News, 10(2), Feb-March : 34-5.

346. DAI, Lummer (1977) Donyi-Poloism : A scientific religion.
Aru. News, 6(4), Aug : 56-8.

347. DALTON, E.T. (1845) On the Miris and Abors of Assam (in a letter to Maj. Jenkins).
Jour. Asiatic Soc. of Beng. (New Series), 14,pt. I :426-30.

348. ———— (1845) On the Miris and Abors of Assam.
India's North East Frontier...Ed. by Verrier Elwin. Bombay, O.U.P. (1959) : 136-59.

349. ———— (1845) Report by Lt. E.J.T. Dalton, Junior Assistant Commissioner of Assam, of his visit to the hills in the neighbourhood of the Sooubanshiri River.
Jr. Asiatic Soc. of Bengal (New Series), 14, Pt. I : 150-267.

350. ———— (1855) Progress in a late visit to a clan of Abors on the Dihong River.
(Selection from the Records of the Bengal Govt. No. 23 : 151-69).
India's North East Frontier...Ed. by Verrier Elwin. Bombay, O.U.P. (1959) : 249-69.

351. ———— (1856) A visit to Membu...An Abor village near the Dihong River.
Bengal Judicial proceedings, January 3 and Selection from the Records of the Bengal Govt. XXIII.

352. ———— (1960) Descriptive Ethnology of Bengal.
Calcutta, Firma K.L. Mukhopadhyay (Reprinted in 1960 : 1st Published in 1872), Dophlas : 40-2, Khampti : 9-13, Aka/Hrusso : 42-4.

353. ———— (1872) Descriptive Ethnology of Bengal.
*India's North East Frontier...*Ed. by Verrier Elwin.
Bombay, O.U.P. (1959) : 41-2, 65-7, 179-80, 331-39, 363-69, 404-08.

354. DAPORIJO, Larbin Nachi (1980) Tagin mythology and celebration of Si-Donyi festival.
Aru. News, 9(1), Feb-March : 19-21.

355. DAS, Achintya (1984) Weight and measures amongst some Arunachal tribes.
The Tribes of North East India. Ed. by S. Karotemprel.
Calcutta, Firma K.L.M. Pvt. Ltd : 429-35.

356. DAS, Arun Kumar (1980) A note of finger prints of the Adis of Arunachal Pradesh.
Bull. Dept. of Anth. : Dibrugarh Uni. 9 :190-96.

357. DAS, Ashit Kumar (c. 1971) Fish in Arunachal.
Pines, 1(III), Arunachal Number : 24-9.

358. DAS, A.K. (1965) NEFA Textiles.
Assam Tribune (Gauhati), Aug. 22 (Magazine Section).

359. ———— (1969) NEFA Textile.
Shillong Sahitya Kavan Journal, Shillong.

360. ———— (c. 1971) Indigenous transport system in Arunachal Praesh.
Pines, 1(III), Arunachal Number : 8-12.

361. ———— (1972) Anthropological museums of Arunachal.
Aru. News, 1(9), Nov : 18-20.

362. ———— (1973) Archaeological sites and Historical monuments of Arunachal.
Aru. News, 2(2), May : 11-7.

363. ———— (1973) The Art forms of Arunachal. *Aru. News*, 2(8), Nov : 1-5.

364. ————(1973) A brief study of basketry in Arunachal. *Aru. News*, 1(12), Feb : 18-21.

365. ———— (1974) Indigenous textile patterns of Lower Siang. *North Eastern Affairs* (Shillong), 2(4), Jan-March : 37-41.

366. ———— (197.) Style and symbolism in the Art of Arunachal. *Resarun*, 1, Jan : 16-22.

367. ———— (1976) Women Artists of Arunachal. *Resarun* '75, Cum. Vol : 86-91.

368. ———— (1976) Two rare ornaments from Lower Siang. *Resarun* '75, Cum. Vol : 11-15.

369. ———— (1976) Revival of traditional art through functional change, a new approach for Arunachal. *Research Arunachal* : 58-61.

370. ———— (1976) Revival of traditional art through functional change : A new approach for Arunachal. *Jour. Indian Anth. Society* (Calcutta), 11(2), May : 183 (Abstract).

371. ———— (1976) Prospect of exchange of cultural materials from North Eastern India. *Resarun*, 2(2),April : 1-6.

372. ———— (1977) Prospect of exchange of cultural materials from North Eastern India. *Research in Arunachal* : 34-41.

373. ———— (1979) Tribal Art and Craft. Delhi, Agam Kala Prakashan, 190 p.

374. ———— (1982) Tribal Arts and Crafts of North East India. *Fabric of our culture*. New Delhi, Ministry of Education.

375. DAS, A.R. *and* PATHAK, R.D. (1978) Linguistic traits of some Arunachal languages. (1978). Submitted to the Central Institute of Hindi, Shillong (Unpublished).

376. DAS, A.R. *and* PAL, Surendra (1982) Folk songs of Arunachal Pradesh.
Proceedings of a Seminar on "*Folklore*" of NEICSSR, Shillong.
Folklore in North East India. Ed. by Soumen Sen. New Delhi, Omsons (In Press).

377. DAS, B.M. (1984) Some aspects of physical anthropology of the tribes of Northeast India.
The Tribes of North East India. Ed. by S. Karotemprel. Calcutta, Firma KLM. Pvt. Ltd. : 39-57.

378. DAS, B M. and BHAGABATI, A.C. (1962) Investigations of the finger prints of the Khamyang.
Jour. Uni. of Gauhati, 13(2) Science : 75-8.

379. ———— (1963) Somatometic characters of the Khamyang.
Jour. Uni. of Gauhati, 14(2), Science : 49-54.

380. ———— (1964) Investigation on the palm prints of the Khamyang.
Jour. Uni. of Gauhati, 15(2), Science : 80-87.

381. DAS, Bhuban M. *and* DAS, Renuka (1972) A note on the ridge counts of finger patterns of the Khamyang : A Mongoloid population of Assam.
Bull. Dept. of Anth. : Dibrugarh University, 1 : 50-3.

382. DAS, Jogesh (1972) Folklore of Assam. New Delhi National Book Trust, 142 p.

383. DAS, M.M. (1975) Ethnography of the Apatani Society of Arunachal Pradesh.
Report submitted to Anth. Sur. of India (Unpublished).

384. ———— (1975) Ethnography of the Hill Miri Society of Arunachal Pradesh
Report submitted to Anth. Sur. of India (Unpublished).

385. ———— (1975) Ethnography of the Nisi Society of Arunachal Pradesh.
Report submitted to Anth. Sur. of India (Unpublished).

386. ———— (1984) Hill Miri.
Tribal Education in India (*in retrospect*). Ed. by Biman K. Das Gupta *and* Ajit K. Danda. Calcutta, Anth. Sur. of India : 10-1.

387. DAS, N.K. (1947) Agricultural Economy of the Apatanis.
Indian Farming, 8 : 294-98.

388. DAS, Nagendra Narayan (1941) Sword of the East. Shillong. 10 p.

389. DAS, Priya Bala *and* BURAGOHAIN, Satyendra (1972) A study of some genetic traits in two tribes of Arunachal Pradesh.
Bull. Dept of Anth. : Gauhati Uni, 1, December : 28-37.

390. DAS, P.B. *and* CHOUDHURY, B. (1975) Hand clasping, arm folding, ear lobe attachment and colour blindness of the Gallong of Arunachal.
Bull. Dept. of Anth. : Gauhati Uni. 4 : 65-70.

391. DAS, P.B. CHOUDHURY, B. *and* DUARAH, D.K. (1977) A study of hand clasping arm folding and tongue rolling among the Nocte, Wancho and Tangsa of Tirap, Arunachal Pradesh.
Bull. Dept. of Anth. : Gauhati Uni. 5.

392. DAS, P.K. (1979) Mineral resources and possibilities of economic development of Arunachal Pradesh.
Aru. News, 8(2) : 4-6.

393. ——— (1981) Mineral resources of Arunachal Pradesh.
Himalaya : Man and Nature, 5(1), June.

394. DAS, T.C. (1953) Land Tenure among the tribal populations of Assam.
Vanyajati (Delhi), 1(1) : 12-9.

395. ——— (1953) Social organisation of the tribal peoples.
Indian Jour. of Social Work (Bombay), 14(8) : 245-62.

396. ——— (1956) Religious beliefs of the Indian Tribes. *The Cultural Heritage of India*, Vol. IV : The Religions. Ed. by Haridas Bhattacharyya. Calcutta, Ramakrishna Mission Institute of Culture : 421-32.

397, DAS, Tarak Chandra (1962) The Problem of the tribal community of India.
Bull. Dept. of Tribal Culture and Folklore Gauhati Uni. 1-22.

398. ———— (1962) Nature and extent of Social change in tribal society of eastern India.
Sociological Bulletin, XI : 112,221-38.

399. ———— (1963) Aspects of tribal culture under modern impact in Eastern India.
Anthropology on the March : Recent Studies of Indian beliefs, attitudes and Social Institution. Ed. by Bala Ratnam. Madras, The Book Centre and the Social Sciences Association : 137-54.

400. DAS, T.R. (1973) Town Planning : A necessity in Arunachal.
Aru. News, 2(5), Aug : 10-6.

401. DAS GUPTA, B.K. (1976) Demography and society in Lower Siang, Arunachal.
Report submitted to Anth. Surv. of India (unpublished).

402. DAS GUPTA, Biman Kumar (1978) Tribal women in North East India.
Tribal Women in India. Ed. by Committee. Calcutta, Indian Anthropological Society : 80-5.

403. DAS GUPTA, J. (1983) Importance and problems of human resource development in Arunachal Pradesh.
Proceedings of a Seminar on "*Planning in North East India (Retrospective and Perspective)*" organised by NEI-CSSR, Shillong.

404. DAS GUPTA, K. (1963) An Introduction to the Gallong language. Shillong, T.P. Khaund, NEFA, DIPR, 122 p.

405. ———— (1963) Galo language guide. Shillong, Res. Dept. Dir. of Inf. & Pub. Relations, Govt. of NEFA, 68 p.

406. ———— (1967) A brief note on the NEFA language.
The Hornbill (Shillong) 26-32.

407. ———— (1969) An Introduction to the Central Monpa. Shillong, Research Dept., DIPR, Govt. of A.P. 167 p.

408. ———— (1969) Some names, surnames and names of places in NEFA.
NEFA Information, 3(1), Feb : 15-7.

409. ———— (1969) Dafla language guide. Shillong, NEFA, 114 p.

410. ———— (1969) A Brief Note on the Grammatical categories in some of the languages of NEFA.
Bull. Cultural Research Institute (Calcutta), 8(3-4) : 11-16.

411. ———— (1969) Some faiths and customs of the Singphos.
NEFA, Information, Dec : 19-21.

412. ———— (1971) Some faiths and beliefs among the Mijus.
NEFA, Information, May : 10-2.

413. ———— (1971) An Introduction to the Nocte language.
Shillong, Research Dept., Directorate of Inf. & Pub. Relations, 127 p.

414. ———— (1971) A few concepts in the Moklum dialect.
Pines, 1(I), March : 81-4.

415. ———— (1972) A Phrase Book in Miju.
Shillong, Res. Dept., Directorate of Inf. & Pub. Relations, Govt. of A.P. 103 p (Reprinted in 1977).

416. ———— (1972) A Phrase Book in Singpho.
Shillong, Res. Dept. Dir. of Inf. & Pub. Relations, 95 p (Reprinted in 1979).

417. ———— (1973) Singphoas.
North Eastern Affairs (Annual), Shillong, 2(1), April-June : 94-6.

418. ———— (1975) Language and Culture.
Resarun, 1(1), Jan : 45-53. *and Resarun' 75* (Cam. Vol. (1976) : 31-5,

419. ———— (1976) Affinity of a few words in some of the dialects of Arunachal Pradesh.
Resarun, 2(2), April : 1-6.

420. ———— (1976) Speech and social life.
Resarun, 2(3), July : 18-22.

421. ———— (1977) Speech and social life.
Resarun' 76, Cum. Vol : 115.

422. ———— (1976) A few aspects of the Grammatical features in some languages of Arunachal Pradesh.
Aru. News. Republic Day Issue.

423. ———— (1977) Agglutination in some languages of Arunachal Pradesh.
Resarun '76, Cum. Vol : 156-60.

424. ———— (1976) Agglutination in Adi languages of Arunachal.
Resarun, 2(4), Oct : 18-21.

425. ———— (1977) A few features in some of the languages of Arunachal Pradesh.
Resarun, 3(3), July : 31-5.

426. ———— (1977) A few aspects of the Minyong language.
Resarun, 3(4) Oct : 16-22.

427. ———— (1977) Pattern of Inter-relationship among the language of Arunachal.
Resarun, 3(2), April : 13-25.

428. ———— Problem of teaching Hindi in Arunachal. Agra, Central Hindi Institute.

429. ———— (1977) The Tagins and their language.
Resarun, 3(1), Jan : 6-11.

430. ———— (1978) A note on the Tangsa language.
Resarun, 4(2), Aut-Winter : 6-16.

431. ———— (1978) Language in Adi culture.
Resarun, 4(1), Jan-March : 36-41.

432. ———— (1879) A note on the Wancho language of Arunachal Pradesh.
Resarun, 5(1), Spring-Summer : 25-37.

433. ————(1980) Tangsa language : A synopsis. Shillong, Dir. of Research, Govt. of A.P., 77 p.

434. ———— (1980) A note on Milang language.
Resarun, 6(2), Aut/Win : 14-8.

435 ———— ( ) Galo language guide. Shillons, Research Dept., Dire. of Inf. & Pub. Relations, Govt. of A.P. 68 p.

436. ———— (1980) Suggestion for affiliation of the Khasi language to the Tibeto-Burman family.
Resarun 6(1), Spring-Summer : 49-64.

437. ——— (1981) Suggestion for affiliation of Khasi (Mon-Khmer) and Arunachal Pradesh languages to a super family (Part-III).
Resarun, 7(1-2) : 17-26.

438. ——— (1982) A few aspects of some of the languages of Arunachal Pradesh.
Linguistic Situation in North East India, Ed. by Mrinal Miri. Shillong, North East Indian Council for Social Science Research : 97-102.

439. ——— (1982) A brief note on Sherdukpen language.
Resarun, 8(1), Spring-Summer : 8-13.

440. ——— (1983) A few folk songs of Arunachal Pradesh.
Resarun, 9(2), Aut-Win : 36-40.

441. ——— (1983) An outline on Tagin Language.
Shillong, Dir. of Res. Govt. of A.P.

442. DAS GUPTA, K.R. (1983) Need for agricultural resource planning in the North Eastern region with a view to boosting agricultural production.
Social Research : Journal of Institute of Social Research (Shillong), 3(3-4), July-Dec : 13-22.

443. DAS GUPTA, P.K. (1980) Book Review : The Ramos of Arunachal by M.M. Dhasmana. New Delhi, Concept Publishing Company, 1979, 298 p, Rs 80/-
Jour. NEICSSR (Shillong), 4(2), Oct : 30.

444. DAS GUPTA, Pradeep (1958) The core of the Problem.
The Outlook on NEFA. Comp. by Parag Chaliha.
Jorhat, Assam Sahitya Sabha : 18-31.

445. DAS SHASTRI, Bibhabasu (1958) A tentative alphabet for NEFA language (Adi).
Bull. Research Deptt., NEFA (Shillong), 1(1), Jun : '64-91.

446. DATTA, Bhupendranath (1938) A note on the presence of light coloured eye-iris amongst the population of North Eastern India.

Man in India, XVIII(1), Jan-March : 1-8.

447. DATTA BARUA, B.N. (1957) Asamar Parbat Vaiamor Bhaisakal (in Assamese). Gauhati, Lawyers Book Stall, 60 p.

448. DATTA CHOUDHURY, S. (1970) The Ahom and the Northern Tribes of NEFA.
NEFA Information, 4(8), March : 15-8.

449. ———— (1968) Archaeological exploration in NEFA : A Prelude.
NEFA, Information, Oct : 19-24.

450. ———— (1973) Arunachal tribes and the Ahoms : A History of friction and friendship.
North Eastern Affairs (Shillong), Annual, 2(1), April-June : 17-23.

451. ———— (*Ed*) (1978) Arunachal Pradesh District Gazetteers : Lohit District. Shillong, Dir. of Inf. & Pub. Relations, A.P., 262 p.

452. ———— (*Ed.*) (1980) Arunachl Pradesh District Gazetteers : Tirap District. Shillong, Dir. of Inf. & Pub. Relations, 238 p.

453. ———— (*Ed.*) (1981) Arunachal Pradesh District Gazetteers : Subansiri District. Shillong, Govt. of A.P., 338 p.

454. DATTA CHAUDHURY, S.S. (1983) Indigenous health practices among Idu Mishmis, Wanchos and Singphos of Arunachal Pradesh.
Report submitted to Anth. Sur. of India.

455. ———— (1984) A note on hand clasping, arm folding and tongue rolling among the Miji of Arunachal Pradesh (India).
Vanyajati, 32(2), April : 12-3.

456. DATTA CHAUDHURY, S.S. and GHOSH, G.C. (1984) Indigenous health practices among the Idu Mishmi of Arunachal Pradesh.
Human Science (old name was Bulletin : Anth. Survey of India), Calcutta, 33(1), March : 24-34.

457. DATTA RAY, B. (1975) Book Review : Hill Politics in North East India by S.K. Chaube.

North Eastern Affairs (Shillong), 3(4), Jan-March.

458. ———— (c. 1971) The Inner Line Policy, a Historical Survey.
Pines, 1(III), Arunachal Number : 55-65.

459. ———— (*Ed.*) (1978) Social and Economic Profile of North East India. Delhi, B.R. Publishing Co., 356 p.

460. DE, S K. (1978) Ixodid tick fauna of Arunachal Pradesh: Acarina Metastigmata.
Indian Vetenary Journal, 55(12), Dec : 1018-19.

461. DEB, D.B. (1964) A new species of Terra forest from North East Frontier Agency, India.
Ind. For., LXXXX : 241-43.

462. ———— (1965) Plants new to India.
Ind. For., LXXXXI : 193-94.

463. ———— (1967) A new species of Petasites Gaertn, (Compositae), from India.
Ind. For., LXXXXIII : 255-57.

464. DEB, D.B. *and* DUTTA, R. (1965) Interesting plants from Eastern India-II.
Bull. Bot. Sec. Bengal, 19 : 37-8

465. DEB, Papia *and* DUTTA, R. (1965) A remarkable new genus and species from Tirap Forntier Division, NEFA.
Ind. For., LXXXXI : 363-66.

466. DEBI, Nalinibala *et al.* (1958) The position of the Assamese language in the North East Frontier Agency.
The Outlook on NEFA. Comp. by Parag Chaliha.
Jorhat, Assam Sahitya Sabha : 42-7.

467. DEKA, H. (1958) Trip to Bomdila (Tourist's Diary).
The Outlook on NEFA. Comp. by Parag Chaliha.
Jorhat, Assam Sahitya Sabha : 72-83.

468. DEKA MAHAPATRA, Usha (1962) Aka (in Assamese).
Asamar Janajati. Ed. by Pramod Chandra Bhattacharya.
Jorhat, Assam Sahitya Sabha : 1-9.

469. ———— (1962) Apatani (in Assamese).
Asamar Janajati. Ed. by Pramod Chandra Bhattacharya.
Jorhat, Assam Sahitya Sabha : 290-93.

470. ———— (1962) Monpa (in Assamese).
Asamar Janajati. Ed. by Pramod Chandra Bhattacharya. Jorhat, Assam Sahitya Sabha : 304-07.

471. ———— (1962) Kameng Simanta bivagar janajati (in Assamse).
Asamar Janajati. Ed. by Pramod Chandra Bhattacharya. Jorhat, Assam Sahitya Sabha : 308-11.

472. DELMAR, Walter (1906) The Romantic East : Burma, Assam and Kashmir. London, Adam and Charles Black, 211 p.

473. DEORI, D.K. (1984) The People and Forest of Arunachal Pradesh.
Arunachal Review (Itanagar), 1(1), March-June ; 9-10.

474. DEORI, M.L. (1979) Potassium (K) status of the soils of Arunachal Pradesh.
Aru. News, 7(9) : 30-5.

47. DEORI, Omen (1978) Twenty Five years of social welfare in retrospect.
Aru. News, 7(4), Aug : 33-7.

476. DEURI, R.K. (1970) Chhekar festival of the Sherdukpens.
NEFA Information, 4, June : 5-10.

477. ———— (1971) The accounts of the tribes such as Monpas, Sherdukpens, Akas, Khowas, Mijis, Bangnis and Sulungs.
Census of India (1971) : Arunachal Pradesh, District Census Handbook, Town and Village Directory, pt.-B, Primary Census Abstract, Kameng District. Shillong, Dir. of Census, Govt. of A.P.

478. ———— (1971) 'Kshyat-Sowai' festival of Khowas.
NEFA Information, 6(3), Oct : 18-21.

479. ———— (1975) 'Khan' festival of the Mijis.
Aru. News, 3(9), Dec-Jan : 10-2.

480. ———— (1975) The place of women in Khowa society.

Resarun, 1(3), July : 20-6 *and* '*Resarun*' 75, (Cum. Vol. 1976) : 79-83.

481. ———— (1976) Marriage system of the Khowas of Kameng District.
Resarun, 2(3), July : 11-7.

482. ———— (1976) A note on some popular Sherdukpen traditions about their conversion from Animism to Buddhism.
Resarun, 2(1), Jan : 1-6 & Cum. Vol. : 24-7.

483. ———— (1976) The Akas of Kameng, their origin, migration, present distribution with an account of Thagje Raja.
Aru. News, 5(1), Feb : 12-6.

484. ———— (1977) The costumes and ornaments of the tribes of Kameng District.
Resarun, 3(1), Jan : 18-42.

485. ———— (1977) The Khowas of Kameng.
Aru. News, 6(3), June and July : 2-5.

486. ———— (1977) The Sulungs of Kameng.
Aru. News, 6(7), Nov : 15-20.

487. ———— (1977) The Fung-glin festival of the Mijis of Kameng District.
Resarun, 3(4), Oct : 23-25.

488. ———— (1978) The Mlokom-Yulo' festival of the Bangnis of Kameng District.
Resarun, 4(2), Aut-Win : 25-7.

489. ———— (1978) A brief note on the inter-relationship of the Sulungs and the Bangnis of Kameng District, Arunachal Pradesh.
Research in Arunachal 1951-1976. Shillong, Directorate of Research, Govt. of A.P. : 79-84.

490. ———— (1981) Marriage system of the Mijis of West Kameng District.
Resarun, 7(1-2) : 56-61.

491. ———— (1982) Festivals of Kameng. Shillong, Dir. of Research, Govt. of A.P.

492. ———— (1982) The Sulungs. Shillong, Dir. of Res., Govt. of A.P. 106 p.

493. ———— (1983) Ritual beliefs and practices of the Miju Mishmis of Lohit valley.
Resarun, 9(2), Aut-Win : 1-4.

494. ———— (1983) Land tenure system of the Mishmis of Lohit valley.
Aru. News, 12(5), Aug-Sept : 13-4.

495. ———— (1983) Festivals of Kameng. Shillong, Dir. of Res., Govt. of A.P.

496. ———— (1984) A few aspects on ritual beliefs and practices of the Miju Mishmis.
Arunachal Review, 1(1), March-June : 11-12 & 4.

497. DEVI, Lakshmi (1968) Ahom Tribal Relations : A Political study. Gauhati, Mrs. L. Devi. 301 p.

498. DEWAN, Vijay Kumar (1976-78) North Eastern Region Local Acts of Assam, Nagaland, Meghalaya, Manipur, Tripura, Mizoram & Arunachal Pradesh, Vol. I-VII. Allahabad, Orient Law House.

499. DEY, Jatin (1967) A scheme for a zonal Government in the Eastern Region.
A Common Perspective for North East India. Ed. by Rathin Mitra *and* B. Das Gupta. Calcutta, Pannalal Das Gupta : 148-52.

500. DHAR, Bibhas (1982) Chhos Kor : The festival of the Monpa and the Sherdukpen.
Jour. of the Indian Anth. Society (Calcutta), 17 : 265-68.

501. ———— (1982) Monpas of West Kameng : A study into Tsangla sub-culture.
Resarun, 8( ) Aut-Win : 18-26.

502. ———— (1984) The Monpas of Khalegthang Area, alias, the Tsanglas : A brief ethnographic accout.
The Tribes of North East India. Ed. by S Karotemprel. Calcutta, Firma KLM Pvt. Ltd. : 295-306.

503. DHASMANA, M.M. (1979) The Ramos of Arunachal. New Delhi, Concept Publishing Co., 298 p.

504. DIRECTORATE of Information (1957) A brief account of administrative and development activities in North East Frontier Agency since Independence. Shillong, Dir. of Inf. & Publicity, NEFA, Supdt. Govt. Press, 44 p.

505. ———— (1964) NEFA on the March. Shillong, Dir. of Inf. & Pub. Relations, NEFA, 44 p.

506. ———— (1968) Brochure on the Seminar of the Research Dept., NEFA. Shillong, Dir. of Inf. & Pub. NEFA, 49 p.

507. ———— (1968) NEFA : The Land and the People. Shillong, Dir. of Inf. & Pub. Relations, NEFA, 31 p.

508. ———— (1971) Festival of folk dances of NEFA. Shillong (NEFA), 21 p.

509. ———— (?) Arunachal (Land of the Sun Rise Mountain) Pradesh. Shillong, Directorate of Inf. & Pub. Relations.

510. ———— (1972) Arunachal Pradesh on the March. Shillong (A P.), 20 p.

511. ———— (1972) Arunachal's rich heritage. Shillong (A.P.), 13 p.

512. DIRECTORATE of Economics (1974) Statistical Hand-book of Arunachal Pradesh, 1971-72. Shillong, Dir of Eco. & Sta., A.P. Administration, 162p.

513. DIRECTORATE of Research (1958) Bulletin of the Research Department, Vol. I, no. I. (June), 113p. Shillong (NEFA [Mimeographed].

514. ———— (1972) Arunachal Research Bulletin. Shillong, Res. Dept., Govt. of A.P.

515. ———— (1976) Resarun '75. Shillong, Res. Dept. Govt. of A.P. 183 p.

516. ———— (1977) Resarun '76. Shillong, Res. Dept. Govt. of A.P., 174 p.

517. ———— (1977) Malinithan : Heritage of Arunachal. Shillong, Dir. of Res., Inf. & Pub. Rela., 18p.

518. ———— (1977) Research in Arunachal Pradesh. (Proceedings of a Seminar of the Directorate of Research, Govt of A.P., Shillong, 14th & 15th Nov '75). Shillong, Res. Dept., Govt. of A.P., 55 p.

519. ———— (1978) Research in Arunachal Pradesh. (Proceedings of a Seminar for Silver Jubilee of the Dir. of Research, Govt. of A.P., Shillong, 7th Sept. '77). Shillong, Res. Dept., Govt. of A.P., 88 p.

520. DOIG, Desmond (1963) NEFA tribals welcome return of Indian Administration.
March of India (Delhi), 15(6), June : 3-4.

521. DOLEY, D. (1975) Socio Economic life of the Miri tribe.
North Eastern Research Bulletin, 4, Summer : 49-61.

522. ———— (1975) Arunachal tribes and the Ahoms.
North Eastern Affairs, 3(4), Jan-March : 38-48.

523. ———— (1984) The Religious beliefs and practices among the Mishing of Assam.
The Tribes of North East India. Ed. by S. Karotemprel. Calcutta, Firma KLM Pvt. Ltd : 87-94.

524. DORJI, Phunso (1981) 'Duba' festival.
Aru. News, 10(7), Sept-Oct : 24-5.

525. DUARAH, D.C. (1972) The Apatanis : A profile.
Sugar Uni. Unpublished Disser. (Masters' Degree).

526. DUARAH, D.K. (1979) Neolithic celts from Subansiri District.
Aru. News, 8(9), Aug : 13-4.

527. ———— (1979) Festivals of the Apatanis (in Assamese).
Asom Bani (Newspaper, Gauhati), Special Bangali Bihu Issue, April.

528. ———— (1979) Festivals of the Arunachal (in Assamese).
Na Lekhani (an weekly newspaper), Oct. '79.

529. ———— (1979) Hand clasping, arm folding and ear lobe attachment among the Monpas of Kameng, Arunachal Pradesh.
Resarun, 5(1), Spring-Summer : 53-61.

530. ———— (1979) Distribution of ABO, MN, Rh Blood Groups among the Mishmis (Taraon) of Lohit, Arunachal Pradesh.
Resarun, 5(2), Aut-Winter : 22-8.

531. ———— (1980) A study of ABO Blood Groups and some genetic traits of the Sulungs of Subansiri District, Arunachal Pradesh.
Resarun, 6(2), Aut-Winter : 19-29.

532. ———— (1980) Frequency of colour blindness in Arunachal.
Aru. News, 9(1), Feb-March : 22-5.

533. ———— (1981) Food habits of the tribes of Arunachal Pradesh.
Resarun, 7(1-2) : 37-41.

534. ———— (1981) Socio Cultural Aspects of the Solungs (in Assamese).
Na Lekhani (Weekly newspaper), Nov. 13th, 20th and 27th.

535. ———— (1981) Two folk tales of the Apatanis.
Aru. News, 10(5), July : 35-7.

536. ———— (1982) Notes on land tenure system of the Nishis, Hill Miris and Tagins of Arunachal Pradesh.
Resarun, 8(2), Aut-Win : 41-54.

537. ———— (1982) The kinship and friendship system of the Apatanis of Arunachal Pradesh.
Resarun, 8(1), Spring-Summer : 22-7.

538. ———— (1983) Incidence of colour blindness among the Monpas of West Kameng, Arunachal Pradesh.
Resarun, 9(2), Aut-Win : 10-4.

539. DUARAH, D.K., DAS, P.B. *and* CHOUDHURY, B. (1976) A study on hand clasping, arm folding and tongue rouling among Nocte, Wancho and Tangsa of Tirap, Arunachal Pradesh.
Bulletin Anth. Dept. : Gauhati Uni., 5, December : 54-8.

540. DUARAH, D.K. *and* DAS, P.B. (1978) A study of some genetic traits of the Tagins of Arunachal Pradesh.
Resarun, 4(2), Aut-Winter : 39-47.

541. DUARAH, D.K. *and* DUTTA, P.C. (1978) A calender of the festivals of the Arunachal Pradesh.
Aru. News, 7(4), Aug : 41-9.

542. DUARAH, Dweigendra Kumar *and* SHARMA, Hem (1979) Hand clasping, arm folding and ear lobe attachment of the Monpas of Kameng, Arunachal.
Resarun, 5(1), Spring-Summer : 53-61.

543. DUBE, S.C. (Ed.) (1977) Tribal Heritage of India, Vol. I : Ethnicity, Identity and Interaction. New Delhi, Vikas Publishing House.

544. DUBEY, S.M. (1975) Modernisation and elites in Arunachal Pradesh.
(Report of a Research Project sponsored by the Census Organisation of India and Directorate of Census, Arunachal Pradesh, 1971). Delhi, Controller of Publications, 167 p.

545. ———— (Ed) (1978) North East India : A Sociological study. Delhi, Concept Publishing Co., 424 p.

546. DUFF, B. (1912) Report on the Miri country and the operations of the Miri Mission. Simla, Govt. Press.

547. DUFF-SUTHERLAND-DUNBAR, George (1938) Other men's lives : A study of primitive peoples.
London : 230-4 (Dafla and Abors).

548. ———— (1916) Personal narrative of a visit to Pemakoichen : Part III, Abor and Galongs.
Memoir of the Asiatic Society of Bengal (Calcutta), 5, Extra No. : 93-113.

549. DUKPE, Tarin (1980) The Bori Boot Festival.
Aru. News, 9(1), Feb-March : 29-31.

550. DUN, G.M. (1897) Preliminary notes on Daphlas.
Simla.

551. ———— (1897) Preliminary notes on Daphlas.
India's North East Frontier... Ed. by Verrier Elwin.
Bombay, O.U.P. (1959) 185-88.

552. DUN, G.W. (?) (1897) Preliminary notes on Miris.
India's North East Frontier... Ed. by Verrier Elwin.
Bombay, O.U.P. (1959) : 159-64, 199-200.

553. DUNBAR, G.D.S. (1915) Abors and Galongs.
Memoir of Asiatic Society of Bgngal, Calcutta, Vol. 5, (Baptist Mission Press) : 1-91.

554. DUNBAR, G. (Duff-Sutherland-Dunbar) (1915) Tribes of the Brahmaputra valley.
J.R. Soc. Arts, LXIII : 189-303. (Abors).

555. DUNCAN, W.M. David : (1970) On the marriage customs of the Bangni.
Bulletin of Tibetology (Gangtok) 7(1) Feb : 21-8.

556. DUTTA, B.B. (Ed.) (1981) Land and land relations in the Hills of North East India. Delhi, Peoples Pub. House (in Press).

557. DUTTA, Bimal, C. (1979) Book Review : Anthropometry of Adis of Siang District, NEFA by Sachin Roy.
Jour. NEICSSR (Shillong), 3(1) : 16.

558. DUTTA, Deepanjana (1973) Finger prints of the Singpho females.
Bulletin Anth. Dept., Dibrugarh Uni., 2 : 44-9.

559. ——— (1974) Palmar dermatoglyphics of the Singpho females.
Contemporary Anthropological Research in North East India. Ed. by B.M. Das.
(*Bull. Anth. Dept., Dibrugarh Uni.*, : 67-72).
Dibrugarh, Dibrugarh Uni., Dept. of Anth. : 67-72.

560. ——— (1978) A note on the finger prints of the Daflas of Assam.
Cultural and Biological Adaptability of Man with special reference to North East India. Ed. by A.C. Bhagabati and R.K. Kar.
(*Bull. Anth. Dept. Dibrugarh Uni.*, 6, 1977). Dibrugarh, Dibrugarh Uni , Dept. of Anth. : 200-03.

561. DUTTA, D.K (1979) A legend of the origin of the Lisus.
Resarun, 5(2), Aut-Win : 29-30.

562. ——— (1979) A little known tribe of Tirap.
Resarun, 5(1), Spring-Summer : 61-7.

563. ——— (1980) A prehistoric artifact at the Nao Dihing, Tirap District.
Resarun, 6(2), Aut-Win : 33-4.

564. ——— (1981) How the Bulbul became the king of the birds : A Nocte myth.
Aru. News, 10(5), July : 43.

565. ——— (1981) Land Tenure system of the Noctes of Tirap District.
Resarun, 7(1-2) : 27-9.

566. ——— (1982) Lisus of Gandhigam : Their origin, migration and settlement.
Resarun, 8(2), Aut-Win : 27-9.

567. ——— (1982) Folk songs of the Singphos of Tirap District.
Resarun, 8(1), Spring-Summer : 31-2.

568. ———— (1983) Sajolang : The Ancestor of the Mijis.
Resarun, 9(2), Aut-Win : 34-5.

569. DUTTA, J.C. (1982) Notes on the ruins of Naksaparvat in Arunachal Pradesh.
Resarun, 8(2) Aut-Win : 30-4.

570. DUTTA, Mahendra Nath (1980) A,B,O, Blood Groups among the Wancho and some Mongoloid populations of North East India.
Bull. Dept. of Anth., Dibrugarh Uni, 9 : 197-99.

571. ————(1983) A note on vertex whorl of the Wancho of Arunachal Prdaesh.
Vanyajati, 31(1), January : 27-8.

572. ———— (1983) Variation of Ear lobe attachment among the Wanchos of Tirap District, Arunachal Pradesh.
Vanyajati, 31(4), Oct. : 3-5.

573. DUTTA, Mahendra Nath *and* SEN GUPTA, Sarthak (1983) Finger dermatoglyphic study of the Wanchos of Arunachal Pradesh.
Vanyajati, 31 (4), Oct : 18-24,

574. DUTTA, M N. (1979) An investigation on the fingre prints of the Wanchos of Arunachal Pradesh.
The Anthropologist (Delhi), 23 (1-2) : 1-3.

575. DUTTA, M.S. (1977) Land and the Mishing economy : A study in change.
Proceedings of a Seminar on "*Tribal Economy*" held in Calcutta, Anth. Sur. of India.

576. ———— (1978) The Mishing Economy : A study in transformation.
Proceedings of the *Xth ICAES*, New Delhi.

577. ———— (1982) Land and the Mishing Economy : A study in change.
Proceedings of a Seminar on "*Agrarian Situtaion in India*", organised by Anth. Sur. of India, Mysore, Nov. 23-25.

578. DUTTA, Pradesh Chandra (?) A peep into social and economic conditions of the Gallongs in Arunachal Pradesh.

North Eastern Affairs (Shillong), 2 (2), July-Sept.
579. ———— (1972) Agriculture in a tribal village. *Yojana* (Delhi), Oct. 15 : 797-99.
580. DUTTA, Parul (1959) The Tangsas of the Namchik and Tirap Valleys (The People of NEFA). Shillong, DIPR, 98 p. (Reprinted in 1969).
581. ———— (1960) The Khunboo : A Nocte chief. *The Hornbill* (Shillong). April.
582. ———— (?) Problems of changes among the Noctes. Shillong, Research Dept., Govt. of Arunachal Pradesh.
583. ———— (1965) Folklore of NEFA. Radio Talk Broadcasted by AIR, Shillong.
584. ———— (1967) Wood carving in NEFA. *NEFA Information*, 1 (12), July : 9-14.
585. ———— (1967) The Institution of Lawang and Wangham of the Tirap District of NEFA. *Bull. Cul. Res. Inst.* (Calcutta), Govt. of West Bengal, 1 & 2 : 12-4.
586. ———— (1968) Revival of arts and crafts in the border area of NEFA. *NEFA Information*, 3 (1), Aug ; 7-10.
587. ———— (1968) India's North East Frontier and its people. Shillong, Research Dept., NEFA.
588. ———— (?) Cultural trait and ethnic types in NEFA. Shillong, Research Dept., NEFA.
589. ———— (?) Preservation and revitalisation of the traditional handicraft of NEFA. Shillong, Res. Dept., NEFA.
590. ———— (1669) Trends of socio cultural development in NEFA. *NEFA Information*, 3 (12), July ; 3-7 & 4 (1), Aug : 22-7.
591. ———— (1969) Solung, a festival of the Adis of NEFA. Shillong, Research Dept. Govt. of A.P., 61 p.
592. ———— (1969) Origin of the tribes of North Eastern India.

The Hornbill : 19-23.

593. ———— (c. 1971) Arunachal Tatoo. *Pines*, 1 (III). Arunachal Number : 1-7.

594. ———— (1971) The Tangsas. Shillong, Dir. of Res., NEFA, 98 p.

595. ———— (1972) Trends of socio economic development in NEFA. *Aru. News*, March.

596. ———— (1973) Ornaments and costume of Tirap tribes. *Aru News*, 2 10, March : 1-6 ; 2(2), May : 4-7.

597. ———— (1974) Socio Political Economic set up of Arunachal : People vis-a-vis development schemes, a discussion. *North Eastern Affairs* (Shillog), 2(4), Jan-March : 19-21.

598 . ———— (1975) Loku festival of the Nocties. *Resarun*, 1(1), Jan : 12-5 *and Resarun '75* (Cum. Vol. 1976) : 8-10.

599. ———— (1975) Folk songs of the Noctes. *The Statesman* (Calcutta), Sunday, Nov. 29 and *Aru. News* 4(9).

600. ———— (1975) Jauban Chuam : A religious festival of the Noctes. *Resarun*, 1(4) *and Resarun '75* (Cum. Vol. 1976): 99-101.

601. ———— (1975) Role of women in the various aspects of life of the Arunachalis. *Aru. News*, 4(5), July : 22-4.

602. ———— (1975) Nocte women and their life in the Society. *Aru. News*, 4 (5).

603. ———— (1975) Belief and rituals of the Noctes of Arunachal Pradesh. *Aru. News.*

604. ———— (1976) Women in Arunachal and their Status in Socio Cultural life. *Resarun* '75, Cum. Vol : 68-76.

605. ———— (1976) Local institutions of Tirap District. *Aru. News*, 5(5) Sept : 27-8.

606. ———— (1979) Mopin : A festival of the Adis of

Arunachal Pradesh. Shillong, Research Dept., Dir. of Inf. & Pub. Rela., Govt. of A.P. 25 p.

607. ———— (1976) The Noctes on the path of progress. *Aru. News*, 5 (2), March : 15-20.

608. ———— (1976) The story of origin and migration of the Noctes. *Resarun*, 2(2), Apr.l : 1-11.

609. ———— (1976) The material culture of the Noctes of Arunacal Pradesh. *Resarun*, 2(4), Oct : 2-10.

610. ———— (1976) The story of origin and migration of the Noctes. *Resarun '75*, Cum. Vol : 52-9.

611. ———— (1976) The material culture of the Noctes of Arunachal Pradesh. *Resarun '75*, Cum. Vol : 135-46.

612. ———— (1976) Folk stories of Arunachal. *The Mail*, Sunday, Aug. 26.

613. ———— (1976) Arunachalis Folk Stories. *Patriot*, March.

614. ———— (1976) Cultural Heritage of Arunachal Pradesh and its continuity. *Aru. News*, 5(6), Aug-Sept : 35-42.

615. ———— (Ed. & Comp.) (1976) Mopin, a festival of the Adis of Arunacal Pradesh. Shillong, Dir. of Inf. & Pub. Relations, 9 p.

616. ———— (1976) Folk songs of the Noctes of Arunachal Pradesh. *Aru. News*, 4(9), Repub. Day Issue : 16-9.

617. ———— (1977) About a heritage in Subansiri District of Arunachal Pradesh. *Aru. News*, 6(7), Nov : 1-6.

618. ———— (1977) The Wanchos, their legendary beliefs regarding origin and migration. *Resarun*, 3(4), Oct : 2-9.

619. ———— (1977) About a hermitage in Subansiri District of Arunachal Pradesh. *Aru. News*, 6(7) Nov : 1-2.

620. ——— (1977) Socio-Cultural life of the people of Arunachl Pradesh,
Resarun, 3(2), April : 1-7.

621. ——— (1977) The People and their socio-cultural life.
Yojana (Delhi), 22(1), Nov. : 114-91.

622. ——— (1977) Institution of Chieftainship of the Noctes of Arunachal Pradesh.
Proceedings of a Seminar on "*Social and Political Institutions*" organised by NEICSSR, Shillong.

623. ——— (1978) Social organisation of the Wanchos of Tirap District, Arunachal Pradesh.
Resarun, 4(1), Jan-March : 14-35.

624. ——— (1978) Dormitory institution in Arunachal with special reference to the Wanchos of Tirap District.
Aru. News, 6(9) Jan, Rep. Day Issue : 17-22.

625. ——— (1978) The Noctes. Shillong, Res. Dept. Directorate of Inf. & Pub. Relations Govt. of A.P., 317p.

626. ——— (1978) Calender of the festivals of Arunachal Pradesh.
Aru. News, 7(4), Aug : 41-9.

627. ——— (1978) Socio-cultural pattern in Arunachal Pradesh.
Resarun, 4(2), Aut-Winter : 1-5.

628. ——— (1978) Cultural patterns and trends of socio-cultural development in Arunachal.
Research in Arunachal : 15-22.

629. ——— (1978) Cultural Research in Arunachal Pradesh : An appraisal.
Research in Arunachal : 47-9.

630. ——— (1980) Cultural and Historical Background of the Wanchos of Arunachal Pradesh.
Resarun, 6(2), Aut-Win : 1-13 and also Proceedings of a Seminar on "*Development Strategies in Historical Perspectives in North East India.*" Shillong, School of Social Science.NEHU.

631. ——— (n.d.)Arts and Crafts of NEFA.
Shillong, Directorate of Research, Govt. of A.P.

632. ——— (1981) Dialectical Problems in Arunachal Pradesh. Radio Talk broadcasted by AIR Dibrugarh on 30.3.81.

633. ——— (1981) Arunachal's Socio Cultural Patterns. *Jour. of North Eastern Council* (NEC, Shillong), 4(1), Jan-June.

634. ——— (1981) Arunachal Pradesh : Land and the People.
North East Times (Gauhati), 2(10), Aug.

635. ——— (1981-82) Dormitory institution in Arunachal with special reference to the Wanchos of Tirap District.
North East Times, 2(12), Aug. 28 and 2(13), Sept.4, 1982.

636. ——— (1981) Arunachal Pradesh from tradition to modernity.
Resarun, 7(1-2) : 14-6.

637. ——— (1981) The Wanchos of Arunachal Pradesh.
North East Times, 2, Nov. 21. and 23.

638. ——— (1982) Agricultural system of the Wanchos.
Resarun, 8(2), Aut-Win : 1-10.

639. ——— (1982) Folk stories associated with the origin and migration of the People of Tirap, Arunachal Pradesh.
(Proceedings of a Seminar on "*Folklore*" of NEICSSR, Shillong).
Folklore in North East India. Ed. by Soumen Sen.
New Delhi, Omsons (in Press).

640. ——— (1983) Socio Cultural Spectrum of Arunachal Pradesh.
Souvenir : Anthropological Society of North East India.
Ed. by H.C. Sharma and B. Choudhury.
Gauhati Uni., Dept. of Anth. : 29-36.

641. ——— (1983) The Wanchos. Shillong, Research Dept., Govt. of A P.

642. ——— (1984) Cultural and Historical background of the Nocte of Arunachal Pradesh.
The Tribes of North East India. Ed. by S. Karotemprel.
Calcutta, Firma KLM Pvt. Ltd : 366-75.

643. ——— (1985) The Singphos. Shillong, Dir. of Res., Govt. of A.P.

644. ———— (?) Reasons of backwardness : Wancho area in Tirap District.
Shillong, Research Dept., Govt. of A.P.

645. ———— (?) Story of origin and migration of the Nocte. Shillong, Research Dept., Govt. of A.P.

646. ———— (?) The Hill Miris.
Shillong, Res. Dept., GOAP.

647. ———— (1980) Nocte chieftainship : It's genesis, structure and function. Gauhati University. (Ph. D. Thesis. Unpublished).

648. ———— (?) Tirap Frontier Division and its people. Shillong, Research Dept., Arunachal Pradesh.

649. ———— (?) The Institution of Chieftainship of the Noctes of Arunachal Pradesh.
Shillong, Research Dept., Arunachal Pradesh.

650. ————(?) Socio Political Economic set up of Arunachal people vis-a-vis development chaines.
Shillong, Research Dept., Arunachal Pradesh.

651. DUTTA, Priyamboda (1975) Nocte women and their life in the society.
Aru. News, 4(5), July : 49-51.

652. DUTTA GUPTA, Jaya (1960) Ponung : Girls' Association among the Padam Abor in the Lower Abor Hills.
Bull. Dept. of Anth. (Anthropological Survey of India, Calcutt), 9 (2) : 71-3.

653. ECONOMIC And Political Weekly (1978) Arunachal Pradesh : Keeping out trouble makers.
Economical and Political Weekly, (Bombay), 13(27), July: 1086.

654. ECONOMIC Times (1971) NEFA.
Economic Times (Bombay). Sept. 3.

655. EDITORIAL (1964) NEFA Khetro men Kalayan Karya (in Hindi).
Vanyejati. 12(1), Jan : 1.

656. ———— (1981) Education in Arunachal
Aru. Newsletter, Sept. 16 : 2.

657. ———— (1983) Coverage of Scheduled Tribe Population under Tribal Sub-Plan strategy.
Vanyajati (Delhi), 31(4), Oct : 1-2.

658. ELWIN, Verrier (1956) Tribal Art.
The Assam Tribune, June 10.

659 ———— (1956) The North East Frontier Agency of India.
The Geographical Magazine (London), 29(8) : 405-16.

660. ———— (1956) The People of NEFA (i) A Pilgrimage to Tawang.
Illustrated Weekly of India (Bombay), 77(40), Sept. 30.

661. ———— (1956) The People of NEFA (ii) In Subansiri.
Illustrated Weekly of India, 77(41), Oct. 7.

662. ———— (1956) The People of NEFA (iii) In Siang.
Illustrated Weekly of India, 77(42), Oct. 14 : 32-4.

663. ———— (1956) The People of NEFA (iv) In Lohit.
Illustrated Weekly of India, 77(43), Oct. 21 : 23-5.

664. ———— (1956) The People of NEFA (v) In Tuensang.
Illustrated Weekly of India 77(44), Oct. 28 : 31-3.

665. ———— (1956) The People of NEFA (iv) In Tirap.
Illustrated Weekly of India, 77(45), Nov. 4 : 25-7.

666. ———— (1957) The NEFA of India.
Tribal Welfare (West Bengal Weekly), Supplement, July 18.

667. ———— (1957) Poetry in NEFA mythology.
March of India (Delhi), 9(9), Sept : 5 & 22-3.

668. ———— (1957) Ten years of progress in NEFA.
Shillong, North East Frontier Agency.

669. ———— (1957) Myths of North East Frontier of India. Shillong, Dir. of Inf. & Pub. Rels., Govt. of NEFA, 448p. (Reprinted in 1968).

670. ———— (1958) Tribal Art of Assam.
Akashvani, 23(18), May 4 : 6-8.

671. ———— (1958) Tribal Women.
The Tribal Women of India. Ed. by Tara Ali Baig.
Delhi, Publication Division, Ministry of Inf. & Broadcasting, G.O.I. : 200-07.

672. ———— (1958) A frontier of hope.
Bull., Research Dept. (NEFA, Shillong), 1(1), June: 3-25.

673. ———— (1959) Tribal life in other plants.

Illustrated Weekly of India, 80(28), July 12 : 14-5.

674. ——— (1959) A Philosophy for NEFA. Shillong, Sachin Roy on behalf of the North East Frontier Agency (2nd edition published in 1959), 296 p.

675. ——— (1959) Tribal administration in other planets. *Illustrated Weekly of India*, 80(29), July 19 : 31-2.

676. ——— (1959) Art of North East Frontier of India. Shillong, Sachin Roy on behalf of the North East Frontier Agency, Research Dept. 211 p.

677. ——— (*Ed.*) (1959) India's North East Frontier in the Nineteenth Century Bombay, Oxford University Press, 473 p.

678. ——— (1960) Report of the Committee on special multipurpose tribal blocks. New Delhi, Ministry of Home Affairs, 453 p.

679. ——— (1961) The Beauty of tribal Assam. *Folklore*, 2(4), July-Aug : 209-12.

680. ——— (1961) When the world was young : Folk tales from India's hills and forests. Delhi, Pub. Division, 82 p. (National Book Trust Book).

681. ——— (*Ed*) (1963) A new deal for tribal India. New Delhi, Manager of Publications, 146p (Abridgement of the Xth Report of the Commissioner for Scheduled Castes and Scheduled Tribes for the year 1960-61.

682. ——— (1964) The Tribal World of Verrier Elwin : An Autobiography. London, Oxford University Press : 225-86.

683. ——— (1965) Democracy in NEFA. Shillong, Research Dept., NEFA, 195p.

684. ——— (1965) Field Work in Tribal World. *Folklore* (Calcutta), 6(2) : 480-81.

685. ——— (Ed) (1969) The Nagas in the Nineteenth century. London, Oxford Uni. Press : Abor : 343, 503, 6 1 : Khampti : 98, 611.

686. ——— (1970) A new book of tribal fiction. Shillong, Research Dept., Direc. of Inf. & Pub. Rela., 376p.

687. ELWIN, Verrier and COVERLEY-PRINCE, Victor (1960) The Hill People of North East India (People of the World.) London, Oxf rd Uni. Press, 32 p.

688. ELWIN, Verrier, SHASTRI, B. and SIMON, I. (Ed) (1967) Important directive on administration of NEFA. Shillong, DIPR, North East Frontier Agency, 297p.

689. ERING, D. (1972) The North East Frontier Agency. *Tribal Situation in India : Proceedings of a Seminar*. Ed by K. Suresh Singh. Simla, Indian Institute of Advanced Study : 51-71.

690. ERING, Oshong (1970) The Tanis and the Donyi : Polo cult.
NEFA Information, 4(8), March : 22-5.

691. ———— (1970) Adi marriage and divorce.
NEFA Information, 5(2), Sept : 14-7.

692. ———— (1970) Marriage system of the Adis.
NEFA Information, 5(1), Aug : 19-23.

693. ———— (1971) Adi dom nitom.
NEFA Information, 5(12), July : 15-8.

694. ———— Spirit of the Adi land
NEFA Information, 6(2), Sept : 24-8,

695. ———— (1971) Trial of murder case in the Kebang.
NEFA Information, 6(3), Oct : 1 -6.

696. ———— (1971) Some traditional usages of the Adis.
NEFA Information, 6(4) Nov : 9-14.

697. ———— (1971) Adi belief.
NEFA Information, 6(5) Dec : 15-7.

698. ———— (1972) Sikpabo and the two boys : An Adi myth.
Aru. News, 1(2), March : 26-30.

699. ———— (1972) Sikipabo and the two boys : An Adi myth.
Aru. News, 1(5), July : 8-10

700. ———— (1972) Songs and dances in Adi society.
Aru. News, 1(7), Sept : 29-30.

701. ———— (1972) Nyany, Myete : The most beautiful bride.
Aru. News, 1(10), Dec : 7-9.

702. ———— (1973) Traditional culture of Arunachal. *Aru. News*, 2(1). March : 10-4.

703. ———— (1973) Communing hunity and fishing of the Adis. *Aru. News*, 1(12), Feb : 24-7.

704 ———— (1973) Yalo of the Adis. *Aru. News*, 2(4). July : 11-5.

705. ———— (1973) Traditional housing system of Adi villages. *Aru. News*, 2(7), Oct 9-11.

706. ———— (1974) Taboo in Adi life. *Aru. News*, 3(1). Feb-March : 10-2.

707. ———— (1974) Fads and fallacies of Arunachal. *Aru. News*, 3(7), Oct 9-16.

708. ———— (1975) Pasighat. *Aru. News*, 4(1), Feb : 3-8.

709. ———— (1975) Ayit Miri or ode for the soul. *Aru. News*, 4(8), Nov : 18-21.

710. ———— (1976) Adi belief : From infiniteness to physical emergence (As reflected through the Aabang). *Aru. News*, 5(8), Nov.-Dec. : 48-55.

711. ———— (1976) Jungles and junglees of Arunachal. *Aru. News*, 5(2), March : 25-7.

712. ———— (1977) Adi beliefs as reflected through the Aabang. *North Eastern Spectrum* (Gauhati), 2(1), July : 7-11.

713. ———— (1978 My education in traditional Adi society. *Aru. News*, 7(3), June-July : 18-23.

714. ———— (1978) Adi myth and belief. *Aru. News*, 7(7), Nov. : 21-6.

715. ———— Adi Kebang : An introduction of popular rural democracy. *Aru. News*, 7(4). Independence Day : 25-8.

716. ———— (1979) Boleng. *Aru News*, 8(6), Sept. : 7-10.

717. ———— (1979) Nobo-Robo story. *Aru. News*, 8(8), Nov.-Dec. : 11-3.

718. ——— (1979) Destruction of an early civilization and emergence another civilization. *Aru. News*, 8(7), Oct. : 9-13.

719. ——— (1980) An Adi myth: Destruction and survival of the monkeys. *Aru. News*, 9(6), Oct.-Nov. : 17-20.

720. ——— (1980) Religion of the Adis. *Aru. News*, 8(9), Repub. Day Issue : 31-4.

721. ——— (1981) Concept of Donyi : Poloism and religion thereon. *Aru. News*, 10(7), Sept.-Oct. : 19-20.

722 ——— (1981) Child marriage in Adi society and plight of girls. *Aru. News*, 10(6), Aug. : 9-12.

723. ——— (1981 Festivals of Arunachal tribes and their channelisation. *Aru. News*, 10(4), June : 6-10.

724 ——— (1983) Adi belief and faith. *Aru. News*, 12(5), Aug.-Sept. : 25-6.

725. ERING, Tapi (1972) Changing faces of Arunachal. *Aru. News*, 1(10), Dec. 28-30.

726. ETE, Tumpak (Ed) & (Tr) : (1974) Pume Dada Hoi Dade. Along, Adi Folk literature Research Centre, 320p.

727 ——— (n.d.) Urom Pak Nam. Shillong, Directorate of Research, Govt. of A.P.

728. FICK, Richard (1920) The Social Organisation in North East India in Buddha's time. Calcutta, Calcutta Uni. Press, 365p.

729. FORBES, C.J.F.S., (1878) On Tibeto-Burman languages. *JRAS* : 210-27.

730. FRANK & BROWN, Marie (1962) Mission to the head hunters. London, Hodder & Stoughton, 252p.

731. FUCH, Stephen (1973) The Aboriginal Tribes of India. Delhi, The Macmillan Company of India Ltd. : 201-41.

732. FURER-HAIMENDORF, C. von. (1907) Religious beliefs and rituals practices of the Minyong Abors. Anthropos, XLIX.

733 ———— (n.d.) Tribal India.
Bombay. Mayfair, Littlegibs, Road, Malabar Hill, 54p.

734. ———— (1938) Through the unexplored mountains of the Assam-Burma border.
Geographical Journal (London), 91, March : 201-19.

735. ———— (1946) Agriculture and land tenure among the Apa Tanis.
Man in India, 26(1), March : 20-49.

736. ———— (1946) Notes on tribal justice among the Apa Tanis.
Man in India, 26(3-4), Sept.-Dec. : 181-95.

737. ———— (1946) Culture types in the Assam Himalayas.
Indian Geographical Journal (Madras), 21 : 1-9 (It has description on Sulung Dafla, Apetanis).

738. ———— (1947) Exploration in the Eastern Himalayas (Diaries of Travel in the Subansiri Region, 1944 and 945) Shillong Assam Govt. Press, 131p.

739. ———— (1947) Ethnographic notes on the tribes of the Subansiri region. Shillong, Assam Govt Press, 61p.

740 ———— (1949) Anthropology and administration in the tribal areas of North East Frontier.
Eastern Anthropologist (Lucknow), 3(1) : 8-14.

741. ———— (1950) Ethnographic notes on the tribes of the Subansiri region. Shillong, Assam Govt., 66p. (Reprinted).

742. ———— (1953) The after-life in Indian tribal belief.
Jour. of the Royal Anthropological Institute (London), 83, pt. 1 : 37-49.

743. ———— (1954) Religious beliefs and ritual practices of the Minyong Abors.
Anthropos, 49 : 588-604.

744. ———— (1955) Himalayan Barbary. London, John Murray, 41p.

745. ———— (1956) Gluckliche Barbaren. Wiesbaden, F.A. Brockhans, Bei unbekannten volkern an der Nordostgrenze Indiens, 75p. (1956).

746 ———— (1961) Book Review : The Daflas of the Subansiri region by B K. Shukla, Shillong, NEFA, 1959, Pp. 139, 8 half tone illus, 19 line drawings, 1 map. *Man (London)*, 61, Article 183-199, Sept. : 166-67.

747. ———— (1962) The Apa Tanis and their neighbours : A primitive civilization of the Eastern Himalayas. London, Routledge & Kegan Paul, 66p.

748. ———— (1965) Book Review : The Gallongs by L.R. N. Srivastava, Shillong, Research Dept. Adviser's Secretariat, 1962, Pp. XII-128, plates, line drawings. *Man* (London), 65, Articles 1-28, Jan..Feb. : 32.

749. ———— (1967) Morality and the social order among the Apa Tanis. *Gods and Rituals : Readings in religious beliefs and practices*. Ed. by John Middleton. New York, Garden City, National History Press for American Museum of National History : 1-19.

750. ———— (1972) Recent development in Nagaland and NEFA. *Asian Affairs : Jour. of the Royal Central Asian Society*, 59(1), Feb. 3-13.

751. ———— 1978) Resurgent Apatanis. *Aru. News*, 7(3), June-July : 4-5.

752. ———— (1980) Arunachal to-day as Prof. Haimendorf sees it. *Aru. News*, 9(3), June-July : 1-5.

753. ———— (1980) Comparing the fortunes of tribal populations in Nagaland, Arunachal Pradesh and Andhra Pradesh. *Eastern Himalayas : A study on Anthropology and Tribalism*. Ed. by T.C. Sharma and D.N. Majumdar. New Delhi, Cosmo Pub. : 206-21.

754. ———— (1981) Asian Highland societies : An anthropolegical perspective. New Delhi, Sterling Publishers Pvt. Ltd, 265p.

755. ———— (1980) Himalayan Tribe: From Cattle to cash. Delhi, Vikas House Pvt. Ltd. 224p.

756. ————(1982) Highlanders of Arunachal Pradesh : Anthropological research in North East India. New Delhi, Vikas Pub. House Pvt. Ltd. 185p.

757. ———— (1982) Tribes of India : The struggle for survival. Delhi, Oxford Uni. Press, 342p.

758. GAIT, E A. (1892) Census cf India 1891, Vol. I ; Assam, pt. I, Report. Shillong, Govt. Press : 183-84, 186, 221-22, 213.

759. ———— (1926) History of Assam. Calcutta, Supdt. Govt. Ptg. India, 383p.

760. GALIE, A. (1913) Account of an expedition among the Abors in 1853 by Rev. Fr. N.M. Krick. (A foreign mission of Paris and superior of the South Tibetan Mission). *Jour. of the Asiatic Society of Bengal*, 9 : 107-22.

761. GANGULI, B.N.(1976) An integrated research approach to the problems of shifting cultivation with particular reference to Arunachal Pradesh (Abstract). Proceed ngs of a Seminar on "*Shifting Cultivation*" organised by NEICSSR, Shillong.

762. GANGULY, J.B. (1971) Solung, a great festital of the Adis. *NEFA Information* (Shillong), 6(2), Sept. : 21-4.

763. GANGULY, Pranab *and* HUSAIN, Zahid (1984) Relative proportions of tribals and non-tribals in North East India. *The Tribes of North East India*. Ed. by S. Karotemprel. Calcutta. Firma KLM Pvt. Ltd. : 30-5.

764. GAZETTER (1906) Provincial Gazetteers of Assam : Eastern Bengal and Assam. Oxford, Horace Hart, Printer to the University : 147-51.

765. GEE, E.P. (1965) Wild animals and plant life in NEFA. *The Hornbill* (Shillong) : 6-11.

766. ———— (1966) Orchids in North East India. *The Hornbill* : 7-12.

767. GHATAK, Indu Bhushan: (1945-46) Abor, Aka, Daphla. *Ethnology of India : The Quarterly Journal of the Mythic Society* (Bangalore), 36(1) : 25.

768. GHATE, Muralidhar (1968) NEFA ke Adivashi (in Hindi).
Vanyajati, 16(4), Oct. : 145-50 and 17(1), Jan. : 22-7.

769. GHOSE, A.K. (1971) Aphids (Insecta) or plant lice of economic crops of Arunachal.
Pines, 1 (III), Arunachal Number : 66-9.

770. GHOSH, J.N. (1955) Health measures in NEFA.
The Adivasis.
Delhi, Publication Division, Ministry of I. & B, Govt. of India ; 73-9.

771. GHOSH, L.K. (1971) New records and new sub-species of aphids (Homoptera) from India.
Oriental Insects, 5(1) : 129-33.

772. GHOSH, Sailendra Kumar (1951) Clouds over Assam. Calcutta, One India Society, 75p.

773. GHOSH, Samir Kumar (1968) The Mishmi world view.
Man in India (Ranchi), 48 4), Oct.-Dec. : 327-36.

774. ———— (1969) The Mishmis of the North East Frontier Agency (NEFA) of India : Between stability and change.
Bulletin of International Committee on Urgent Anthropological and Ethnological Research (Vienna), 11 : 35-40.

775. ———— (1969) Education and social change, NEFA.
Ethnos, 34 : 118-29.

776. ———— (1969) Education and social change.
Jour. of Social Research (Ranchi) 12(1) : 27-37.

777. GHOSH, S.K. *and* CHOPRA, Prabha (1930) Echoes from North Eastern India. New Delhi, S. Chand & Company : 110-11.

778. GHOSHAL, Hiranmoy(1958) The Nagari script in NEFA
Bulletin of the Research Dept., NEFA (Shillong), 1(1), June : 26-35.

779. GILLE, A (1913) An account of expedition among the Abors in 1853.
JRASB, 9 (N.S.) : 107-22.

780. GODDEN, G.M. (1897) Nagas and other Frontier Tribes of North East India.
J.A.I., XXVI (2) & XXVII.

781. GODWIN-AUSTEN, H.H. (1875) Notes on the Geology of part of the Dafla Hills, Assam.
JASB, 1 : 35 & 139.

782. ———(1876) Extract from the narrative report of the Daphla Military Expeditionary Survey.
Calcutta, *General Report on the Topographical Survey of India for the season 1874-75 : 68-82.*

783. ——— (1876) List of the Birds collected on the expedition into the Dafla Hills, Assam, together with those obtained in the adjacent Darrang Terai.
JASB, 2 : 64.

784. ——— (1882) Notes on the wild tribes inhabiting the so-called Naga Hills on our N.E. Frontier of India.
J.A.I. XI : 56-73 & 196-214.

785 GOGOI, Lila (1858) The Age old amity of the Hills and the plains.
The outlook on NEFA. Comp. by Parag Chaliha.
Jorhat, Assam Sahitya Sabha : 12-7.

786. ——— (1963) The Adis of NEFA.
Folklore, 4(1) Jan. : 1-7.

787. ——— (1963) Simantar mati aru manuha.
Gauhati, Lawyers Book Stall, 98p.

788. ——— (1971) Tai Sanskritir ruprekha (in Assamese).
Calcutta : 226p.

789. ——— (Comp.) (1971) The Tai Khamtis.
Chowkham (NEFA), Chowkhamoon Gohain (Namsoon), 210p.

790. GOGOI, Padmeswar (1968) The Tai and Tai Kingdom.
Gauhati Uni., Dept. of Publications, 552p.

791. GOGOI, P.D. (1975) Political structure of Adi people of Arunachal Pradesh.
Indian Jour. of Local Self Govt., 14(4-5), April-Sept. : 467-76.

792. GOHAIN, A.K. (1966) Some place names of Tirap.
The Hornbill (Shillong, DIPR, Arunachal Pradesh), 41-3.

793. ——— (1979) On the Lissus of Vijaynagar.
Aru. News, 8(5), Aug. : 37-8.

794. ———— (1979) Khomong and Khamtis.
Aru. News, 7 (9), Repub. Day Issue : 24-9.

795. ———— (1979) Interesting stones at Long-Veih and Teng-Pum village.
Aru, News. 8(4), June-July : 14-5.

796. GOHAIN. B.C. (1953) Shifting cultivation among the Abors.
March of India (Delhi), 6(2), Nov-Dec : 39-43.

797. ———— (1953) Shifting cultivation among the Abors. *Report of the second conference for Tribes and Tribals (Scheduled) Areas, Lohardonga* (Bharatiya Adimjati Sevak Sangh), New Delhi, November :250-58.

798. ———— (1959) Agricultural organisation among the Abor.
Bulletin of the Dept. of Anthropology. (Anthropological Survey of India, Calcutta), 3(2 , July(1954) : 34-47.

799. ———— (1967) & (1971) Tribal Map of India (1967) and Annexure (1971). Calcutta, Anthropological Survey of India.

800. ———— (1977) Human sacrifice and head hunting in North Eastern India, Gauhati, Lawyer's Book Stall. 106p

801. GOHAIN, C. B. (1971) Food production in Lohit.
NEFA information, 6(2), Sept : 21-4.

802. ———— (1971) The Khampti tradition.
NEFA information, May : 14-6.

803, ———— (1972) Approach to Agricultural development.
Aru. News. 1(3), April : 10-2.

804. ———— (1972) Hayi or Jhum : A traditional mean of living.
Aru. News, 1(7), Sept. : 27-8.

805. GOHAIN, D. (1979) Apple cultivation in Kameng district of Arunachal Pradesh.
North Eastern Economic Review (Gauhati), 3(2) : 75-83.

806. GOHA N, D. *and* SAIKIA, D. (1970) Khonsa, a socio economic survey of Nocte Naga village in NEFA.
Jorhat, Agro—Economic Research Centre (1970).

807. GOHAIN, Hiren (1980) Tangled theories.
Economic and Political Weekly (Bombay), 15 (16), April : 733-35.

808. GOHAIN, U.N. (1958) Ahom relations with the Neighbouring Hill Tribes and the tributary chiefs.
The Outlook on NEFA, Comp. by Parag Chaliha. Jorhat, Assam Sahitya Sabha : 5-12,

809. GOSWAMI, B.B. (1953) Shifting cultivation among the Abors.
Man in India, 2,

810. ———— (1973) The tribes of North East India : A few comments on their social and culturalties with the non-tribes.
North Eastern Research Bulletin (Dibrugarh), 4, Summer: 41-8.

811. ———— (1983) Book Review : Gazetteer of India, Arunachal Pradesh : Subansiri District, edited by S. Dutta Choudhury, Govt. of Arunachal Pradesh, pages 338-XXI, Rs. 78/-.
Jour. of Indian Anthropological Society, 18(2), July : 199.

812. GOSWAMI, M.C. SHARMA, H.C. and DAS, R. C. (1972) A typological study of some prehistoric tools from Kameng district of NEFA (Arunachal).
Jour. Assam Science Society (Gauhati), 15(1), June : 29-35.

813. GOSWAMI, M.C. and ROY, S.K. (1975) A short note on Tanga Hoe.
Bulletin Dept. of Anth., Gauhati University.

814. GOSWAMI, P.C. (1977) Problems of economic development in tribal areas.
North Eastern Economic Review (Gauhati), 1(1), Jan-March : 8-14.

815. GOSWAMI, P.C. and SAIKIA, P.D. (1971) Problems of economic development in tribal areas with special reference to Dafla and Gallong tribes of NEFA.
North Eastern Research Bulletin (Dibrugarh), 2, Summer 33-41.

816. GOSWAMI, P.D. (1929) Abor tales.
Man in India, 29(3-4) : 209-11.

817. ——— (1978) Book Review : Puma Dada Hoi Dada, Adi folklore.
Resarum, 4(2), Aut-Win : 48-50.

818. GOSWAMI, Praphulladatta (1982) Essays of the folklore and culture of North Eastern India,
Gauhati. Spectrum Pub., 174p.

819. GOSWAMI, Praphulla (1949) Abor tales.
Man in India, 29 (3-4), July-Dec. : 209-11.

820. ——— (1959) Miri Folk Songs.
Folklore, 2(2), April-June : 103-06.

821. ——— (1969) Folk tales of the Miris.
Folkolore, 10(10), Oct. : 390-92.

822. GOVT. of India (1913) Frontier and overseas expeditions from India : Official account of the Abor expedition, 1911-12.

823. ——— (1957) Bench mark survey report : Arunachal (Assam), Delhi, Govt. of India, Planning Commission. Programme Evalution Organisation, July.

824. GOYI, Taba Tani (1981) The Nishings.
Aru. News, 10(8) : 14-16.

825. GRAY, J. Errol (1893) Diary of a journey to the Bor Khamti country and sources of the Irrawady made by Mr. J. Errol Gray, session 1892-93, from Assam. Simla.

826. ——— (1893) Diary of a journey to the Bor Khamti country, 1892-3,
India' North East Frontier. Ed. by Verries Elwin.
Bombay, O.U.P. (1959) : 346, 372-82, 416-17, 419 26

827. GRIERSON, George A. (1909) : Linguistic Survey of *India, Vol. III, pt. I, Tibeto—Burman family : General* Introduction, specimens of the Tibetan dialects, the Himalayan dialects and the North Assam Group.
Calcutta, Supdt. of Govt. Printing, 641p.

828. GRIFFITH, William (1836) Journal of a trip to the Mishmi mountain. (Selection of Papers).

India's North East Frontier....Ed. by Verrier Elwin. Bombay, O.U.P. (1959) : 311-13, 421.

829. ———— (1838) Visit to the Mishmee Hills in Assam. *Jour, Asiatic Society of Bengal, New Series*, 25 : 233-44.

830. ———— (1847) Journals of travels in Assam, Burma, Bootan, Afganistan and the Neighbouring countries. Calcutta, (Reprinted in 1984).

831. GRILL, A. (Tr) (1913) An account of an expedition among the Abors in 1853 by N.M. Krick. *Jour. Asiatic Society of Bengal*, 9(5) : 107-22.

832. GUIDE (DUTTA, Gita and DUTTA, Mrinal) (1982) Bhraman Sangi (in Bengali). Calcutta, Asia Publishing Company : 483-87.

833. GUHA, B.S. (1951) The Indian aborigines and administration. *Jour. Asiatic Society of Bengal, Science* (Calcutta), 17(1) : 19-44.

834. ———— (1953 Indian aborigines and who they are. *March of India* (Delhi), 6(2), Nov.-Dec. : 9-13.

835. ———— (1953) The Abor Moshup as a training centre for youth. *Vanyajati*, 1(4), Oct. : 83-95.

836. ———— (1959) Medicine man of Abor Hills. *The Times of India* (Delhi), Oct, 25.

837. ———— (1964) Moshup legape doying agonu lunnue (i.e. Mythological origin of the Abor [Adi] dormitory system). Shillong, Research Dept., Govt. of NEFA, 66p.

838. ———— (1964) Mosup Abang. Shillong, Dir. of Inf. & Pub. Rela., 66p.

839. GUHA, K (1960) Tribal handicrafts in India. *Vanyajati*, 8(3) July : 117-23.

840. GUPTA, Karunakar (1984) : Book Review : Problem of the Hill Tribes : North East Frontier by H.K. Barpujari. Spectrum Publications, Gauhati, Assam, 1981. *Jour, NEICSSR* (Shillong), 8(1), April : 44-6.

841. GUPTA, S. (1948) British Policy on the North East Frontier of India, 1826-86. London, Oxford University (Unpublished Dissertation).

842. GURDON, P.R.T. (1895) On the Khamtis (Assam). *Jour. of the Royal Asiatic Society*, 27 : 157-64.

843. HAGDA. S.N. (1984) Orchids of Arunachal Pradesh. Shillong, Dir. of Res., Govt. of A.P. (in Press).

843A. HALDIPUR, Krishna (1985) Around the Hill and Dales of Arunachal Prcadesh. Shillog, NEHU, 82p.

844. HALDIPUR, R.N. (1972) Policy towards and administration of the Tribes of North East India. *Tribal Situation in India: Procedings of a Seminar*. Ed. By K. Suresh Singh Simla, Indian Institute of Advanced Study: 305-15.

845. HALLIDAY, H.I. (1928) The Abors of Assam. *United Empire* XIX ; 339-42.

846. HAMILTON, Angus (1912) In Abor Jungles. London, Eveheigh Nash, 352p.

847. ———— (1912) In The Mishmi Mission. *Fortnightly Review*, XCI; 552-65.

848. ———— (1983) Abor Jungles of North East Iadia. Delhi, Mittal pub., Reprinted), 352p.

849. HAMILTON, Francis (1940) An account of Assam. Edited by S.K. Bhuyan. Gauhati, Govt. of Assam in the Dept. of Historical & Antiquarian Studies, 104p.

850. HAMILTON. Robert C. (1900) An outline grammar of the Dafla language, as spoken by the tribes immediately south of the Apa Tanang country. Shillong, Assam Secretariat Printing Office. 127p.

851. HAMILTON. W. (1984) East India Gazetteer, 2 Vols. Delhi. (Reprinted).

852. HANNAY, S.F. (1847) Sketch of the Singphos or the Kakhyens of Burma. the position of the Tribe as regards Baumo and the Inland Trade of the Irrawaddy with Yunnan, followed by an account of the Shans. Calcutta.

853. HARMMAN, H.J. (1876) Narrative Report of Lt. H.J. Harman in charge Daphla Military Expeditionary Survey (General Report on the topographical Surveys of India for the season 1874-75). Calcutta.

854. ———— (1876) Narrative Report of Lt.H.J. Harman in charge Daphla Military expeditionary Survey. *India's North East Frontier*...Ed. by Verrier Elwin. Bombay: O.U.P. (1959) : 181-83.

855. HARRISS, Barbara (1983) The North East Frontier of India Delhi.

856. HASTINGS, James (Ed) (1978) Encyclepaedia of Religion and Ethics, Vol.I. Edinburg, T & T Clark (Reprinted in 1921 from London).

857 HAZARIKA, K.C. (1979) Traditioal textile industry of Taraons. *Resarun*, 5(1),Spring-Summer : 84-51.

858 ———— (1983) Reh and Idu religion : A nanthropological glance to the process. *Resarun*. 9(2), Aut-Win : 25-30.

859. HAZARIKA, Kirtinath (Tr) (1958) The N bula of the North East Frontier. *The Outlook on NEFA. Comp.* by Parag Chelihe. Jorhat. Sahitya Sabha : 52-66.

860, HAZARIKA. Munindra Prasad : (1974) Arunachal : From Kebang to Penchayat an experiment in decoratic decentralization. *North Eastern Affairs* (Shillong), 2(4), Jan-March : 27-30

861. ———— (1976) Cultural development in Arunachal. *North Eastern Spectrum* (Gauhati), 1(1 , 7uly : 39-40.

862. ———— (1976) An era of socio cultural awakening in Arunachal. *Aru, News*, 5(5), Sept : 7-9.

863. ———— (1978) Donyi-Polo : A Philosophy of religion. *Aru. News*, 7(3). June-July : 8-10.

864. HEGDE, M R. (1978) Liming of acid soils. *Aru News*. 7(4).Aug : 53-4.

865. HESSELMEYER, C.H. (1868) The Hill Tribes of the Northern Froniier of Assam. *Jour Asiatic Society of Bengal*, 37, p. 2: 192-208.

866. ———— (1868) The Hill Tribes of the Northern Frontier of Assam.
India's North East Frontier... Ed. by Verrier Elwin. Bombay, O.U.P. (1959) : 435-46.

867. ———— (1972) The Hill Tribes of the North East Frontier.
Indian Antiquary, 1 : 62-3.

868. HIMALAYA (1980) Arunachal Pradesh : A glorious example of an idealist youth.
Himalaya : Man & Nature. 4(7). Dec. : 15-6.

869. ———— (1981) New round in Arunachal inaugurated.
Himataya: Man & Nāture, 5(3), March,: 10.

870. ———— (1981) Land develepment in Arunachal.
Himalaya : Man & Nature, 4(4). April : 11.

871. ———— (1981) Local Institutions of Tirap District : The Dormitory system.
Himalaya : Man & Nature, 5(9), Sept : 10-1.

872. ———— (1984) Polygamy system of the Wanchees Call
Himalaya : Man and Nature, 8(5-6), Oct-Nov. : 9-11.

873. HODGSON, B.H. (1849) On the Aborigines of the Eastern Frontier.
Jour Asiatic Society of Bengal, 18, pt. II ; 967-75.

874. ———— (1850) Aborigines of the North Eastern Frontier. *Jour. of the Royal Asiatic Society of Bengal*, 19 : 309-16.

875. (1853) On the Indo-Chinese borders and their connextion with the Himalayans and Tibetans.
Jour. of the Asiatic Society of Bengal, 22 : 1-25.

876. ———— (1880) Miscellaneous essays relating to Indian subjects London.

877. HODSON, T. C. (190') Head-Hunting among the Hill Tribes of Assam.
Falklore (London), 20 : 132-43.

878. HOLDICH, T.H. (1912) The North Eastern Frontier of India.
J.R.Soc.Arts, XC: 379-92.

879. HORE.W.B. (1913) Report on the Abor country. Simla.

880. HOUGHTON, B. (1896) Outlines of Tibeto-Burman Linguistic Palaeontology.
JRAS: 23-55.

881. HUDSON, B.H. (1850) On the aborigines of eastern frontier. *Jour.Royal Asiatic Society of Bengal*, pt. I & II.

882. HUSSAIN, Imadad (1980) Book Review : British Policy in the North East Prontier Agency by M.L. Bose, Concept Pub. House, New Delhi, 1979, 236p, Appendices, Bibliography, Index, price Rs.90.00.
Jour. NEICSSR (Shillong), 4(1), April : 22-3.

883. HUSAIN, Zahid (1983) Human adaptation to extreme climate : A case study of Arunachal Himalya Kameng District).
Workshop paper on "*Human Adaptation to extreme climte*", July 27, Anthropological Survey of India, Calcutta.

884. ———— (1984) Settled plough farming in the alluvlial flat land of mountain ecosystem : Problems and prospects in Yangse Valley.
Proceedings of a seminar on *Land Reforms*, organised by NEICSSR, Shillong.

885. HUTCHINSON, Walter (Ed.) (1984) Customs of the World : A popular account of the manners, rites and ceremonies of men and women in all countries, Vol. I. Delhi, Concept Pub. (Reprinted)

886. HUTTON J.H. (1936) Headhunters of the North East Frontier.
J.R. Soc. Arts, LXXXV, 134-44.

887. ———— (1945) Problems of reconstruction in the Assam Hills. London, Institute of Great Britain & Ireland, 7p.

888. ———— (1946) Caste in India. London, Combridge University Press : 274,278 (Glossary).

889. ———— (1961) Book Review : India's North East Frontier in the Nineteenth Century. Edited by Verrier Elwin, Bombay, Oxford University Press, 1959, pp. xxx +473.

Man (London), LXI, Articles 1.25, Jan : 29-30.

890. HUNTER, W.W. (1975) A Statistical Account of Assam. (in two Vols.) B. R. Publishing Corporation (Reprinted) (1st Published in 1879), Delhi.

891. ICAR (1978), Research on shifting cultivation. *News Letter* : *ICAR* (Shillong), 1(3), July-Sep. 1-3. 2

892. ———— (1980) Proceedings of workshop on Agricultural Research in North Eastern Hill region of India. Shillong. Director ICAR Region. 263p.

893. IMPERIAL Gazetteer (1909) The Imperial Gazetteer of India.

(Provincial series : Eastern Bengal and Assam), Calcutta, Supdt., Govt. Printing, India, 66p.

894. INDIA Census (1892) Census of India 1891: Assam, Vol. I, Report by E. A. Gait. Shillong, Assam Secretariat Printing Office, 311p.

895. ———— (1902) Census of India 1901, Vol. 4, Assam, pt. I, Report by B.C. Allen. Shillong, Assam Secretariat Printing Office, 179p.

896. ———— (1912) Census of India 1911, vol. 3 : Assam, pt.I, Report by J.McSwiney. Shillong, Assam Secretariat Printing Office, 183p.

897. ———— (1923) Census of India 1921, Vol. : Assam. Shillong, Govt. Printing, 199p.

898. ———— (1932) Census of India 1931, Vol. 3 : Assam. pt. I, Report by C. S. Millan. Calcutta, Central Publication Branch, Govt. of India, 227p

999. ———— (1954 Census of India 1951, Vol 12 : Assam, Manipur and Tripura, pt I-A, Report by R.B. Vaghaiwalla. Sh llong, Municipal Printing Press, 431p.

900. ———— (1967) Census of India 1961 Vol. 3 : Assam, pt. VI : Village Survey Monograph 14 : Laisong. Delhi, Manager of Pub., 56p.

901. INDIAN Army (1887) Military report on the Khampti Singpho countries by C.R. Macgregor. Calcutta, Supdt., Govt, Ptg., 71p.

902. INDIAN Folklore (1958) NEEA Highlander.
Indian Folklore, 1(1), Jan-March : 85-8.

903. INDIAN, Administrative (1969)Report on administration of Union territories and NEFA. Delhi, Indian Administrative Reforms Commission, Manager of Publication, 55p.

904. INDIA, Constitution Assembly (1948) India, Constituent Assembly Subcommittee on North East Frontier (Assam) Tribal and excluded areas : Report (July,1947).
Constituent Assembly Debates. Official Report, 7(1), Nov. Appendix-C : 103 42.

905. INDIA, Govt. of (1913) Frontier and overseas expeditions from India : Official account of the Abor expedition, 1911-12, Simla.

906. INDIAN Labour Statistics (1972) NEFA.
Indian Labour Statistics : 108.

907. INDIA, National Council (1962) Techno-Economic Survey of Assam. New Delhi, National Council of Applied Economic Research : 273-74.

908. INTERNATIONAL Journal (1961) A seventh Indian Sociological conference (news).
International Journal of Comparative Sociology, 2(1) : 115.

909. IZZARD, Ralph (1951) The Hunt for the Buru. London, Hodder and Stoughton, 176p.

910. JAFRI, S.S.A. (1980) Industrial classification and hierarchical order of towns in the North Eastern Region of India.
Jour. NEICSSR (Shillong), 4(2), Oct : 19-25.

911. JASWAL, I.J.S. (19 5) Anomalous colour vision among three tribes of Arunachal Pradesh, India.
The Anthropologist, 32(1-2), March-Sept : 60-4.

912. ———— (1976) Prospects of Palaeoanthropogical studies in Siwaliks, Arunachal Pradesh .
Proceedings of a Seminar of Geology and Mineral Resources of Eastern Himalayas (A Publication of Geological Survey of India).

913. ———— (1976) Search for early man in North East India.
Man in India, 56 : 276-77.

914. ———— (1976) Tribes of North East India, Fthnic and population aspects.
Report submitted to Anth. Survey of India. (Unpublished)

915. ———— (1983) PTC testingability among Apatanis.
Report submitted to Anth. Survey of India (Unpublished).

916. ———— (1983) Socio-anthropology of Apatanis,
Report submitted to Anth. Survey of India. (Unpublished).

917. ———— (1984) Ecology in Anthropological studies.
Status of Ecology. Ed. by I.J.S. Jaswal. Patiala, Punjab Pub. House : 9-16.

918. ———— (1984) Tribes of Northeast India : Ethnic and population aspects.
The Tribes of North East India. Ed. by S. Karotemprel. Calcutta, Firma KLM Pvt. Ltd. : 27-9.

919. ———— (Ed) (1984) Status of Ecology. Patiala, Punjab Publishing House.

920. JASWAL, I.J S. and JASWAL, Sushma (1983) Mental retardation and tribal society.
Jour. NEICSSR (Shillong), April : 26-30.

921. JASWAL, I.J.S. and PADMNABHAM, P B. S.V (1983) Sero-anthroplogy of Apatanis of Arunachal Pradesh.
Human Science (Anth. Sur. of India, Calcutta), 32(2), June : 120-24.

922. JASWAL, S & JASWAL, I J.S.(1983) Anthropometry of Apatanis.
Report submitted to Anth. S.I. (Unpublished).

923. JASWAL Sushma & JASWAL, I. J. S. (1983) Anthropometry of the Apatani of Arunachal Pradesh.
Human Science (Anth. S.I. Calcutta), 32(4), Dec. 292-302.

924. JAYAKAM, K. C & MAJUMDAR, N. (?) On a collection of fish from Kameng Frontier Division, NEFA.
Jour. Bombay Nat. Hist. Soc. (Bombay), 61(2): 264-80.

925. JENKINS, F. (1869) Notes on Burmese route from Assam to Hookong Valley.
Proceedings of A.S.B.

926. JENKINS, H.L. (1870) Notes on a trip across the Patkoi Range from Assam to the Hookong Valley.
Proceedings A.S.B. : 230-7.

927. JHA, S.D. (1976) Socio Econmic study of Arunachal Pradesh.
Gauhati Uni., Ph. D. Thesis (Unpublished).

928. ———— (1983) Study of growth oriented problems for industrial development in Arunachal Pradesh.
Aru. News, 12(5), Aug-Sept : 1-5.

929. ———— (1984) Focus on agrarian structure in the perspective of Socio-economic development in Arunachal Pradesh.
Proceedings of a Seminar on *Land Reforms* organised by NEICSSR, Shllong.

930. JOHRI, Sita Ram (1962) Where India China and Burma meet. Calcutta, Thacker Spink, 302p.

931 ———— (1964) Our borderlands. Lucknow, Himalaya Publications, 376p.

932. ———— (1967) Integrated study of the Hillmen of Assam.
A Common Perspective for North East India. Ed. by Rathin Mitra and B. Das Gupta. Calcutta, Punnalal Das Gupta : 180-90.

933. ———— (1968) Chinese invasion of NEFA. Lucknow, Publications, 263p.

934. JOMOH, Abeng (1972) Significance of festival : Cultural Heritage.
Aru. News, 1(4), May : 33-4.

935. J.R.Soc. (1936) Head hunters of the East Frontier.
J R. Soc. Arts, LXXXV.

936. JOSHI, Changanlal (1958) Tour impressions of North East Frontier Agency.
All India Congress Committee, *Economic Review* : 9(24), April 15 : 21.

937. JOSHI, M.C. & JHA, S. D. (1977) Vocationalisation under 10+2+3 pattern of education in Arunachal Paradesh.
Aru. News, 6(4), Aug : 58-65.

938. ———— (1977) Suitable scale of production and technology in the Hills of North East India.
Aru. News, 6(6), Oct : 15-23.

939. ———— (1981) Livestock in Arunachal Pradesh.
Himalaya : Man and Nature, 5(4), Sept : 3-6.

940 JOSHI, M.C. (1977) Study of Arunacha' Pradesh Admistration.
Gauhati Uni., Ph. D. Thesis (Unpublished).

941. ———— (1978) Electorates and the first assembly election in Arunachal Pradesh.
Aru. News, 7(4), Aug. : 30-2.

942. ———— (1978) Dimensional study of manpower in relation to agricultural production in Arunachal Pradesh.
Aru. News, 7(5) : 13-8.

943. ———— (1979) Development of horticulture in Arunachal Pradesh.
Aru. News, 7(9) : 416.

944. ———— (1979) Rural development in Arunachal Pradesh : Integrated approach.
Aru. News, 8(6) : 33-8.

945. JOSEPH, A.N.T. and PARU, P. (1969) Notes on styringomyia subobscura Alexander (Diptera : Tipulidae).
Oriental Insects, 3(3) : 311-12.

946. JOSEPH, J. and CHOWDHURY, S. (1966) Oberonia sulcata Joset Chowd, a new orchid from Kameng Frontier District, NEFA, Assam.
Jr. Bombay Nat. Hist. Soc, LXIII : 54-6.

947. JOSEPH, J. and ROLLA, S.R.(1968) Aneilema Glanduliferum Joseph et Rolla Rao, a new species from NFFA.
Jr. Indian Bot. Soc., XLVII : 367-70.

948. ———— (1972) Rubus Ghanakantus Joseph et Rolla Rao : A new species from NEFA.
Bull. Bot. Survey of India, 12.

949. JOUNSARI, Bhatan Singh (1970) NEFA Lohit ke Msshmi adivashiyon ka jivan (in Hindi).
Vanyajati, 18(4), Oct : 101-05.

950. ——— (1974) NEFA Lohit khetro ke adivashi Mishmi in Hindi).
Vanyajati, 22(1), Jan : 21-3.

951. JOURNAL NEC (1976) Factors affecting Industrial development in North Eastern Region.
Jour, North Eastern Council (Shillong), 1(4), Jan : 39-49.

952. KAKATI, Satis Chandra (*Comp*) (1954) Discovery of Assam. Gauhati, the author, 179 p.

953. KAMAT, J. (1979) Survey of intestinal parasites infesting population of Itanagar with special mention to hookworm.
Aru. News, 8(2) : 10-4.

954. KAMAT, Prabhakar (1978) Programme of adult education in Arunachal Pradesh, 1978.
Aru. News, 7(4), Aug. : 78-80.

955. KANI, M. (1983) The Dree festival of the Apatanis.
Resarun, 9(2), Aut-Win : 31-3.

956. KAPADIA, K.M (1954) Changing patterns of Hindu marriage and family.
Sociological Bulletin.

957. KAR, P.L. & KHARLUKI, A.T. (1981) Mishmi teeta of Arunachal Pradesh and its cultivation practices.
Aru. News, (10(5), July : 16-20.

958. KAR, R.K. (1969) Social changes among the Adis.
Tribe (Udaipur, Rajasthan),6(3), Dec. : 35-41.

959. ——— (1975) The Rh blood groups among the Adi of Pasighat, Arunachal Pradesh.
Eastern Anthropologist (Lucknow).
28(2), April-June : 165-68.

960. ——— (1980) Arunachal Pradesh and her peeple : A preliminary appraisal.
Vanyajati, 28(3), July : 23-5.

961. ————(1981) A note on the A, A_2 BO and MN Blood Groups among the Adis of Pasighat, Arunachal Pradesh. *Bull. Dept af Anth. : Dibrugarh Uni.*, 7-8(1978-79) : 38.45.

962. KAR, R. K. & MAHANTA, Shyamali (1975) Menarche and menopause among the Singpho women of Arunachal Pradesh.
Indian Jour of Physical Anth. and Human Genetics, 1(1), June : 51-7.

963. KAR, S.K. & PANIGRAHI, G. (1963) The Rubiaceae in Assam and North East Frontier Agency.
Bulletin Bot Survey of India, 5 : 227- 7.

964. KAR CHOUDHURY, Amalendu Bikash (1984) Tribal songs of Northeast India. Calcutta, Firma KLM Pvt. Ltd.

965. KATAKI, S.K. and PANIGRAHI, G. (1964) Ranunculaceae in Assam and North East Frontier Agency.
Ind. For, LXXXX : 393-400.

966. KATAKI, S. K. & SASTRY. A. R. K. (1965) Notes on the distribution of Bulleyia yunanensis Schltr.
Ind For., LXXXXI : 862-63.

967. KAUL, Ikbal (1977) Carpet weavers of Tawand.
The Hindusthan Times. Sept. 11 : 1.

968. KAUL, Prem Nath (1976) Frontier callings. Delhi, Vikas Publishing House : 54-91.

969. KAULBACK, R. (1938) Salween.
London (It has description on Mishmis).

970. KEISAING, Rishang (1956) The problem of India's North Eartern tribals.
Indian Affairs Record, 2, June : 1-4.

971. KENNEDY, R. S. (1914) Ethnological report on the Akas, Khoas and Mijis and the Monpas of Tawang.
Shillong.

972. KHANNA, K. C. (1969) Stability in the North East ; New problems and challenges.
Times of India (Delhi), Aug. 22 : 6.

973. KHOUND, T. P. (1964) NEFA on the march. Shillong, NEFA Publications, 44p.

974. KINGDON-WARD, F. (1930) Plant hunting on the edge of the world. London (Having description on Mishmis).

975. ———— (1930) The Seingkin and Delei valleys, North Eastern Frontier of India.
Geographical Journal (London), LXXV : 412-35(Mishmi).

976. ———— (1934) A plant hunter in Tibet. London.

977. ————(1941) Assam Adventure. London. (Regarding Monpa).

978. KINGDOM-WARD, Jean (1952) My hill so strong.
London, Jonathan Cape, 240p.(It contains a vivid account of the earthquake of 1950 as it affected the Lohit Frontier Division).

979. KOHLI, Y. P. (1980) Our scientific heritage.
Aru. News, 9(4), Aug. : 35-7.

980. ———— (1981) Our scientific heritage.
Aru News, 10(2), Feb-March : 29-31.

981. KOJEEN, Hage (1973) The Myoko festival.
Aru News, 2(6), Sept : 3-7.

982. KONDINYA, Bhikshu (1975) Ashom Rajya ki Misid janajati ki bibaha paddhati ebong samaj me nari ka sthan. (in Hindi).
Vanyojati, 23(2-3), April-July : 16-20.

983. ———— (1975-76) Monasticism in Khamti society.
Jour. of the University of Gauhati (Arts), 26-27(1).

984. ———— (1975-76) Role of religion in Khamti society.
Jour. of the Uni. of Gauhati (*Arts*), 26-27(1).

985. ———— (1976) Monasticism in Khamti society.
Aru. News, 5(2), March : 3-9.

986. ———— (1977) Buddhist ceremony and festivals in Khamti Society.
Aru. News, 5(9), Jan-Feb. : 11-17 *and* 22.

987. ———— (1977) Nibbana and Kamti Society.
Aur. News, 6(1), April : 1-5 *and* 6(2), June : 5-8.

988. ———— (1977) Role of religion in Khamti society.
Aru. News, 6(3), June-July : 5-14.

989. ———— (1977) Thirty Eight types of Buddhist Mangala.
Aru. Fews, 6(4), Aug : 43-55.

990. ———— (1978) Monastic life and the Buddhist Sangha.
Aru. News, 6(9), Jan (Republic Day Issue): 23-31.

991. ———— (1978) Monastic social structure in Khamti Society.
Aru.News, 7(4), Aug(Independence Day) : 37.40. :

992. ———— (1978) Misind Janjati : Ek Parichaya. (In Hindi).
Himalaya : Man & Nature, 1(10), March : 35-40.

993. ———— (1978) Apa-Tani janajati of Arunachal Pradesh.
Himalaya : Man and Nature, 2(4), Sept : 15-21.

994. ———— (1979) Buddhist magical protection practices in Khamti society.
Resarun, 5(2), Aut-Winter : 31-40.

995. ———— (1980) Monpa janajati of Arunachal Pradesh.
Himalaya : Man and Nature, 3(8-9), Jan-Eeb: 45-8.

996. ———— (1980) Aka janajati of Arunachal Pradesh.
Himalaya : Man and Nature, 3(10), March : 4-7.

997. ————(1980) Wancho Janajati of Arunachal Pradesh.
Himalaya : Man and Nature, 4(2), July : 6-9.

998. ———— (1980) The monkhood and the rules of conduct in Khamti society.
Resarun, 6(1), Spring-Summer : 12-41.

999. ———— The sacred words in Buddhist ritual chants among the Khamti monks.
Resarun, 7(1-2) : 1-13,

1000. ———— (1982) Primary concepts and cosmological belief in Khamti village.
Resarun, 1(1), Sprsng-Summer : 1-7.

1001. KONOW, Sten (1902) Notes on the languages spoken between the Assam valley and Tibet.
J.R.A.S. : 127-37 (Aka, Dafla, Abor, Mishmi).

1002. KOUL, Pramod (1981) Mishings (Miri).
Aru. News, 10(4), June : 21.

1003. KRICK, N.M. (1913) An account of an expedition among the Abors in 1853 (Translated by Rev. A. Gille .
Jour. Asiatic Soc. of Bengal, 9(5) : 108-22.

1004. ———— (1913) An account of an expedition among the Abors in 1853.
India's North East Frontier in the Nineteenth Century. Ed. by Verrier Elwin. Bombay, Oxford University Press (1959) : 227, 236-49,

1005. KUMAR, B. (1981) A resume on the provisional population totals 1981.
Aru. News, 10(5), July : 1-9; 10(4), June and 10(6), Aug: 1-9.

1006. KUMAR, K. (1967) Mopin (A Gallong Festival).
Souvenir of the Mopin festival, Cultural Society (Along) : 3-9.

1007. ———— (1976) Pailibos.
Resarun, 2(2), April : 1-18.

1008. ———— (1976) The Boris.
Resarun '75, Cum. Volume : 11*-22.

1009. ———— (1976) Social organisation among the Boris.
Research in Arunachal : 72-8.

1010. ———— (1977) Pailibos.
Resarun '76, Cum. Volume : 72-84.

1011. ———— (1978) The Boris. Shillong, Research Dept., Dir. of Inf & Pub. Relations, Govt. of A.P., 397p.

1012. ———— (1979) The Pailibos. Shillong, Res. Dept., DIPR, Govt. of A.P., 374p.

1013. ———— (1983) The traditioal economic life of the Bokars.
Resarun, 9(1) : 15-24 *and* 9(2), 10(1).

1314. KUMAR, N. (1955) Middle-Phalangeal hair and occipital whorls among Nocte Naga.
Bull. Anth. Surv. of India (Calcutta), 4(2) : 61-7.

1015. ———— (1958) Blood group and secretor frequency among the Galong.
Bull. of the Dept. of Anth. (Anthropological Survey of India, Calcutta), 3(1), Jan(1954), : 55-64.

1016. KUMAR, Paramjit (1964) Till God wakes, immortal story of Sino-Indian War in NEFA. Chandigarh. Peoples Guardian Press, 261p.

1917. KURUP, G.U. (1968) Mammals of Assam and adjoining areas, 2. Distributional list.
Proc. Soc, 21(1), : 79-99.

1018. LAL, P.N. (1981) Shifting cultivation in Arunachal Pradesh. Proceedings of a Seminar on *Shifting Cultivation*, Sept. 25-26, 1981, Anth. Survey of India, Calcutta.

1019. LAL, Parmanand and DAS GUPTA, Biman Kumar (1979) Lower Siang People : A study in ecology and society (Memoir no. 50). Calcutta, Anth. Sur. of India. 158p,

1020. LAMA, Ratan (1970) Booriboot festival of the Hill Miris.
NEFA Information, 4(9), April : 13-4.

1021. LAMA, Tashi (1981) Tawang at a glance.
Resarun, 7(1-2) : 30-6.

1022. ———— (1983) Dungyru : A reilgious festival of Tawang Monpa.
Resarun, 9(2), Aut-Win : 4-9.

1023. LA TOUCHE, T.D. (1912) Notes on the Geology of the Aka Hills.
Rec. Geo. Surv. India, XVIII : 121.

1024. LEACH, E R. (1954) Political systems of Highland Burma.
Cambridge, Mass : (Champti & Singpho).

1025. LEPPER, C.H. (1882) Notes on the Singpho and Khampti country, North Eastern Frontier.
Proceedings of the Asiatic Society of Bengal, Calcutta ; 64-70.

1026. LEWIN, T.H. (?) The wild races of South Eastern India, London, W.A. Allen.

1027. LINDSAY, A.B. (1913) Expedition against the Abors, 1911-12.
Army Review, 4 : 343-58.

1028. LITTLE, W.R. (1895) Report on the Abor expedition, 1884. Simla, Govt. Central Printing Office, 41p.

1029. LLOYD, G. and HUTTON, J.H. (Ed) (1923) Census of 1921, Vol. III, Assam, pt. I : Report.

Shillong, Govt. Printing Press : Appendix-B, XI-XIII, 150p.(Aka, Dafla, Khamti, Abor).

1030. LOKANATHAN, P.S. (1967) Techno-Economic Survey of NEFA. New Delhi, National Council of Applied Economic Research, 197p.

1031. LONGCHANG, C. (?) Long Chang jatir chamu buranji (in Assamese). Shillong, 26p.

1032. LORRAIN, J. Herbert (1907) A dictionary of the Abor Miri language, with Illustrative sentences and Notes. Shillong. Printed at the Eastern Bengal & Assam Secretariat Printing ffice, 572p.

1033. LOWANG, P.W. (1968) The Morung of Tirap. *NEFA Information*, March : 9-10.

1034. LOWANG, Wangpha (1981) Namsang Pang. *Aru. News*, 10(7), Sept-Oct : 23-4.

1035. LOWIS, C.C. (1902) Census of India, 1901, Vol. 12 : Burma, pt. I, Report. Rangoon. (Akkas : 129).

1036. LUMSDEN, D.M. and WILLIAMSON, Noel (1911) A journey into the Abor country, 1909. *Geogrgphical Journal* (London), 37 : 621-29.

1037. LUTHRA, P.N. (1963) Mishmis of Lohit Frontier Division. *Modern Review*, 114(5), Nov : 376-78.

1038. ———— (1964) The Mishmis of Lohit Frontier Division. *Folklore*, 5(2), Feb : 62-6.

1039. ———— (1971) Constitutional and administrative Agency. Shillong, North East Frontier Agency Administration, 173p.

1040. ———— (1971) North East Frontier Agency Tribe : Impact of Ahom and British Policy. *Eco. and Pol. Weekly*, June 5 : 1143-9.

1041. MACFARDANE, Elieer and ERLANSON, W. (1937) Eastern Himalayan Blood Groups. *Man*, 37(158) : 127-29.

1042. MACGREGGR, C.R. (1884) Notes on Akas and Akaland.
Proceedings Asiatic Society of Bengal, No. 11 : 198-212.

1043. ———— (1884) Notes on Akas and Akaland.
India's North East Frontier in the Nineteenth Century. Ed. by Verrer Elwin. Bombay, Oxford University Press (1959) : 446-54.

1044. ————(1887) Military report on the Kampti-Singpho countries. Calcutta, Supdt., Govt. Ptg., 71p.

1045. ———— (1887) Military report on the Kampti-Singpho countries.
India's North East Frontier in the Nineteenth Century. Ed. by Verrier Elwin. Bombay, O.U.P. (1959) : 357-81, 414-16,419.

1046. ———— (1887) Journey of the expedition under Col. Woodthorpe R.E, from Upper Assam to the Irawadi and return over the Patkoi Range.
Proceedings of the Royal Geographical Society (London), 9 : 19-42.

1047. ———— (1894) Rough notes on the traditions, customs etc. of the Singpho and Khamptis.
Babylonian and Oriental Record. 7 : 172-76.

1048. MACKENZIE, Alexander (1869) Memorandum on the North East Frontier of Bengal. Calcutta, Bengal Secretariat Press, 78p.

1049. ————(1884) History of the relations of the Government with Hill Tribes of the North East Frontier of Bengal. Calcutta, Home Dept., 586p. (NEFA : 27-32, 537-5J).

1050. ————(1884) History of the relations of the Govrnment with Hill Tribes of the North East Frontier of Bengal.
India's North East Frontier in the Nineteenth Century. Ed. by Verrier Elwin. Bombay, O.U.P. (1959) : 15-25, 88, 91, 167-74, 207-18, 286-88, 597-302, 385-95,429-35.

1051. ———— (1979) The North East Frontier of India. Delhi, Mittal Publications, 586p. (Reprinted) (1st Published in 1884).

1052. MADAN, T.N. and SARANA, Gopala (1962) Indian Anthropology : Fssays in memory of D.N. Majumdar. Bombay, Asia Publishing House : (Dafla).

1053. MAHANTA, K. C. (1977) Socio-Economic aspects of the Nocte marriage system. *Vanyajati*, 25(1), Jan : 1-9.

1054. MAHANTA, Sarat (1961) Noga Noruttam Gosain Sri Ram (in Assamese). *Asam Bani* (Gauhati), Sept. 1.

1055. MAHAPATRA, L.K. (1962) Daphla and the Miji Society : A preliminary ecological analysis. *Sociologus*, 12(2) : 158-67.

1056. ———— (1974) Determining social types on the tribe peasant continuum. *Jour. of the Anthropological Society* (Calcutta), 9(1), April.

1057. MAIR, Lucy (196) Book Review : The Tangsas of the Namchik and Tirap valleys by Parul Dutta, Shillong, NEFA, 1959, p. 98, end paper maps, illus. *Man* (London), LXI, Articles 48-79, March : 6 .

1058. MAITRA, A. (1983) The Lisus : A little known ethnic group. *Report* submitted to Anth. Survey of India (Unpublished).

1059. MAITRA, Sunilranjan (1976) Bachelor's dormitories of the tribes of Eastern India. *Bulletin : Anth. Survey of India* (Calcutta), 19(2), April, 1970 : 61-5.

1060. MAJUMDAR, D.N. (1969-70) An appraisal of administrative Policies for Economic Development of the people of the Hill Areas of North Eastern India. *Tribe* (Udaipur, Rajasthan), 6(1) : 24.

1061. ———— (1973) Size-shape categories in the languages of North East India : An exploration of the Sapirwhorft Hypothesis.

Bull. Dept. of Anth., Gauhati Uni., 2, Dec : 41-61.

1062. ——— (1980) North East India : A Profile.
Eastern Himalayas : A Study on Anothropology and Tribalism. Ed. by T.C. Sharma and D.N. Majumder. New Delhi, Cosmo Pub. : 27-32.

1063. MAN (?) A note on the derivation of Miri, *Man* (London), 11(56).

1064. MANN, R.S. (1984) Research ventures and trends : Case of tribal North East India.
Proceedings of a Seminar on *Tribal Research in North Eastern Region*, organised by Nor h Eastern Council Secretariat, Shillong.

1065. MARAK, Joseph D. (1978) Preserving indigenous faiths. *Frontier*, Oct. 21 : 9-12

1066. MARCH of India (1953) Tribal administration in the North East Frontier Agency.
March of India (Delhi), 6(2), Nov-Dec : 24-8.

1067. MATHUR, K.S. (1972) Tribes in India : A problem of identification and Integration.
Tribal Situation in India : Proceedings of a Seminar. Ed. by K. Suresh Singh. Simla, Indian Institute of Advanced Study : 457-61.

1068. MCCABE, R.B. 1897 R.B. Mc Cabe's Report.
India's North East Frontier in the Nineteenth Century. Ed. by Verrier Elwin. Bombay, Oxford University Press (1959) : 191, 2-1-06.

1069. M'COSH, J. (1837) Topography of Assam.
India's North East Frontier in the Nineteenth Century. Ed. by Verrier Elwin. Bombay, O.U.P. (1959) : 3-4, 223.

1070. ——— (*Comp*) Account of the mountain tribes on the extreme North East Frontier of Bengal. (Compiled from the original manuscripts of Capt. Jenkins, Maj. White and Mr. Bruce)
Jour. of the Asiatic Society of Bengal, 5 : 193-208.

1071. MCLEISH, Alexander (1983) The Frontier People of India. Delhi, Mittal Publications, 212p (Reprinted).

1072. MCSWINEY, J. (1912) Census of India, 1911, Vol. III : Assam, pt. *I Report*. Shillong, Govt. Printing Press: (Aber, Aka : 128, Dafla : 130, Khamti : 132).

1073. MEDHI, Birinchi Kumar (1980) Akhan Desh, Alekh Manuh (in Assamese). Mangaldai, J.N. Chakrabarti, Cha. Bro. (Apatani : 29-32 ; Nisi : 33-37 ; Sherdukpen : 38-43 ; Idu Mishmi : 44-47 ; Adi : 48-52 ; Mishing : 53-57.)

1074. MEGHDOOT (1979) Arunachal News : Plan for Educational facilities.
Meghdoot (Shillong), Biweekly Newspaper, 4(22), June 9 : 5.

1075. MEGU, A. 1982 Dame Lamkang : An extinct social organization of the Padam.
Resarun, 8(1), Spring-Summer : 16-21.

1076. MEHRA, Jai Dayal (1958) Book Review : Myths of the NEFA by Verrier Elwin published by NEFA, Shillong, Assam, 1958, pp. 439.
Vanyajati, 6(4), Oct : 176-77.

1077. MEHRA, Parshotam (?) The McMahon Line and After.

1078. MEHTA, G. (?) Articles on North East Frontier Agency. Gangtok, 25p.

1079. MEHTA, K.L. (1955) Road building in NEFA.
Adivasis.
Delhi, Pub. Div., Ministry of Inf. & Broadcasting, G.O.I. : 8 -5.

1080. ———— (1956) The North East Frontier Agency to day.
March of India, 8(8), June : 8-12.

1081. ———— (1959) New life for NEFA.
March of India, 11(2), Feb : 18-23 *and* 41.

1082. MICHELL, John F. (1973) North East Frontier of India. Delhi, Vivek Publications, (Reprinted), (1st Published in 1883) : 65, 69, 70, 75 & 116.

1083. MILLINGTON, Powell (1912) On the track of the Abor. London, Smith Elder, 218p.

1084. MILLS, A.J. Maffatt (1980) Report on Assam. Delhi, Gian Publications. (Abor : G7, 53, 54, Acxxvi, Acxxvii, FALxv, FALxxv, GI).

1085. MILLS, J.P. (1946) A brief note on Agriculture in in Dirang Dzong Area.
Man in India, 26 (1), March : 8-11.

1086. ———— (1947) Tours in the Balipara Frontier Tract, Assam.
Man in India, 27(1), March : 9-35.

1087. ———— (1947) Notes and Queries : Head hunting among the Mishmis of the Lohit Valley, Assam.
Man in India, 27(1), March : 74-75.

1088. ———— (1948) A preliminary note on the Senji-thongji of the Balipara Frontier Tract, Assam.
Jour. Indian Anthropological Institute, 2 : 1-8.

1089. ———— (1952) The Mishmis of the Lohit Valley, Assam.
Jour. of the Royal Anthropological Institute (Great Britain and Ireland, London), LXXXII, pt. I : 1-13.

1090. MINATTUR, Joseph (1958) The Abors of NEFA.
Vanyajati, 6(2), April : 80-3.

1091. MIPUN, J. (1978) Acculturation, communication and development in a Mishing Village.
North East India : A Sociological study. Ed. by S.M. Dubey. Delhi, Concept Publishing Co. : 165-80.

1092. MIRI, Mrinal (1978) Book Review : Pume dada hoi dada. Edited and translated by Tumpak Ete. Adi Folk Literature Research Centre, Along, 1974, 320p.
Jour, NEICSSR (Shillong). 2(9), April : 16.

1093. ———— (*Ed.*) (1982) Linguistic Situation in North East India. Shillong, NEICSSR, 100p.

1094. MISRA, Bani Prasanna : 1982 : Kirata Karyokinesis : An introduction to the Political Economy of Tribal Societies in North East India.
Economies of the Tribes and their transportation. Ed. by K.S. Singh New Delhi, Concept Pub. Com. : 43-62.

1095. MISRA, P. (1979) Rat controling the granaries in Apatani plateau.
Aru. News 8(8), Nov-Dec : 8-10.

1096. M.K.S. (1958) Review of "Aadiyon ke Nritya Aur Geet" by Sachin Roy.
The Eastern Anthropologist (Lucknow), 11(3-4), March-Aug. 229.

1097. MOOKERJI, R.R. (1940) Combined pattern and Basket specimens from Upper Assam.
Man (London). (About Singpho, Khampti).

1098. MORGENSTIERNE, Georg (1959) Comparative notes on Abor-Miri-Dafla consonance (A Preliminary study in Tibeto-Burman phonology).
Bull. of the Bihar Tribal Research Institute (Ranchi), 1(1) : 143.

1099. MORRISON, T. (1972) Twenty five years of progress : Agriculture, Education, Health.
Aru. News, 1(6) Aug. : 6-13, 13-17, 17-22.

1100. MUKHERJEE, P.K. (1969) Hydrocotyle himalaica, P.K. Mukh sp. Nov. A new Hydrocotyle from India.
Ind. For.. LXXXXV : 470-72.

1101. MUKHERJEE, Ranjit (1971) Mutiple cropping around Pasighat : An asessment.
NEFA Informotion, 6(3). Oct : 4-7 *and* 6(2), Sept : 13-6.

1102. ———— (1972) Multiple cropping around Pasighat : An assessment.
Aru. News, 1(5), July.

1103. ———— (1974) Problems of shifting cultivation.
North Eastern Affairs, 3(1), April-June : 47-54 & 57.

1104. MURPHY, R.F. (1960) Head hunter's heritage.
University of California Press, 202 p.

1105. MURTHI, T.S.R. (1968) The Akas : A tribe in NEFA.
Vanyajoti, 16(1), Jan : 11-4.

1106. MURTY, T.S. (1963) Tribals of Kameng Division (Monpas and Daflas).
Careers and Courses, 15(19), Oct : 900-02.

1107. ———— (1969) A re-appraisal of the Mon legend in Himalayan tradition.

Central Asiatic Journal, 13(4) : 291-301.

1108. ———— (1972) Arunachal Pradesh 1947-72. Shillong, Dir. of Inf. & Pub. Relations, Govt. of A.P. (No page marks).

1109. ———— (197?) The Ramgarh shrine of Subansiri. *Resarun*, 5(1) Spring-Summer : 1-16.

1110. NACHI, Larbin (1980) Tagin mythology and Si-donyi Festival.
Aru. News, 9(6), Oct-Nov : 8-11.

1111. NAG, Amit Kumar (1957) Development of NEFA.
March of India, 9(11), Nov. : 33.

1112. NAG CHOUDHURY, K.K. (1979) A grain storage structure.
Aru. News. 8(4), June-June : 5-6.

1113. NAGALAND Bhasha Parishad (1984 ?) Hindi Adi Dictionary. Kohima, Nagaland Bhasha Parishad.

1114. ———— (1984) Hindi Taraon Dictionary. Kohima, Nagaland Bhasha Parishad.

1115. ———— (1984) Hindi Apatani English Vocabulary Kohima, Nagaland Bhasha Parishad.

1116. ———— Hindi Nishi English Vocabulary. Kohima, Nagaland Bhasha Parishad.

1117. ———— (1984) Hindi Hill Miri English Vocabulary. Kohima, Nagaland Bhasha Parishad.

1118. ———— (1984) Hindi Miri Dictionary. Kohima, Nagaland Bhasha Parishad.

1119. NAIK. V.N. *and* PANIGRAHI, G. (1961) Genus Hedychium in Eastern India.
Bull. Bot. Survey of India, 3 : 67-73.

1120. NAIK, K. (1961) Blossoms in dust. London, 221p.

1121. NAIR, P. Thankappan (1965) Youth dormitories of NEFA, India.
Ethnes (Sweeden), 30 : 57-58.

1122. ———— (1966) Slavery in NEFA.
Vanyajati, 14(1) , Jan : 19-29 & 14(3), July : 113-26.

1123. (1967) Ladies club of NEFA.
Vanyajati, 15(1), Jan : 9-14.

1124. NAMCHOOM, Srimati Khalayna (1974) A humourous folk tale of the Khamtis. *Aru. News*, 3(1), Feb-March : 7-9.

1125. ———— (1975) Progress of female education in Arunachal Pradesh.

1126. NAMPONG, Kengsam Kanglang (1980) Social and Cultural integrity of the Tangsas. *Aru. News*, 9 (1), Feb-March : 17-18.

1127. NANDA, Neeru (1982) *Twang : The land of Mon.* New Delhi, Vikas Pub. House, 156p.

1128. NANDI, D.R. (1970) Daphabum Expedition. *NEFA Information*, March : 1-5.

1129. NANDI, S.B. (1978) Customary laws of the tribes in North Eastern India : A survey. *Report* submitted to Anth. Survey of India. (Unpublished).

1130 NARBU, Rinshing (?) Sherdukpenor saddu (in Assamese). Shillong, Research Dept. Govt. of A.P., 78p.

1131. NARGOLKAR, Kusum (1965) In the wake of the Chinese trust. Bombay, Popular Prakashan, 276p.

1132. NATARAJAN, Nalini (1975) International women's year and Arunachal. *Aru. News*, 4(5), July : 13-7.

1133. NATH, Jogendra (1976) The social ethics of Adi marriage. *The North Eastern Spectrum*, 1(3-4), Sept-Oct. : 22-5.

1134. NATIONAL COUNCIL of Applied Economic Research (1967) Techno Economic Survey of NEFA. New Delhi, National Council of Applied Economic Research, 197p.

1135. NATUN Asamiya (1958) Anti-Assamese activities in the administrative set up of NEFA. *The Outlook on NEFA.* Comp. by Parag Chaliha. Jorhat, Assam Sahitya Sabha : 106-110 *and Natun Asamiya* (Daily, Gauhati), May 15, 1954.

1136. NEEDHAM, J.F. (n.d.) A few Digaro (Taraon), Miju (M'yju), and Thibetian (Sic) words collected by

Needham during a trip from Sadiya to Rima and back in December, 1885 and January, 1886.
No Place of Publication and Publisher's name are there. 29p.

1137. ———— (1884) Report ou the visit of Mr. Needham to the Abor villages beyond the British Frontier.
R.G.S. Suppl. Papers, Vol. II : 485-555.

1138. ———— (1884) Report on the visit of Mr. Needham to the Abor villages beyond the British Frontier.
India's North East Frontier.. Ed. by Verrier Elwin. Bombay, Oxford Uni. Press (1959) : 269-77, 219-94.

1139. ———— (1886) Excursion in the Abor Hills from Sadiya on the Upper Assam and Rima in South Eastern Tibet.
Proceedings of the Royal Geographical Society (New series), 8 : 313-28.

1140. ———— (1886) Outline grammar of the Shaiyang Miri language as spoken by the Miris of that clans residing in the neighbourhood of Sadiya with illustrative sentences, phrase-book and vocabulary.

1141. ———— (1889) Outline grammar of the Singpho language as spoken by the Singphos, Douanniyans and others residing in the neighbourhood of Sadiya with illustrative sentences, phrase book and vocabulary.
Shillong, Assam Secretariat Press, 199p.

1142. ———— (1894) Outline grammar of the Khamti language as spoken by the Khamtis residing in the neighbourhood of Sadiya with illustrative sentences, phrase book and vocabulary. Rangoon (Burma), Supdt. Govt., Printing, 201p.

1143. ———— (1900) Report on the Bebejiya Mishmi expedition, 1899-1900. Shillong. *India's North East Frontier in the Nineteenth Century*. Ed. by Verrier Elwin. Bombay, Oxford University Press (1959) : 346-52, 382-84.

1144. ———— (1895) Report of a trip into the Abor hills. Shillong, Govt. Press.

1145. NEEDHAM, Rodney (1961) Book Review : Aspects of Minyong Culture by Sachin Roy. Shillong, NEFA, 1960. p. XXXI+315, end paper, maps, illus.
Man LXI, Articles 48-79, March : 63.

1146. ——— (1962) Book Review: The Idu Mishmis by Tapan Kumar M. Baruah, Shillong, NEFA, 1960, P. XII+end paper maps, illus.
Man, LXII, Articles 232-257, Oct - 160.

1147. NEFA Communique (1958) No desire to oust Assamese.
The Outlook on NEFA. Comp. by Parag Chaliha. Jorhat, Assam Sahitya Sabha : 111-130.

1148. NEFA Information (1968) Mithun, facts and myths.
NEFA Information, 2(11), June : 23-7.

1149. ——— (1970) Reh festival, myth and celebration.
NEFA Information, 4(8), March : 12-4.

1150. ——— (1971) Khiksaba festival of the Sherdukpen.
NEFA Information, 6(5), Dec : 18-9.

1151. ——— (1971) Nechido festival of the Akas.
NEFA Information, 6(5), Dec : 9 12.

1152. ——— (1971) Dree festival of the Apatanis.
NEFA Information, Independence Day Issue, 6(1), Aug : 22-4.

1153. NEFA Publicity (1957) A brief account of administrative and development activities in North East Frontier Agency since Independence. Shillong, NEFA Publicity Office, Supdt., Govt. Press, 44p.

1154. ——— (1964) NEFA on the march. Shillong, Cultural Research Officer, NEFA Publicity, 44p.

1155. ——— (?) Ten years progress in NEFA. Shillong, Govt. of NEFA, 44p.

1156. NEGI, Balbir Singh (1964) Tribes of the North East Frontier Region.
Anthropogeography : A study of races and people of the world Geographical series No. 1. Allahabad, Kitab Mahal : 237-69.

1157. ———— (n.d.) Human Geography : An ecological approach. Meerut, Kedar Nath Ram Nath : 353-66.

1158. NEHRU, Jawaharlal (1953) The Tribal Folk. *March of India* (Delhi), 6(2), Nov-Dec : 5-8.

8159. ————(1964) Speech on return from tour of North East Frontier Agency in 1952. *Vanyajati*, 12(3), July : 127-28.

1160. NEOG, Maheswar (?) Tirapar tinge tinge (in Assamese). *Asam Bani* (Gauhati, newspaper).

1161. ———— (?) Lohit agharir chenehar batori (in Assamese). *Asam Bani* (Gauhati).

1162. ———— (1962) Nocte (in Assamese). *Asamar Janajati*. Ed. by Pramod Chandra Bhattacharya. Jorhat, Assam Sahitya Sabha : 236-47.

1163. ———— (1962) Wanchoo (in Assamese). *Asamar Janajati*. Ed. by Pramod Chandra Bhattacharya. Jorhat, Assam Sahitya Sabha : 248-51.

1164. ———— (1962) Tangsa (in Assamese). *Asamar Janajati*. Ed. by Pramod Chandra Bhattacharya. Jorhat, Asam Sahitya Sabha : 252-55.

1165. ———— (1962) Khampti (in Assamese). *Asamar Janajati*. Ed. by Pramod Chandra Bhattacharya.

1166. ———— (1962) Mishmi (in Assamese). *Asamar Janajati*. Ed. by Pramod Chandra Bhattacharya. Jorhat, Assam Sahitya Sabha : 278-83.

1168. ———— (1962) Siang simanta bibhagar annanya janajati (in Assamese). *Asamar Janajati*. Ed. by Pramod Chandra Bhattacharya. Jorhat, Assam Sahitya Sabha : 284-89.

1169. ———— (1962) Parbatar Miri (in Assamise). *Asamar Janajati*. Ed. by Pramod Chandra Bhattacharya. Jorhat, Assam Sahitya Sabha : 294-98.

1170. ———— (1962) Tagin (in Assamese). *Asamar Janajati*. Ed. by Pramod Chandra Bhattacharya. Jorhat, Assam Sahitya Sabha : 300-03.

1172. ———— (1976) Snehar Arunachal : My Hill So Strong, travelogues and essays concerning Arunachal Pradesh (in Assamese). Jorhat, Assam Sahitya Sabha, 97p.

1173. NEVILL, G.A. (1923) Census of India 1921, Vol. III : Assam, pt. I, Report. Ed. by G.T. Llyod. Shillong, Govt. Press : Appendix-B, X-XI.

1174. NEVILL, G.A. *and* BARDOLOI, G.C. (1923) Census of India 1921, Vol. III. Assam, pt. I, Shillong, Govt. Press.

1175. NEVILL, A. Watts (1970) The Half Clad Tribes of India. New Delhi, Orient Longman, 153p,

1176. NEWSLETTER (1972) Research Information : Cultural Anthropology Division, "Ecological Studies in NEFA". *Newsletter : Anthropological Survey of India*, 1(2), May-June : 52-9.

1177. NEUFVILLE, J.B. (1828) On the Geography and Population of Assam 1823.
Asiatic Research, 16.

1178. ———— (1828) On tthe Geography and Population of Assam 1823.
India's North East Frontier in the Nineteenth Century. Ed. by Verrier Elwin. Bombay, Oxford Uni. Press (1959) 4-6, 398-99, 417-18.

1179. NGEMU, Tangam (1975) Tangsa folk legends.
Resarun, 1(2), April : 1-4 *and Resarun '75*. Cum. Vol. 1976). 57-59.

1180. ———— (1976) A Tangsa folk Tales : How the elephant and the ferment for rice-beer came into being.
Aru. News, 5(1), Feb : 18.

1181. ———— (1977) : In quest of social welfare.
Aru. News, 6(7), Nov : 10-5.

1182. ———— (1977) Moklum language guide. Shillong, Research Dept., Dir. of Inf. & Pub. Rela., Govt. of A.P., 66p.

1183. NIGAM, Ramesh Chandra (1953) Abors and myths of their origin.
March of India, 6(2), Nov-Dec : 31-3.

1184. NIGAM, R.G. (1959) A study of Padam (Abor) Phonology.
Bull. Dept. of Anth. (Anth. Survey of India, Calcut'a), 3(2), July (1954) : 48-65.

1185. NORTH EASTERN Council (1980) Plans and perspective. Shillong, North Eastern Council, 42,

1186. NORTH EASTERN Spectrum (1977) The Khamtis.
North Eastern Spectrum, 2(3-4), Sept-Oct : 15-29.

1187. O'CALLAGHAN, T.P.M. (1923) Notes on certain tribes.
Census of India 1921, Vol. III : Assam, pt. I, Report : App.-B. 11-3 (on Khamptis, Singphos & Mishmis).
Shillong, Govt. Press

1188 O'DONEL, J.H. (1863) Notes on the tribes of the Eastern Frontier Nos. I & II.
Jour. of Asiatic Society of Bengal (Calcutta), 32: 400-07.

1189. O'NEILL, J.S. (1912) Native suspension bridge over the Dihong.
Geographical Journal, XL : 213-15.

1190. OSIK, Nagangin (1981) Concept of Donyi-Poloism.
Aru. News, 10(5), July : 12-3.

1191. OSIK, N.N. (1981) Why the dove weeps.
Aru. News, 10(3), April-May : 6-8.

1192. PADMANABHAM, P.B.S.V. (1981) A dermogenetic profile of Singphos.
Report submitted to Anthropological Survey of India (Unpublished).

1193. PADMANABHAM, P.B.S.V. and JASWAL, I.J.S. (1982) A dermogenetic study of Apatanis.
Report submitted to Anth, Sur. of India (Unpublished).

1194. PADUN. N. (1972) Mishing Bhasha.
Bhrignmuni Kagyund. Ed. by Mishing Sanskritir Alekhya. Birubari, Gauhati, Assam.

1195. PADUN, Nahendra (1973) Mishing samaj Paddhati (in Assamese).
Pragati (Pathsala, Assam), Bajali Pragati Sangha : 23-31.

1196. PAKYNTEIN, E.H. (*Ed.*) (1965) Census ofIndia 1961, Vol. III, Assam, pt. V-A, Scheduled Tribes and Scheduled Castes : Reprints from old Census Reports and Special Tables. Delhi, Manager of Pub., 148p.

1197. ———— (*Ed*) (1965) Census of India 1961, Vol. III. Assam, part V-A, Scheduled Tribes and Scheduled Castes : Reprints from old Census Reports and Special Tables. Delhi, Manager of Publications, 428p.

1198. PAMEGAM, Tarun Chandra (1962) Miri ba Mising (in Assamese).
Asamor Janajati. Ed. by Pramod Chandra Bhattacharya. Jorhat, Assam Sahitya Sabha : 155-62.

1199. PANDEY, B.B. (1930) A study of leadership among the Adis of Arunachal Pradesh : Family, marriage and Social change and the Indian Fringe.

1200. ———— (1970) Itanagar.
NEFA Information, 4(6), Jan : 15-8.

1201. ———— (1974) Bangi.
Aru. News, 3(8), Nov : 6-7.

1202. ———— (1974) Nigre lene (Shaman's rock).
Aru. News, 3(7), Oct : 7-8.

1203. ———— Burial in a Minyyong village.
Resarun. 1(2), April : 1-8 *and Resarun 75*, (Cum. Vol. 1976) : 63-7.

1204. ———— (1976) Lopu.
Resarun, 2(2), April : 1-2.

1205. ———— (197) Lopu.
Resarun, '*75*, Cum. Volume : 89-90.

1206. ———— The Hill Miris on the new path.
Aru. News, 5(6), Aug-Sept : 43-50.

1207. ———— A visit to Gyakar Sinyik.
Resarun, 2(1), Jan : 1-5.

1208. ———— (1977) Indigenous leadership, its nature and mechanism.
Aru News, 6(4), Aug : 35-41.

1209. ———— (1977) Cultural pattern among the people of Siang and trends of development.
Resarun, 3(4) : 13-5.

1210. ———— ((1978) *The Hill Miri.*
Shillong, M.P. Hazarika, Dir. of Inf. & Pub. Relations, Govt. of A.P., 176p.

1211. ———— (1978) Leadership among the Adi communities of Arunachal Pradesh.
Social and Economic Profile of North East India. Ed. by B. Datta Roy. Delhi, B.R. Publications : 321-35.

1212. ———— Law of the Adis.
Research in Arunachal : 56-71.

1213. ———— The tribes of Arunachal Pradesh.
Jour. of Social Research, 23(1), March : 105-10.

1214. ———— Festivals of Subansiri District (in Hindi) (and also in English). Shillong, Directorate of Research, Govt. of A.P.

1215. ———— (n.d.) Siang. Shillong, Adm. of NEFA, 33p.

1216. ———— (1981) Land and land use of a Himalaya tribe : '*Adi*' of Arunachal Pradesh.
Land and Land Relations in the Hills of North East India. Ed. by B.B. Dutta. Delhi, Peoples Pub. House (in Press).

1217. PANDEY, D.N. (1982) Kebang : A folktale of the Gallongs. (Proceedings of a Seminar on '*Folklore*' of NEICSSR, Shillong).
Folklore in North East India. Ed. by Sumen Sen. New Delhi, Omsons (in Press).

1218. PANIGRAHI, G. (1960) Studies on tropical evergreen and semi-evergreen forests of Assam and NEFA.
Proceedings of Tropical Forests symposium.

1219. PANIGRAHI, G. *and* JOSEPH, J. (1966) A Botanical tour to Tirap Frontier Division, NEFA (India).
Bull. Bot. Surv, India, 8 : 142-57.

1220. PANIGRAHI, G. *and* KAR, S.K. (1966) The family compositae in Assam and NEFA.
Economic and Political Weekly, ?)

1221, PANIGRAHI, G. *and* NAIK, V.N. (1961) A Botanical tour to Subansiri Frontier Division [NEFA].
Bull. Bot. Surv. India, 361-88.

1222. ———— (1964) A new variety of Smilax griffithii A. D C from NEFA (India).
Cur. Sci, 33 : 500-01.

1223. PAREEK, R.N. (1979) Phakials.
Aru. News, 8(7), Oct : :0-2

1224. PATHAK, R.D. (1979) A study of parental sacred complex of Apatani adolescent girl student.
Proceedings of a Seminar on "*Bio-Culrural Profile af North East India*", Anthropological Survey of India, Shillong 26th April, 1979.

1225. PATNAIK, G.S. (1984) 'Kuh' festival of the Tanggas.
The Assam Tribune (daily, Gauhati), January 22 - 4.

1126. PAUL. Gemini (1958) Sherdukpen (I) : Origin and Historical Background.
Vanyajati, 6(1), January : 22-6.

1227. ———— (1958) Sherdukpen (II): Habitat, Migrations and Tribal Drink.
Vanyajati, 6(2), April : 61-9,

1228. ———— 1958) Sherdukpen (III) : Childhood, Marriage and Medicine Man.
Vanyajati, 6(3), July : 96-102.

1229. ———— (1958) Sherdukpen (IV) : Village Council, Land, Taxes and Food.
Vanyajati, 6(3), Oct : 153-56.

1230 ———— (1959) Sherdukpen (V) : Crime and Festivals.
Vanyajati, 7(1), Jan : 4-10.

1231. PAYENGKATAKI, S. Miri jatir buranji (In Assamese). Dhemaji (Assam), Mornoi Bebejia.

1232. PEAL, S.E. (1872) Notes on a visit to the Tribes inhabiting the Hills south of Sibsagar.
J.A.S.B., XLI : 15.

1233. ———— (1872) : Notes on a visit to the tribes inhabiting the Hills south of Sibsagar.
India's North East Frontier in the Nineteenth Century. Ed. by Verrier Elwin. Bombay, Oxford Uni. Press (1959) : 54-55, 68-70, 89-96.

1234. ———— (1881) Report on a visit to the Nongyang lake on the Burma Frontier, February 1879
Jour. Asiatic Society of Bengal, L, pt. 2 : 130, (on khamptis).

1235. ———— (1881) Report on a visit to the Nongyang lake on the Burma Frontier, February, 1879.
India's North East Frontier in the Nineteenth Century. Ed. by Verrier Elwin. Bombay, Oxford Uni. Press (1969) 96-130.

1236. ———— (1896) Eastern Nagas of the Tirap and the Namtsik.
J.A.S.B. LXV, pt. 3 : 9-17.

1237. PEEL, A.C. (1869) Short notes of a trip into the Hills South of Sibsagar.
Proc. A.S.B. : 76-9 (About Wancho).

1238. PEGU, Nomal C. (1956) The Miris or the Mishings of of the Brahmaputra valley. Majuli (Assam), Dasiram Pegu, Kumarbari, 63p.

1239. PEGU, R.C. (1978) Condition of female in education in Arunachal Pradesh.
Aru. News, 7(8), Dec : 6-7.

1240. PEMBERTON, R.B. (1979) Eastern Frontier of India. Delhi, Mittal Publications, 261p. (Reprinted).

1241. PERME, O. (1969) The Padams : A brief study of the past.
NEFA Information, June : 7-10.

1242. PERTIN, Batem (1982) Social and Political organization of Padam-Minyong. Shillong, Dept, of Anth., NEHU (Unpublished Dissertation).

1243. ———— (1983) The role of moshup in Adi society : An anthropological appraisal.
Aru. News, 12(5), Aug-Sept : 30-31.

1244. PERTIN, Mading (1971) The Padams.
NEFA Information, 6 (3), Oct : 26-8 and 6(2), Sept : 37-9.

1245. ———— (1979) Voluntary family planning programme suitable for Arunachal Pradesh.
Aru. News. 2(3), May : 7-10.

1246. PERTIN, Pejing (1979) Influence of Adi culture on hygiene.
Aru. News, 2(3), May : 7-10.

12 7. ———— (1979) Nibo Robo story (As prevalent in Adi Padam).
Aru. News, 8(1), Feb-March : 19-21.

1248. ———— (1980) The doctrine of Nibo Robo story.
Aru. News, 9(5), Sept : 19-20.

1249. ———— (1981) Adi faith through the ages.
Aru. News, 10(1), Jan : 12-20.

1250. PHILOLOGY Section (1962) A Phrase Book in Idu. Shillong, P. C. Dutta for Research Dept., Philology Section, NEFA, 103p.

1251. ———— (1963) A Dictionary of the Taraon language. Shillong, P. Dutta for Research Dept. Philology Section, NEFA Administrarion, 61p.

1252. ———— (?) Miri Kitap (in Devanagari script). Shillong, Govt. of NEFA, 15p.

1253. PHOOKAN, M.M. (1981) Marriage system of the Miniyong.
Aru. News, 10(1), Jan : 32-6.

1 54. PHUKAN, Umananda (1978) Apatani agriculture of Arunachal Pradesh.
Indian Jour. of Agricultural Economics, 33(4), Oct-Dec: 44-5.

1255. PILLAI, R.S. (1971) The Carnivora of Arunachal : An Assessment.
Pines (Shillong). (III), Arunachal Number : 13-9.

1256. PINGAM, T. (1971) Slaughter of King Tamden.
NEFA Information, Aug : 19-21.

1257. PRINCE PETER of Greece & Denmark (1960) People of the Himalayas.
Geographical Mag., Sept. 33(5) ; 295-308.

1258. PUGH, B.M. (1976) The story of a Tribal : An autobiography. Bombay, Orient Longman Ltd., 150.

1259. PUGH, Marion (1958) Games of NEFA. Shillong, Sachin Roy, Cultural Research Officer on behalf of North East Frontier Agency, 51p.

1260. ——— (1958) Some understandings from a study of the games of NEFA.
Bull. of Research Dept., NEFA (Shillong), 1(1), June 92-8.

1261. PULU, Ahuki (1977) Some traditional customs of the Idu Mishmis.
Aru. News, 6(2), June : 15-5.

1262. ——— (1977) Weaving practice in Idu society.
Aru. News, 6(5), Sept. : 18-9.

1263. ——— (1977) Marriage system in the Idu society.
Aru. News, 6(8), Dec. : 12-4.

1264. ——— (1979) Idu legend on the enmity between man and tiger.
Aru. News, 2(3), May : 5-6.

1265. ——— (1979) Weaver's Valley.
Aru. News, 8(6), Sept. : 11-8.

1266. PULU, Jatan (1972) The Idu Religion.
Proceedings of a Seminar on Idu Religion held at Roing on the occassion of the '*Reh*' festival in February, 11th to 14th.

1267. ——— (1976) The struggle between Anno and Asahme.
Resarun '75, Cum., Volume : 126-27.

1268. ——— (1976) Idu proverbs.
Resarun, 2(3), July : 27-9.

1269. ——— (1976) Two Mishmi Tales.
Resarun, 2(2), April : 1-3.

1270. ——— (1976) Two Mishmi tales.
Resarun '75, Cum. Vol. : 71-89.

1271. ——— (1977) The Bamboo and cane culture of the Idus
Resarun, 3(2), April : 33-42.

1272. ——— (1978) Idu Phrase Book. Shillong, Research Dept., Directorate of Inf. & Pub. Relations, Govt. of A.P., 80p.

1273. ——— (1978) Preparation of yarn by the local method among the Idus.
Resarun, 4(2), Aut-Win : 28-30.

1274. ———— (1979) Plants that are used by the Idus of Lohit District for medical purpose.
Resarun, 2(1) : 10-4 and (2), Aut-Winter : 10-4.

1275. ———— (1979) Ceremonial equipment of the Idus.
Resarun, 5(1), Spring-Summer : 51-3.

1276. ———— (1980) Reh festival flag of the Idus.
Aru. News, 9(3), June-July : 20-1.

1277. ———— (1981) Evolution of tiger, an Idu myth.
Aru. News, 10(5), July : 20-2.

1278. ———— (1982) Folk songs of the Idu Mishmis.
Resarun, 8(1), Spring-Summer : 35-7.

1279. PURI, Rakshat (1972) Towards security in the North East : Transportation and nationalism.
Tribal Situation in India : Proceedings of a Seminar. Ed. by K. Suresh Singh, Simla, Indian Institute of Advanced Study : 98-109.

1280. RAGHAVAN, V. (1951) The Mishmis
Tribes of India. Delhi, Bharatiya Adim Jati Sevak Sangh 2 : 30-4.

1281. RAGLAN, (1964) Book Review : The Akas by Raghuvir Sinha, Shillong, NEFA, 1962, pp. X+144.
Man (London), LXIV, Articles 1-48, Jan-Feb. : 28.

1282. RAHUL, Ram (1969) The Himalaya Borderland. Delhi, Vikas Publications, 157p. (Abor : 25, 47, 49, 50; Aka : 29, 48; Apa Tanis : 26, 29 ; Dafla : 27, 28, 29 ; Mishmi : 24-6, 28, 29, 47, 49).

1283. ———— (1978) The Himalaya as a frontier. Calcutta, Vikas Pub. House, 154p.

1284. RAI, M.B. (1981) Census of India 1981 : Arunachal Pradesh, Provisional Population Totals (Paper - I, Supplement). Shillong, Director of Census Operation Arunachal Pradesh, 96 p.

1285. ———— (1981) Census of India 1981, Arunachal Pradesh Provisional Population Totals, series 25, paper I of 1981. Shillong, Director of Census Operation, Arunachal Pradesh, 31 p.

1286. RAI, Prabha (1963) Life in the lap of the Himalayas.
Social Welfare, 10 (7), Oct. : 31-5.

1287. RAIKAR, Y.A. (1969) An Approach to the Historical Research of NEFA.
The Hornbill (Shillong) : 8-12.

1288. ———— (1969) Archaeology around Bhalukpung.
NEFA Information, Feb. : 9-12.

1289. ———— (1969) Archaeology in the Noa Dihing Valley.
NEFA Information, 4(4), Nov. : 16-9.

1290. ———— (1970) T. Block and Bhishmaknagar.
NEFA Information, 5(2), Sept. : 4-8.

1291. ———— (1971) Rukmini Legend : A critical study.
NEFA Information, 5(12), July : 9-14.

1292. ———— (1972) Death of Bayan.
Aru. News, 1(2), March : 21-3.

1293. ———— (1972) Bhishmaknagar : A forgotten chapter in the History of India.
Aru. News, 1(2), March : 31-6.

1294. ———— (1972) A note on Padam Pukhur near Jia.
Aru. News, 1(10), Dec. : 10-11.

1295. ———— A mud fort near Tezu.
Aru. News, 1(8), Oct. : 10-4.

1296. ———— (1973) A Padam Pukhuri near Jia.
Aru. News, 2(2), May : 9-10.

1297. ———— (1973) The Mud Fort Near Tezu could be Sisupalgarh.
Aru. News, 2(1), March : 7-9.

1298. ———— (1973) Function organisation in the Adli society.
Aru. News, 1(12), : Feb. 13-7.

1299. ———— (1974) Vijaynagar : The forgotten Khomong Shillong, Research Dept., Directorate of Inf. & Pub. Relations, Govt. of A.P., 140 p.

1300. ———— (1974) Operation Bhishmaknagar.
Aru. News, 3(3), May : 3-6.

1301. ———— (1974) Meeting Kuru Hasang.
Aru. News, 3(9), April : 10-11.

1302. ———— (1974) Rukmini Nati : The wedding horizons of Bhishmaknagar.

Aru. News, 3(7), Oct. : 2-6.

1303. ———— (1975) A woman speaks. *Aru. News*, 4(5), July : 45-7.

1304. ———— (1975) A note on Mishmi Tita. *Resarun*, 1(2), April : 1-4.

1305. ———— (1976) A note on Mishmi Tita. *Resarun*, '75, Cum. Volume : 36-8.

1306. ———— (1976) The Twelve Principles of Buddhism. *Resarun*, '75, Cum. Vol. : 102-04.

1307. ———— (1976) Place names in Ring-Dambuk area. *Resarun*, 2(1), Jan : 1-9.

1308. ———— (1976) British explorers of Bhishmaknagar. *Aru. News*, 5(7), Oct : 27-30.

1309. ———— (1976) Ita Fort. Shillong, Research Dept., Dir. of Inf. & Pub. Relations Govt. of A.P., 21p.

1310. ———— (1976) Archaeological sites. *Patriot*, March 21.

1311. ———— (1977) British explorers of Bhishmaknagar. *Resarun*, 3(1), Jan. : 2-4. and Aru. News, 5(7), Oct. : 27-30.

1312. ———— (1977) Khomong in the History of the Khamtis. *Resarun*, 3(3), July : 11-26.

1313. ———— (1977) Place of Khomong in the Khamptis. *Aru. News*, 6(4), August : 27-30.

1314. ———— (1977) Khomong and the Khamptis. *Aru. News*, 6(7), Nov. : 20-1.

1315. ———— (1977) Archaeology in Arunachal Pradesh: Problems and scope. *Research in Arunachal Pradesh* : 52-2.

1316. ———— (1978) Temple and fort architecture in Arunachal Pradesh. *Aru. News*, 7(6), Oct. : 15.

1317. ———— (1979) A note on the Megaiths at Jamiri. *Aru. News*, 8(6), Sept. : 5-7.

1318. ———— (1979) Private records of Mechuka. *Resarun*, 5(1), Spring-Summer : 42-7.

1319. ———— (1979) Khomong in the History of the Khamtis. Shillong, Res. Dept., Govt. of A.P., 16p.

1320. ———— Some forgotten routes in the Lohit district. *Resarun*, 5(2), Aut-Win : 1-4.

1321. ———— (1979) Some forgotten routes in the Lohit district.
Aru. News, 8(8), Nov-Dec. : 6-7.

1322. ———— (1979) Sources of the History of Arunachal Pradesh.
Aru. News. 7(9), Republic Day Issue : 7-12.

1323 ———— (1979) Sources of the History of Arunachal Pradesh.
Resarun, 5(1), Spring-Summer : 16-24.

1324. ———— (1972) A note on the Megaliths at Jamiri.
Aru. News, 8(6), Sept : 5-7.

1325. ———— (1979) Pre-historic Archaeology in Arunachal.
Aru. News, 8(7), Oct. : 2-6.

1326. ———— (1980) Historical Archaeology in the North East India (300 A.D. to 1200 A.D.).
Aru. News, 8(9), Republic Day Issue :28-31.

1327. ———— (n.d) Bijaynagar, the forgotten Khomong.
Dictionary of Indian Archaeology, Vol. II. New Delhi, Ind. Coun. of His. Res.

1328. ———— (n.d.) The Glory that was Bhismaknagar.
Shillong, Dir. of Res., Govt. of A.P.

1329. RAIKAR, Y.A. and CHATTERJEE'S (1979) Private records of Mechuka.
Aru. News, 8(5), Aug. : 27-30 & Resarun, 5(1), Spring-Summer :42-7.

1330. RAIKAR, Y.A. and LANGHAM, P. (1977) Report from the field.
NEFA Information, 5(2), Sept. : 20-1.

1331. RAJA, K.A.A. (1972) Spirit of Arunachal.
Statesman (Calcutta, Daily), Spl. Supplement, Jan. 20 : 10.

1332. ———— (1974) Prospect of Economic growth of Arunachal Pradesh and Fifth Five Year Plan.
North Eastern Affairs, 2(4), Jan-March : 23-6.

1333. ———— (1978) In retrospect.
Aru. News, 6(9) : 1-4.

1334. RAJBNGSHI, D.C.(1956) Nocte Ce. Shillong, Research Dept., Govt. of A.P. 16p.

1335. RAMAN, Govind and BEIERWALTES, W.H. (1959) Correction of goiter, deafinutisn and hormane levels in non-cretinous inhabitants of severe endemic goiter area in India.
J. Clin. Endocrinology and Metabolism, 19(2).

1336. RAO, A.S. and BALKRISHNAN M.P. (1968) Bulbophyllum brachypodum nom. nov with two new varieties.
Bull Bot. Surv. India, 10 : 350-52.

1337. RAO, A.S. and HAJRA, P.K. (1972) Zeylanidium olivaccum/Gardn./Eng. Posostemaceae : First report of its presence in Kameng district, NEEA.
Bult. Bat. Surv. India 12.

1338. RAO, A.S. and JOSEPH, J (1967) Rhynchoglossum, lazulinum : A new species of Gesneria—ceae.
Bull. Bat. Surv. India, 9 : 280-82.

1339. RAO, A.S. and VERMA, D.M. (1969) Notes on Zingiberaceae from Assam.
Bull. Bat. Surv. India, 11 : 24 -48.

1340. ———— (1969) A risaema setosum : A new species of Araceae from Siang District, NEFA.
Bull. Bot. Surv. India, 11 : 196-97.

1341. RAO, M.R.L. (1978) The Panorama of Tawang.
Aru. News, 6(9), Jan, Repub. Day Issue : 35-40.

342 RAO, Rolla S. (1961) Survey of some important medicinal plants from Eastern India.
Proceedings of International Symposium on Plant Resources of the Middle East and Rauwolfia for the Pharmaceutical Industry held at Peshawar.
Pakistan J. Sci. and Ind. Research, Spl. no. (Reprinted), 4 : 219-31.

1343. ———— (1962) The Himalayan flora. Poona Agricultural college Magazine : 57-60.

1344. ———— (1964) New plant records from India.
Curr. Sci., 33 : 120-21.

1345. ———— (c. 1971) Medicinal plants of the Arunachal Pradesh and the prospect of their development.
Pines, (Shillong), 1(III), Arunachal Number : 30-4.

1346. RAO, Rolla S. and AHUJA, K.K. (1968) New and noteworthy plant records from India.
Bull. Bot Surv. India, 10 : 360-66.

1347. RAO,Rolla S. and JOSEPH, J. (1962) Livistona Jenkinsiana Griff.
Principale, 6 : 103-06.

1348. ———— (1965) Observations on the Flora of Siang Frontier Division, NEFA.
Bull Bot Surv. India, 7(1-4) : 138-61.

1349. RAO, V. Venkata (1976) A century of tribal Politics in NorthEast India : 1874-1974. New Delhi, S. Chand & Com., 559p.

1350. RATNAM, Bala (1963) Anthropology on the March. Madras, Book Centre. 390p.

1351. RATNAM, C. (1968) Exploring the NEFA region.
Commerce, Sept. 28(Supplement) : 16A.

1352. RAY, P C. (1955) The tensional feelings among the Abors and Gaylongs as indicated by the Research technique.
Indian Jour. af Psychology, 30, pt. I & II, March-June : 95-103

1353. RAY, Punya Sloka (1967) Dafla Phonology and Morphology.
Anthropological Linguistics (Chicago, USA), 9(8) : 9-14.

1354. RAY, P.C. (1967) Role of superstitions and beliefs among Indian Tribes.
A common perspective for North East India. Ed. by Rathin Mitra and B. Das Gupta. Calcutta, Pannalal Das Gupta : 24-8.

1355. ———— (1959) The children of the Abor and Gallong.
Education and Psychology, Delhi.

1356. RAY, Sukumar (1907) Music of the Hill People of North Eastern India.

A common perspective for North East India. Ed. by Rathin Mitra and B. Das Gupta. Calcutta. Pannalal Das Gupta : 29-40.

1357. RAY BAROOAH, G. (1949) Abor Sikhyak. Pasighat, NEFA Assam.

1358. RESARUN (1979) Archaeological remains along the foothills of Arunachal Pradesh. *Resarun*, 5(1), Spring-Summer : 68-71.

1359. RESEARCH DEPT. (1968) Brochure on the Seminar of Research Dept., NEFA Shillong, Research Dept., Dir. of Inf. and Publicity, NEFA, 49p.

1360. READ, C.H. (1886) Exhibition of ethnological objects from the Akkas, Northern Assam. *Jour. of the Anthoropological Institute*, 15 : 139-40.

1361. REID, Robert (1942) History of the frontier areas bordering on Assam, from 1883-1941. Shillong. Printed at the Assam Govt. Press : 181-303,

1362. ———— (1944) India's North East Frontier. *Royal Central Asian Journal*, 31 : 165-74.

1363. RIBA, J. (1971) Mopin-Ripin. *Pines*, 1(1 , March : 88-9.

1364. RIBA, Tukmar (1979) Mopin : The light of the Adi life. *Aru. News*, 2(3), May : 1-2.

1365. RIME, Jhummar (1983) Agricultural strategy in Arunachal. *Aru. News*, 12(5), Aug.-Sept:29-30.

1366. RIPLEY, Dillon (1948) Exploring the Mishmi Hills. *Natural History*, LVII : 79-85.

1367. RIPLEY, H.H. (1891) The tribes and castes of Bengal, Vol. 1. Calcutta, (Aka : 15).

1368. ROBINSON, (1841) William Descriptrive account of Assam. *India's North East Frontier in the Nineteenth Century*. Ed. by Verrier Elwin. Bombay, Oxford Uni. Press(1959) 26-31, 56-8, 61-3, 313-14, 360-62, 395-98, 409-10.

1369. ———— (1849) Notes on the languages spoken by the various tribes inhabiting the valley of Assam and its mountain confines. *JASB*, XVIII : 183-237 (Abor).

1370 ———— (1851) Notes on the Dophlas and the peculiarity of their language.
Jour. Asiatic Society of Bengal, 20(2) : 126-37.

1371. ———— (1851) Notes on the Dophlas and the peculiarity of their language.
India's North East Frontier in the Nineteenth Century. Ed. by Verrier Elwin. Bombay, Oxford Uni. Press (1959) : 174-79.

1372. ———— (1855) Notes on the languages spoken by the Mishmis.
Jour. Roy. Asiatic Society Bengal, 24 : 307-24.

1373. ———— (1975) A descriptive account of Assam. Delhi, Sanskaran Prakashak, 433p. (reprinted). 1st Published in 1841.

1374. ROKIMI, Miss (1968) Hair style and its significance among the tribes of NEFA.
NEFA Information, July : 9-16; Oct. : 16-9.

1375. ————(c,1971) Tribal Hair-style and its significance, *Pines*, (Shillong), 1(III), Arunachal Number : 35-54.

1376. ROSE, Leo and FISHER, Margaret W. (?) Notes on North East Frontier Agency in India. Washington, Political Dept., Office of the External Research, Dept. of Space, U.S.A.

1377. ROWLATT, E.A. (1845) Report of an expedition into the Mishmee Hills to the North East of Sudyah.
Jour. Asiatic Society of Bengal, 14 : 477-88.

1378. ———— (1845) Report of an expedition into the Mishmee Hills to the North East of Sudyah.
India's North East Frontier in the Nineteenth Century. Ed. by Verrier Elwin. Bombay. Oxford Uni. Press (1959) : 314-25.

1379. ROWNEY, Horatio Bickersataffe (1882) The Wild Tribes of India. London, Thos De La Rue & Co, 224p. (Reprinted by B.R. Publishing Corporation, Delhi in 1974).

1380. ROY, Ajay (1980) Book Review : The Singphos and their religion bv T.K.M. Baruah.
Man and Life (Calcutta), 6(1 & 2), Jan-June : 102.

1381. ROY, J.K. and BISWAS, S.K. (1964) Proteins in the diets of some Indian Tribes.
Science and Culture (Calcutta), 30(3), March : 126-29.

1382. ROY, Nilima (1957) Basketry and domestic utensils of the Adi.
Vanyajati, 5(4 . Oct. : 170-74.

1383. ———— (1957) Habitations of the Adis of Siang Frontier Division.
Vanyajati, 5(3), July : 125-33.

1384. ROY, Sachin (1953) The body build of the Abors.
Bull. Dept. of Anth. (Anth. Surv. of India, Calcutta), 2(2), July : 99 104.

1385. ———— (1957) Abor weapons of War and Chase.
Jour. of the Asiatic Society of Bengal, (Science), 22(2); 139-58.

1386. ————(1957) Adiyon ke Nritya Aur Geet (in Hindi) Shillong. Dept. of Research, Govt, of NEFA, 46p.

1387. ———— (1958) Hunting and fishing among the Adi (Abors).
Vanyajati 6(2). April : 53-60.

1388. ———— (1958) Uttar-Purb seema ke Adi (in Hindi). (Translated by J.H. Chinchalkar).
Vanyajati, 6(2) April : 66-76.

1389. ———— (1958) Domestic animals and their role in the life of Adi (Abors).
Vanyajati, 6(4), Oct : 146-52.

1390. ———— (1957) Rhymes and rhythms of the Abors.
Indian Folklore (Calcutta), 2(2), Oct-Dec. : 81-93.

1391. ———— (?) Hamare NEFA nivasi mitra (in Hindi). New Delhi. Bharatiya Adimjati Sewak Sangh.

1392. ———— (1958) Dress, ornaments and decoration of the Adis of the NEFA.
Vanyajati, 6(1), Jan. : 4-21.

1393. ———— (1958) Lohit Basi Mishmi : Uttar Purb Simanta Anchal (in Hindi).
Vanyajati, 6(3), July : 107-13.

1394. ———— (1958) Shamal "Mashrique" Agency ke Adi in Hindi).
Ajkal, 17(9).

1395. ———— (1960) Aspects of Padam-Minyong culture. Shillong, Resarch Dept., Dir. of Inf. & Pub. Relations, Govt. of NEFA, 3 5p. (2nd edition 1966).

1396. ———— (1966) Anthropometry of the Adis. Shillong, Govt. of NEFA, Cir. of Inf. & Pub. Relations, 101p.

1397. ———— (1967) Adis of the North East Frontier Agency. Delhi University, (Unpublished Ph. D. Dissertation).

1398. ROY, S.K. (1978) Ceramics of Arunachal Pradesh and their nature of Adaptation,
Cultural and Biological Adaptability of Man with special Reference to North East India. Ed. by A.C. Bhagabati and R.K. Kar.
(It is also Bulletin, Dept. of Anth. : Dibrugarh University, 6, 1977). Dibrugarh, Dibrugarh Univ., : 129-37.

1399. ROY, Sankar Kumar (1983) A note on 'Ma' (fire carrying basket) from Talhia, Subansiri district, Arunachal Pradesh.
Human Science (Anth. Surv. of India, Calcutta). 32(4), Dec : 303-05.

1400. ROY BURMAN, B. (1976) Monastic Education.
Resarun, 2(1), Jan. : 1-5.

1401. ROY BURMAN, B.K. (Ed) (n.d.) Census of India 1961, NEFA, Village Survey monograph : Sibuk (Pasighat, Siang). Delhi, Office of the Registrar General, (Mimeograped).

1402. ———— (Ed) (c.1961) A Preliminary appraisal of the Scheduled Tribes of India. New Delhi, Office of the Registrar General, 368p.

1403. ———— (Ed) (n.d.) Census of India 1961, NEFA Village Survey monograph : Jia (Lohit District). Delhi, Office of the Registrar General (Mimeographed).

1404. ———— (Ed) (n.d.) Census of India 1961, NEFA, Village Survey monograph : Momong (District Lohit). Delhi, Office of the Registrar General (Mimeographed).

1405. ———— (Ed) (1961) Census of India 1961, NEFA, Village Survey Monograph : Dalbing (Siang District). New Delhi, Registrar General of India (Mimeographed).

1406. ———— (Ed) (n.d.) Census of India 1961, NEFA, Village Survey Monograph : Ramsing (Siang District). Delhi, Office of the Registrar General (Mimeographed).

1407. ———— (Ed) (1966) Census of India 1961, Vol. I, NEFA, pt. VI, Monograph series, No. 2 : Socio. Economic Survey of Jara, a Dafla village in NEFA. New Delhi, Registrar General of India, Ministry of Home Affairs, 57p.

1408. ———— (1967) Basic facts and figures relating to the Himalaya and problems of development.
Seminar on *"Social Welfare in the Himalyas"*, Delhi School of Social Work, December, (Mimeographed, circulated by the Office of the Registrar General, India).

1409. ———— (1967) Hillmen of North East India and tensions of Socio.-Economic development.
Jour. of Social Research, 10(2), Sept : 37-50 *and Vanyajati*, 15(3) July : 109-119.

1410. ———— (n.d.) Integrated area approach to the problems of the Hill tribes of North East India. New Delhi, Ministry of Home Affairs, 49p.

1411. ———— (1967) Uttar Purb Bharatiya Pahari Jatiyon ki samajik ebang arthik unnati ki samashya (in Hindi). *Vanyajati*, 15(4), Oct-68.

1412. ———— (1970) Demographic and Socio.-Economic Profiles of the Hill Areas of North East India. New Delhi, Office of the Registrar General, 379p. (Census of India 1961 publication).

1413. ———— (1972) Integrated area approach to the problems of the Hill Tribes of North East India.
Tribal Situation in India : Proceedings of a Seminar. Ed. by K. Snresh Singh. Simla, Indian Institute of Advanced Study : 72-97.

1414. ———— (1972) Social Process in the hills of North East India : An Ecological prospective. Simla, Indian Institute of Advanced Studies, 27p.

1415. ———— (1972) Tribal Demography : A preliminary appraisal,

Tribal Situation in India : Proceedings of a Seminar. Ed. by K. Suresh Singh. Simla, Indian Insttute of Advanced Study : 39-50.

1416. ——— (1973) Society and Culture in Arunachal, 1973. New Delhi, Council for Cultural Studies India, International Centre, 14p.

1417. ——— (Ed) (1970) Census of India 1961, NEFA Village Survey Monograph : Koreng (Pasighat, Siang). Delhi. Office of the Registrar General (Mimeographed).

1418. ——— (Ed) (1975) Census of India 1971 : Socio-Economic Survey of Rupa, a Sherdukpen village in Arunachal Pradesh). Delhi, Controller of Publications, 171p.

1419. ——— (1978) Emerging humanity and the tribal women in India.
Tribal Woman in India. Ed. by Committee. Calcutta, Indian Anthropological Society : 21-5.

1420. ——— (1984) Changes in the institution of family among the tribes of North East and problem of codification of customary law.
The Tribes of North East India. Ed. by S. Karotemprel. Calcutta, Firma KLM Pvt. Ltd. : 336-44.

1421. ROY BARUAH, Sarat (1962) Adi (in Assamese).
Asamar Janajati. Ed. by Pramod Chandra Bhattacharya. Jorhat, Asam Sahitya Sabha : 10-18.

1422. ROY CHOUDHURY, Abhijit (1983) Demographic trend in North Eastern Region with special reference Arunachal Pradesh.
Social Research : Journal of Institute of Social Research (Shillong), 3(2), April-June : 27-32.

1423 ROY CHOUDHURI, Bikash (1978) Dormitory among the tribal women in India.
Tribal Women in India. Ed. by Committee. Calcutta, Indian Anthropological Society : 154-65.

1424. R.P.R. (1963) Sentinels of our frontiers.
Social Welfare, 10(2), May : 15-18.

1425. RUKBO, T. (1970) The stone that speaks.
NEFA Information, Nov : 12-6.

1426. ———— (1965) Festivals of Arunachal Pradesh : It's future development.
Aru. News, 4(4), June : 12-21.

1427. ———— (1976) Festivals of Arunachal Pradesh.
North Eastern Review, Nov.

1428. ———— (1976) Preservation enrichment of dancing patterns and musical wealth of Arunachal Pradesh.
Aru. News, 5(5) Sept : 41-43.

1429. ———— (1977) Solung : The central feature of Adi culture.
Aru. News, 6(8), Dec. : 6-9.

1430. RUSTOMJI, Nari (1953) Tribal administration in the North East Frontier Agency.
March of India, 6(2), Nov.-Dec. : 24-8.

1431. ———— (1955) Tribal administration in North East Frontier Agehcy.
The Adivasis.
Delhi, Publication Division, Ministry of Inf. and Broadcasting Govt. of India, : 133-39 (Revised edition in 1960).

1432. ————(1971) Enchanted Frontiers. Bombay, Oxford University Press : 114-38.

1433. ———— (1983) Imperilled Frontiers : India's North Eastern Borderland. Delhi, Oxford Universtty Press, 160p.

1434. SAADULLA, Md. (1972) Chamtok Mol Festival.
Aru. News, 1(10), Dec. : 16-7

1435. SAHA, Nareswar and PATHAK, R.D. (1977) Nature of punishment in Nocte Law : An Ethnographical Analysis.
Proceedings of a Seminar on "*Social and Political Institutions of North East India*," organised by North East Indian Council for Social Science Research, Shillong.

1436. SAHA, Niranjan (1963) Human Factor in Agricultural Development . Study of a Tribal Community.
Economic Weekly, 15 : 1641-43.

1437. SAHNI, K.C. (1969) A Contribution of the Flora of Kameng and Subansiri District, NEFA.
Ind. For, LXXXXY : 330-52,

1438. SAI, Tasso (1983) Apatani Language Guide. Shillong, Directorate of Research, Government of Arunachal Pradesh.

1439. SAIKIA, P.D. (1958-59) Justice by oaths and ordeals among Daflas.
Adivasi, 3(1) : 16-21.

1440. ———— (1963) Village leadership in North East India : Assessment and conclusion on case-studies in six villages.
Man in India, 43(2), April-June : 92-9.

1441. ———— (1664) Studies in Dafla Social and Religious Life. Gauhati, Dept. ot Tribal Culture and Folklore Research Gauhati University, 70p.

1442. ———— (1969) Sccio-Economic Structure of a Dafla Village. Gauhati University, Ph. D. Thesis (Unpub).

1443. ———— (1972) Institutional factors influencing economic development of Dafla and Gallong tribes of NEFA.
Agro Economic Problems of Tribal India. Ed. by M.L. Patel. Bhopal, Progree : 72-7.

1444. ———— (1974) Economic of marriage payments of Daflas.
North Eastern Affairs, 3(1), April-June : 37-38 and 42.

1445. ———— (1980) Kinship system of the Nisis of Arunchal.
Eastern Himalayas : A study on Anthropology and Tribalism. Ed. by T.C. Sharma and D.N. Majumdar. New Delhi, Cosmo Pub. : 163-75.

1446. ———— (1982) A note on shifting cultivation on North East Indla.
Economic of the Tribes and their Transformation. Ed. by K.S. Singh. New Delhi, Concept Pub. Com. ; 228-39.

14 7. SAMANTA, R.K. (1978) Better cattle feed from paddy straw.
Aru. News, 7(3), June-July : 10-11.

1448. SAREEN, H.K. (1980) Insurgency in North East India : A study of the Sino-American Role. New Delhi, Sterling Publishers : 2, 6, 15, 16, 93.

1449. SARIN, Vik (1980) India's North East in flames. New Delhi, Vikas Publishing : 167-79.

1450. SARKAR, J.K. (1975) The Khamti ethnography of a foothill Buddhist tribe.
Report submitted to Anthropological Survey of India (Unpublished).

1451, ———— (1976) The Padam, ethnography of a tribe living between the High Hills and the valleys.
Report submitted to Anth. Surv. of India (Unpublished).

1452. ———— (1975) The Kaman Mishmis, ethnography of a border tribe living in high altitude.
Report submitted to Anth. Surv. of India (Unpublished),

1453. ———— (1976) Ecological adjustment and identity format among the people of Arunachal Pradesh Border.
Report submitted to Anth. Surv. of India (Unpublished).

1454. ———— (1976) Ecology, economy and ethnic consciousness : A study on the impact of ecology on the people of Arunachal Border Area.
Proceedings of a Seminar on "*Border Area Study*" held in Anthropological Survey of India, Calcutta.

1455. ———— (1976) A note on development of identity consciousness ; A formulatory phase of movement in Arunachal Pradesh.
Report submitted to Anth. Surv. of India (Unpublished.

1456. ———— (1979) Terrain, village type and political organisation in Arunachal Pradesh.
Proceedings of a Seminar on "*Bio Cultural Profile of North East India*", organised by Anth. Surv. of India, Shillong, 26th April, 1979.

1457. (1912) Development of identity consciousness in Arunachal Pradesh.
Tribal Movements in India, Vol. I. Ed. by K.S. Singh. New Delhi, Monohar Pub. : 231-39.

1458. ——— (1982) Economic system and social change in Arunachal Pradesh.
Economies of the Tribes aud their Transformation. Ed. by K.S. Singh. New Delhi, Concept Pub. Com. : 287-302.

1459. SARKAR, J.K. and DAS, M.M. (1977) Ethnography of the Wanchoo Society of Arunachal Pradesh.
Report submitted to Anth. Surv. of India (Unpublished).

1460. ——— *Report* submitted to Anth, Surv. of India (Unpublished).

1461. ——— (1977) Ethnography of Singpho society of Arunachal Pradesh.
(*Report* submitted to Anth. Surv. of India (Unpublished).

1462. ——— (1978) Marriage system of the Wanchos.
Proceedings of a Seminar of Indian Anthropological Society, Calcutta.

1463. SARKAR, Jayanta (1977) A note on avoidance of direct exchange of bride among the Khamtis of Arunachal Pradesh.
Man in India, 57(3), July-Sept. : 208-15.

1464. ——— (1982) Ecology as controlling factor of economy village type and political organisation in Arunachal Pradesh.
Proceedings of a Seminar on "*Environmental Anthropology*" organised by Anth. Survey of India, Dehra Dun.

1465. ——— (1983) Ecology, Bride and Buffer Communities in Subansiri Valley of Arunachal Pradesh.
Human Science (Anthropological Survey of India, Calcutta), (32)2, June : 105-05.

1466. SARKAR, N., (c. 1971) Neolithic celts in Arunachal Pradesh and Assam.
Pines, (Shillong), 1 (III), Arunachal Number : 70-5.

1467. ——— (1973) The socalled polyandry among the Gallongs.
Man in India, 53(2), April-June : 128-34.

1468. ——— (1974) Dances of Arunachal Pradesh. Shillong, M.P. Hazarika, Research Dept., Dir. of Inf. & Pub. Relations, Govt. of A P., 181p.

1469. ——— (1975) Historical account of the introduction of Buddhism among the Monpas and Sherdukpens.
Aru. News, 4(7), Oct. : 11-5 *and* 4(8), Nov: 14-7.

1470. ———— (1975) Introduction of Buddhism among the Monpas and Sherdukpens.
Resarun, 1, January : 23-44 *and Resarun*'75 (Cum. Vol. 1976) : 16-30.

1471. (1975) Tsewang Lhamo : Mother of Sixth Dalai Lama. *Resarun*, 1(3), July : 17-9 *and Resarun*'75 (Cum. Vol. 1976) : 77-8.

147. ———— Rise of Buddhist Schools.
Resarun, 2(4), Oct. : 13-6.

1473. ———— (1976) Two stone engravings in Tirap District (Patkai and its History).
Aru. News, 5(3), April-May : 14-7.

1474. ———— (1976) Buddha and his principles.
Resarun, 2(3), July : 30-2

1475. ———— (1977) The Buddhist sects among the Monpas and Sherdukpens.
Resarun, 3(2), April : 26-8.

1476. ———— Rise of Buddhist Schools.
Aru. News, 5(9), Jan.-Feb. : 32-33 and 37.

1477. ———— (1977) Minor religious structure of the Monpas and Sherdukpens.
Resarun, 3(3), July : 27-30.

1478. ———— (1977) An account of Corcham Ghorten, the largest stupa in Arunachal Pradesh.
Resarun, 3(4), Oct. : 10-2.

1479. ———— (1977) Mahayana Buddhism : Its spread to Tibet and sectarian development there.
Resarun, 3(1). January : 13-6.

1480. ———— (1978) A Historical account of Tawang monastery.
Aru. News, 6(9), January, Republic Day Issue : 7-12.

1481. ———— (1978) A Historical account of Tawang monastery.
Resarun, 4(2), Aut,-Winter : 17-24.

1482. ———— (1978) A further note on the introduction of Buddhism among the Monpas and Sherdukpens.
Resarun, 4(1), Jan.-March : 42-3.

1483. ——— Two stone engravings in Tirap District.
Aru. News, 5(3), April-May : 14-6.

1484. ——— (1980) Buddhism among the Monpas and Sherdukpens. Shillong, Res. Dept., Direct. of Inf. & Pub. Relations, Govt. of A.P. 106p.

1485. ——— (1980) Preservation and promotion of folk dances of Arunachal.
Aru. News, 9(3). June-July : 24-6.

1486. ——— (1980) Preservation and promotion of folk dances of Arunachal Pradesh.
Resarun, 6(1), Spring-Summer : 8-11.

1487. ——— (1981) Tawang Monastery. Shillong, Research Dept., Dir. of Inf. & Pub. Relations, Govt. of A.P., 55p.

1488. ——— (1982) Neolithic celts from Arunachal Pradesh.
Resarun, 8(2), Aut-Win : 11-15.

1489. SARKAR, S.S. (1960) Clan Demography in an Abor village.
Proceedings of National Institute of Science, India, B. 26 : 221-32.

1490. SARMA, Jyotirmoyee (1960) Puberty, Marriage and Child Birth among the Panggi and the Minyong Abor women
Anthropos (W. Germany), 55 : 93-113.

1491. SARMA, J.L. (1983) Wanchoo janajati (in Hindi).
Manav (Lucknow), XI(2), April-June.

1492. SASTRY, A.R.K. (1969) Maesa truncata : A new species of Myrsinaceae from Subansiri District, North East Frontier Agency.
J. Sen Memorial volume (Botanical Survey of India) : 433-36.

1493. SASTRY, A.R.K. *and* CHOWDHURY, S. (1969) Arthroneris jarretti : A new species of Polypodiaceae from Subansiri District, NEFA, India.
Bulletin : Botanical Survey of India, XI : 442-43.

1494. SASTRY, A R.K. *and* DEKA, H. (1967) Nertera sinensis Hemsl. : A new find from Subansiri District, NEFA, India.

1495. SASTRY, A.R.K. *and* KATAKI, S.K. (1967) On some species of Rhododendron from Subansiri District, North East Frontier Agency.
Ind, For.. LXXXXIII : 264-65.

1496. SCHUBERT, J. and SCHINDLER, M. (1960) Roter Fluss and Blausc Berge. Leipzig, 101 p.

1497. SELECTIONS From the Records (1855) Selections from the Records of Bengal Government, 1851-69, No. XXIII. Calcutta. (It contains papers by Neufville, "*On the Geography and Population of Assam;* Wilcox,"*Memoir of a Survey of Assam and the neighbouring countries, executed in 1825-6-7-8*" : Dalton, "*Correspondence and Journal of his visit to a clan of Abors on the Dihong River.*"

1498. SELECTIONS of Papers : (1873) Selections of Papers regarding the Hill Tracts between Assam and Burma and on the Upper Brahmaputra, 1825-70.
Calcutta. (It contains papers by Wilcox, "*Memoir of a Survey af Assam*" ; Griffith, "*Journal of a Trip to the Mishmi Mountains*" ; Griffith, "*A Journey from Upper Assam towards Hockhoom* ; Bayfield, "*Narrative of a Journey from Ava to the frontiers of Assam and Back*"; Jenkins, "*Notes on a Trip across the Patkoi Range*"; Report of a visit by Capt. Vetch to the Singpho and Naga Frontier ; Reports of Lt. Brodie's Dealings with the Nagas; Peal, "*Notes on a visit to the Tribes inhabiting the Hills South of Sibasagar*".

1499. SEINDENFADEN, Erik (1958) The Thai Peoples. Bangkok.

1500. SEN, Biswajit (1965) The Khamptis: An outline of their culture.
Man in India, 45(3), July-Sept.: 237-43.

1501. ———— (1965) The Monpas of Tawang.
Vanyajati, 13(1), Jan: 23-6.

1502. ———— (1967) NEFA, its history of administration and the problem of integration.
A Common Perspective for North East India. Ed. by Rathin Mitra and B. Das Gupta. Calcutta, Pannalal Das Gupta: 164-72.

1503. SEN, Bosi (1972) Crop production at high altitude. *Aru. News*, 1(4), May: 18-22.

1504. SEN, Gertrude Emerson (1960) Sortie over NEFA. *Economic Weekly*, 12: 139-44.

1505. SEN, Sipra (1985) The Tribes of Meghalaya. Delhi, Mittal Publications.

1506. SEN, Seumen (Ed) (1985) Folklore in North East India. New Delhi, Om Sons.

1507. SEN, S.N. (1977) Geology and mineral wealth of Arunachal Pradesh: A challenge to the explorer.
Yojna, 26 January: 46-52.

1508. SEN GUPTA, P.N. (19.2) Investigation on the dietary habits of the Aboriginal tribes of Abor Hills (NEFA), part I: Padam tribe.
Indian Journal of Medical Research, 40(2): 203-18.

1509. ——— (1953) The dietaries of the primitive tribes of India.
March of India (Delhi), 6(2), Nov.-Dec.: 60-3.

1510. ——— (1955) Studies in the vital capacity of Nocte Nagas of Tirap Frontier Division, NEFA.
Proceedings, National Inst. of Science of India. 21(B), No. 1: 18-20.

1511. ——— (1955) Dietaries of Primitive Tribes.
The Adivasis. Delhi, Publication Division, Ministry of Inf. & Broadcasting, Govt. of India: 89-98.

1512. ——— (1956) Population studies and living conditions of the tribes in the Padam and Minyong areas of Abor Hills (Assam).
Bull. Dept. of Anth. Surv. of India), Govt. of India, 2(1), Jan. (1953),: 91-112.

1513. ——— (1959) Investigations into the Dietary habits of the aboriginal tribes of Abor Hills (NEFA), Part II, Minayongs and Pangis.
Bull. Dept. of Anth (Anth. Surv. of Indian, 3(2), July, (1954) . 155-73.

1514. ————(1959) The Investigations into the dietary habits of the Aboriginal tribes of Abor Hills, (NEFA) part III : Galong Tribe.
Bull. Dept. of Anth. (Anth Surv. of India), 4(2), (1955): 69-97.

1515. ———— (1960) Notes on the nutritional index and body build of the Nokte tribes of Tirap Frontier Division. NEFA.
Bull. Dept. of Anth. (Anth. Surv. of India), 9(1) : 79-80.

1516. ———— (1960) Investigation into the diet and nutrition of the Nokte tribe, Tirap Frontier Division, NEFA.
Bull. Dept. of Anth. (Anth. Surv. of India), 9(2): 25-37.

1517. SEN GUPTA, Sarthak *and* DUTTA, M.N.: (1980) ABO Blood Groups in the Kaibarta, Ahom and the Wancho of North East India.
Acta Anthropogenetica (Delhi), 4: 545-46.

1518. SHAKESPEAR, L.W (1914) History of Assam, Upper Burmah and North Eastern Frontier. London, Macmillan & Co. Ltd, 272p.

1519. ———— (1929) History of the Assam Rifles. London, Macmillan, 301p.

1520. SHARMA, J.L. (1980) A note on family structure of the Wancho of Arunachal Pradesh.
Bull. Dept. of Anth., Dibrugarh University, 9: 208-13,

1521. SHARMA. Lalit *and* DUARAH, Dwijendra K. (1981) Ordeal by fire: A study among the Apatanis of Arunachal Pradesh.
Resarun, 7(1-2): 50-5.

1522. SHARMA, L. (1969) Michimi Paharar Rangsinga. (in Assamese). Shillong, Smt. Pranita Devi, Balmik (3rd edition), 174p.

1523. SHARMA, R.R.P. (1961) The Sherdukpens (The People of NEFA). Shillong, P.C. Dutta for Research Dept., Advisers' Secretariat (2nd edition, 1966), 101p.

1524. SHARMA, S.N. (1968) Background of Miju-Mishmi culture.
NEFA Information, August 6-9.

1525. ———— (1970) The Meyors of Lohit.
NEFA Information: 30-1.

1526. SHARMA, T.C. (1961) Physical characters of the Miri.
Jour. of Gauhati University.

1527. ———— (1962) Finger prints of the Miri.
Bulletin: Dept. of Tribal Culture and Folklore Research (Gauhati University), 1: 65-73.

1528. ———— (1984) Some observations on the status of Ecology in North East India.
Status of Ecology. Ed. by I.J.S. Jaswal. Patiala, Punjab Publishing House: 43-53.

1529. ———— (1984) North East India in prehistoric times.
The Tribes of North East India. Ed. by S. Karotemprel. Calcutta, Firma K.L.M. Pvt. Ltd.: 1-21.

1530. SHARMA, T.C. *and* MAJUMDAR, D.N. (1980) Eastern Himalayas: A study on Anthropology and Tribalism. New Delhi, Cosmo Publications, 221p.

1531. SHASHI, S.S. (1978) Night Life of Indian Tribes. Delhi, Agam Prakashan: 65-72 (Adi).

1531. SHASTRI, B. (1972) Legends of Ita.
Jour. of Assam Research Society, 20: 43-8.

1533. ———— (Ed) (1972) Arunachal Research Bulletin (Independence Silver Jubilee issue, August). Shillong, Research Dept., Director of Infor. & Pub. Relations, Govt. of A.P., 101p.

1534. ———— (1974) Growth of administration in Arunachal.
North Eastern Affairs, 2(4), Jan-March: 35-6.

1535. SHASTRI, Bibhabasu Das: (1958) A tentative alphabet for NEFA Language (Adi).
Bull. of the Research Dept, NEFA (Shillong), 1(1), June: 64-91.

1536. SHASTRI, V.N. (1992) Asamor Janajatir Sadhu (in Assamese). Jorhat : 360p.

1537. SHRIKANT, L.M. (1963) Notes: Welfare work in NEFA area.
Vanyajati, XI (4), Oct.: 145-46 and 84.

1538. SHUKLA, B.K. (1958) Dafla dreams and their significance.
Bull. of the Research Dept., NEFA, (Shillong), 1(1), June: 99-113.

1539. ———— (1959) The Daflas of the Subansiriri region. (The People of NEFA). Shillong, Research Dept., (NEFA), 139p. (Reprinted in 1980, 106p).

1540. ———— (1976) (?) The Daflas of the Subansiri regiog,
Man (London), LXI: 194.

1541. ———— (1976) The Daflas of the Subansiri region.
Resarun, 1(3), Oct. : 22-3.

1542. SHUKLA, S.P. (1983) Physico-Biotic environment and agricultural development in Siang Region: Arunachal Pradesh.
Social Research: Journal of Inst. of Social Research (Shillong), 3(3-4), July-Dec. 23-31.

1543 SHUKLA, S.P. *and* AGARWAL, A.K. (1983) The magnitude of the problem of agricultural labour in the North East Region.
Jour., NEICSSR (Shillong), 7(1), April: 34-8.

1544. SIKDAR, Sudatta (1981) Trade fairs in Arunachal: Assam Border.
Proceedings of the North East India, History Association, (1980). Ed. by Jayanta Bhusan Bhattacharjee. Shillong, North East India History Association, Dept. of History, NEHU : 158-73.

1545. SIMON, I.M. (1962) Apatani language guide. Shillong, 44p.

1546. ———— (1970) Aka language guide. Shillong, Philological Section, (NEFA), 91p.

1548. ———— (1675) Array of languages and dialects.
The Statesman (Daily, Calcutta), Saturday, Nov. 29.

1549. ———— (1976) The status of women in some North East Indian tribal communities.
Aru. News, 4(5), July : 34-9.

1550. ———— (1976) Reflections from the past.
Aru. News, 5(4), June: 19-23.

1551. ———— (1976) From Birth to Death among the Mijis.
Resarun, 2(1), Jan.: 1-7.

1552. ———— (1976) From Birth to Death among the Mijis.
Resarun '75, Cum. Volume: 37-42.

1553. ———— (1976) The Khoa language.
Resarun, 2(3), July: 8-10.

1554. ———— (19`6) The Khoa language.
Resarun '75 , Cum, Volume: 100-03.

1555. ———— (1976) The mithun as a prestige symbol.
Aru. News, 5(6), Aug.-Sept.: 20-4.

1556. ———— (1976) A note on the languages of Arunachal.
Resarun '75, Cum. Volume: 60-3.

1558. ———— (1976) Hill Miri language Guide. Shillong, DIPR, Govt. of A.P., 80p.

1559. ———— (1976) Array of languages and dialects.
Aru. News, Republic Day Issue, 4(9): 9-10.

1560. ———— (1977) Affinity among the language group of Arunachal.
Research in Arunachal Pradesh, Research Dept., Govt. of A.P.: 42-6.

1561. ———— The Mithun as a prestige symbol.
Resarun, 3(2), April: 8-12.

1562. ———— (1978) The largest language group in Arunachal.
Resarun, 4(1), Jan.-March: 7-13.

1563. ———— (1978) The Role of Philological Research in Arunachal Pradesh.
Research in Arunachal Pradesh: Research Dept., Govt. of A.P.: 38-41,

1564. ———— (1964) Miji Language Guide. Shillong, Research Dept., Govt. of A.P. ι9p.

1665. ———— (1981) Hill Miri language Guide. Shillong, Research Dept, DIRP, Govt. of A.P., 79p.

1566. SIMOON, F.J. (1968) A ceremonial ox of India: The Mithun in Nature, Culture and History.
Madison.

1567. SINGH, Harminder (1960) Progress in the Frontier.
March of India (Delhi), 12(9), Sept: 12.

1568. SINGH, J.P. (1969 Gadis towns of North East India: A study in population growth and occupational structure.
National Geographical Journal of India (Varanhsi), 15 (3-4), Sept.-Dec.: 235-41.

1569. ———— (1980) Levels of human resources in North Eastern India.
Jour. NEICSSR, 4(?), Oct.: 1-6.

1570. SINGH (Ed.) (1972) Tribal Situation in India : Proceedings of a Seminar. Simla, Indian Institute of Advanced Study, 639p.

1571. SINGH, K.S. (Ed.) (1982) Tribal Movements in India, Vol. I. New Delhi, Monohar Publications.

1572. ———— (Ed.) (1982) Economies of the Tribes and their transformation. New Delhi, Concept Publishing Company.

1573. SINHA, R. (1958) The conception of an ideal individual in Aka society.
Bull. of the Res. Dept., NEFA, 1(1), June: 64-89.

1574. ———— (1961) The significance of village community studies in NEFA.
Vanyajati, 9(1), Jan.: 22-5.

1575. ———— The Akas. Shillong, Res. Dept., NEFA Adviser's Secretariat, 144p.

1576. ———— An analysis of the kinship terminology of the Buguns of NEFA.
Bull. of the Tribal Research and Training Institute (Chhindwara), 4(1), June: 22-6.

1577. ———— (1976) From the Akas.
Resarun '75, Cum. Volume; 93.

1578. ———— (1977) Religion and Culture of North East India. New Delhi, Abhinav Publications. 12p.

1579. SINHA, R.P. (1976) The Akas.
Resarun, 2(4), Oct.: 30-1.

1580. SINHA, Surajit (1972) Tribal solidarity movements in India:

A review.
Tribal Situation in India : Proceedings of a Seminar. Ed. by K. Suresh Singh. Simla, Indian Institute of Advanced Study : 41-23.

1581. SOCIAL WELFARE (1963) Winds of change across NEFA. *Social Welfare*, 10(6), Sept; 28-9.

1582. SONAR, Daniel (1979) Structure, characteristics and behaviour of Mithuns.
Aru. News, 2(3), May: 13-4.

1583. SONI, Bholaprasad (1972) NEFA ke Minyong adivashi (in Hindi).
Vanyajati, 20(2), April: 74-94 *and* 20(3-4), July: 127-43 also 21(2), April: 40-53.

1584. SRIKANT, L.M. *et al* (n.d.) Tribal Souvenir. New Delhi, Bharatiya Adimjati Sevak Sangh, 195p.

1585. SPECTRUM (1977) North Eastern Spectrum, Vol I: 1976-77. Gauhati, North Eastern Spectrum.

1586. SRINIWAS, M.N. *and* SANWAL, R.D. (1970) Some aspects of political development in the North Eastern Hill areas of India.
North Eastern Research Bulletin (Dibrugarh), 1, Summer: 1-10.

1587. SRIPEECEE (1958) Lest there be misgivings and misapprehensions.
The Outlook on NEFA, Comp. Ed. by Parag Chaliha. Jorhat, Assam Sahitya Sabha: 131-34.

1588. SRIVASTAVA, J.M. (1983) Traditional system of adjudication of disputes : contemporary changes and some suggestions.
Aru. News, 12(5), Aug.-Sept.: 19-20.

1589. SRIVASTAVA, L.R.N. (1958) Marriage among the Korka Galongs.
Bull. of the Research Dept., NEFA, 1(1): 36-58.

1590. ——— (1962) The Gallongs. Shillong, Research Dept., Govt. of NEFA, 128p.

1591. ——— (1966) Hair-style, head dress and their social significance among some of the Tribes of North East Frontier of India.

Bull. Cultural Research Institute (Calcutta), 5: 110-25.

1592. ———— (1969) The problem of modernization of the tribes of North East India.
Bull. Cultural Research Institute (Calcutta), 8(-12): 21-5.

1593. ———— (1973) Among the Wanchos of Arunachal Pradesh. Shillong, Director of Inf. & Pub. Relations, Govt. of A.P., 188p.

1594. ———— (1985) Social organisation of the Minyong. Shillong, Directorate of Research, Govt. of A.P.

1595. SRIVASTAVA, R.P. (1969) Fingerprints, colour blindness and other features in the Miris of Assam.
Man in India, 49(4), Oct.-Dec.: 398-403.

1596. ———— (1969) Impact of community development programme and cultural change among the Miris of Dhamaji Subdivision of Assam. Dibrugarh, Dept of Anth., Dibrugarh University (U.G.C. Project).

1597. ———— (1969) Progress and problems of tribal education in Passighat, North East Frontier Agency. Dibrugarh University, Deptt. of Anth., 2p. (Mimeographed).

1598. ———— (1971) Taste sensitivity to P.T.C. in two groups of NEFA tribes.
Man in India, 51(3), July-Sept.: 241-44.

1599. STACK, E. (1885) : Assam, Report. Shillong, Govt. Printing Press (Miri, Dapla, Abor : 86-90).

1600. STAPLETON, H.E.: (1910) Contributions to the History and Ethnology of North Eastern India.
Jour. of the Asiatic Society of Bengal (New Series), 6: 141-66, 619-49.

1601. ———— (1922) Contributions to the History and Ethnology of North Eastern India.
Jour. of the Asiatic Society of Beugal (New Series), 18: 25-60.

1602. STATES (1970) Socio-Economic Progress.
States, Jan., 13: 29-31.

1603. STONOR, C.R, (1948) Notes and Queries: Abor multilation of the slain.
Man in India, 28(3), Sept.: 179.

1604. ———— (1948) On the use of tree-fern sago in the Assam Himalayas.
Man (London), 48 (156).

1605. ———— (1950) The feasts of merit among the northern Sangtam Tribe of Assam.
Authropos (W. Germany), XLV.

1606. ———— (1952) The Sulung tribe of the Assam Himalayas.
Anthropos (W. Germany), 47(5-6): 947-62.

1607. ———— (1957) Notes on religion and ritual among the Dafla tribe of the Assam Himalayas.
Anthropos, LII, (1-2): 1-23.

1608. STRACY, P.D. (1966) Bringing NEFA's Forests alive.
The Hornbill (Shillong), DIPR, Govt. of NEFA: 35-40.

1609. SHUKLA, A.P. (1983) Spatio-Temporal organisational Dimensions of Agriculture in Siang Region: Arunachal Pradesh.
Hill Geographer: The Geographical Society of the North Eastern Region (Shillong), North Eastern Hill University, 1(1-2), 1982: 14-22.

1610. SUKLA, B.K. (1959) The Daflas of the Subansiri region. Shilong, Research Dept., Govt. of NEFA, 139p.

1611. ———— (1962) Apatani Love-Song.
The Hornbill (Shillong).

1612. ———— 1976 From "The Daflas".
Resarun '75, Cum. Volume: 94-8.

1613. SWAMY, M.M. *and* HAZARIKA, B.C.: (1983) A Monograph on Mithun.
Aru. News, 12(5), Aug.-Sept.: 6-12.

1614. SYAMCHOUDHURI, N.K.: (1967) Anthropology and the Tribes of Assam.
A Common Perspective for North East India. Ed. by Rathin Mitra and B. Das Gupta. Calcutta, Pannalal Das Gupta: 58-63.

1615. SYKES, Marjorie (1963) The North East Frontier. Varanasi, Sarva Seva Sangh Prakashan, 39p.

1616. TAHBILDER, S (1969) A Study of Finger and Palm Prints of the Wanchoo of Tirap District of NEFA. Gauhati University, M.Sc. Dissertation, (Unpublished).

1617. TAID, Tabu (1982)A Short Note on Missing Phonology. *Linguistic Situation in North East India.* Ed. by Mrinal Miri. Shillong, NEICSSR: 86-96.

1618. TAIT, Kaleen (1979) Ali Aye Ligang Kaleen Tait. *Aru. News*, 8(4), June-July: 4.

1619. TAKI, Calong Tagang (1962) Abarar Grisma Utsav (in Assamese).
Asamor Janajati. Ed. by Pramod Chandra Bhattacharya. Jorhat, Assam Sahitya Sabha : 19-25.

1620. TAKKA Hfge (1979) Need for common language in Arunachal Pradesh.
Aru. News, 8(4), June-July: 13-4,

1621. TALUKDAR, G.C. (1972) Vasudev Than
Aru. News, 1(5), July: 6-7

1622. ———— (1972) Problem of flood control in Assam and Arunachal Pradesh.
Aru. News, 1(10), Dec : 12-5.

1623. ———— (1973) Vijaynagar.
Aru. News, 2(3). June: 9-13.

1624. ———— (1973) The Naksa Parbat Ruins.
Aru. News, 2(5), Aug : 3 8.

1625. TANA, Padi (1972) Arunachal needs social education.
Aru. News, 1(9), Nov.: 12-4.

1626. TANDON, R.N. (1981) Manpower development in North Eastern Region of India.
Aru. News, 10(6), Aug. 21-4.

1627. TANGDONG, S. (1980) Some admirable customs of the Nocte society.
Aru. News, 9(6), Oct. Nov.: 13-14.

1628. TANGDONG, Kej (1980) Folk Tales of the Apatanis.
Aru. News, 9(3), June-July: 15-8.

1629. ———— (1980) An Apatani Folk tale : Karsiimi and Durk Yalang.

Aru. News, 9(4), Aug.: 38-40.

1630. TASHI, Tsering (1976) Significance of Losen festival. *Aru. News*, 5(3), April-May: 28-9.

1631. TATUM, Michi (1980) Mopin festival of Adis. *Aru. News*, 9(2), April-May: 13-4.

1632. ———— (1980) The tiger and monkey, an Apatani myth. *Aru. News*,9(5), Sept.: 21-2.

1633. ———— (1980) Buru: Fact or fiction? *Aru. News*, 9(6), Oct.-Nov.: 4-5.

1634. ———— Myoke festival of Apatains. *Aru. News*, 10(2), Feb.-March: 16-8.

1635. TAYENG, Aduk (1967) A charm to cure. *The Hornbill* (Shillong), DIPR, Govt. of A.P.: 4-5.

1636. ———— (1975) Adi in vocations, spells and chants. *Resarun*, 1(2), April: 1-4. *and Resarun'74*, (Cum. Vol. 1976): 60-2.

1637. ———— (1976) The Milangs. *Resarun '75*, Cum. Volume: 128-30.

1638. ———— (1976) Two creation myths of the Adis (1) creation of the world (2) creation of the Mithun. *Resarun '75*, Cum. Volume.: 16 -70.

1639. ———— Proverbs (Miri, Kebang Gomru). *Resarun*, 2(1), Jan. 1-6 *and Resarun '75*, Cum. Volume: 18-23.

1640. ———— (1976) Milang Phrase Book. Shillong, Directorate of Research, DIPR, Govt. of A.P., 106.

1641. ———— (1976) Adi creation myths. *Resarun*, 2(4). Oct.: 24-7.

1642. ———— (1976) Creation of the Mithun. *Resarun*, 2(4), Oct. 28-9.

1643. ———— (1982) Leyo-Gokkunam A ritual of Adis. *Resarun*, 8(2), Aut.-Win.: 16-7.

1644. ———— (1983) A Phrase book in Padam. Shillong, Directorate of Research, Govt. of A.P.

1645. TEWARI, A.S. (1984) Book Review: Resarun, Research Department, Government of Arunachal Pradesh, 1977. *Eastern Anthropologist* (Lucknow), 37(2), April-June: 181-82.

1646. THANGA, L.B. (1961) Census of India (1961: North East Frontier Agency, General Economic Tables. Delhi, Manager of Publications.

1647. ———— (1961) Census of India 1961: North East Frontier Agency, Cultural and Migration Tables. Delhi, Manager of Publications.

1648. ———— (1961) Census of India 1961: North East Frontier Agency, Household Economic Tables. Delhi, Manager of Publications.

1649. ———— (1961) Census of India 1961: North East Frontier Agency. Housing and Establishment tables. Delhi. Manager of Publications.

1650. ———— (1961) Census of India (1961) North East Frontier Agency, Tables on Scheduled Caste and Scheduled tribes. Delhi, Manager of Publications.

1651. ————(n.d.) Census of India (1961), Vol. XXIV, pt. II-B, II-C, III, IV, V: North East Frontier Agency. Delhi, Manager of Publications, 543.p.

1652. ———— (1966) Census of India 1961: Vol. XXIV. pt. II-A, General Population Tables and NEFA, Special Tables. New Delhi. Manager of Publications, 289.

1653. THANGAM, E.S. (1976) Forest development programme in Arunachal Pradesh. Proceedings of a Seminar on "*People and Forests*" in the North Eastern Region," organised by Himalaya Seva Sangh, Himalaya, in collaboration with North Eastern Hill University, Shillong, Oct. 18-19, 1976.

1654. ———— (1977) Forest development programme in Arunachal Pradesh. *Himalaya: Man and Nature*, 1(4), Sept.: 31-6.

1655. ———— (1978) Forests of Arunachal Pradesh. *Aru. News*, 6(9): 40-4.

1656. ———— (1979) Forestry activities. *Aru. News*, 7(9) : 37-40.

1657. ———— (1979) Social Forestry in Arunachal Pradesh. *Aru. News*, 8(5) : 20-3.

1658. ———— (1979) Shifting cultivation in Arunachal Pradesh.
Proceedings of a Seminar on "*Agroforestry*" held at Imphal.

1659. ———— (1981) Anchal Forest Reserve of Arunachal Pradesh.
Aru. News, 10(6), Aug.: 15-9.

1660. ———— (1981) Shifting cultivation control programme in Wanchoo area.
Aru. News, 10(7), Sept.-Oct.: 5-14.

1661. (1982) Social forestry round up: Arunachal Pradesh.
Himalaya: Man and Nature, 5(9-10), Feb.-March.

1662. THONGCHI, Yeshe Dorjee (1981) The rituals relating to child birth amongest the Sherdukpens.
Aru. News, 10(8): 7-9.

1666. TIKHAK, Y (1975) Nongyang (The lake of no return): A Tangsa Folk Tale.
Aru. News, 4(4), June: 23-8.

1667. ———— (1976) Impact of modern culture on the traditional cultures of the local tribals of Tirap District.
Aru. News, 5(5), Sept.: 10-3.

1668. TIMES Of India (1968) NEFA Boundary.
Times of India (Dailp newspaper, Delhi), Oct. 29: 8:3.

1669. ———— (1972) Arunachal.
Times of India, Jan. 22. 4:1 1.

1670 TRENCHPRD, O.B.H. (1915) The Abor expedition survey detachment 1911-12, and of the Abor exploration survey detachment 1912-13.
Royal Engineers' Journal, 21:221 41, 268-92 (Reproduced from Records of the Survey of India, 1914, Vol. 4).

1671. TRIBAL Student of NEFA (1958) Memorandum submitted to the Governor of Assam.
The Outlook on NEFA. Comp. by Parag Chaliha. Jorhat, Assam Sahitya Sabha: 67-71.

1672. TROTTER, H. (1877) Account of the Pandit's journey in Great Thibet from Leeh in Ladakh to Lhasa, and of his return to India via Assam.

J.R.G.S., XLVII: 86-136. (Monpa).

1673. TURNER, William (1899) Contributions to the cranimetry of the peoples of the empire of India, pt. I: The Hill Tribes of North East Frontier and the people of Burma with three plates.
Translation of the *Royal Society of Edinburg*, 39(28), pt. III: 703-47.

1674. TYAGI, M.S. (1978) Education in Arunachal Pradesh. *Aru. News*, 6(9): 44-9.

1675. TYSON, Geoffrey (1945) *Forgotten Frontier.* Calcutta, W.H. Tongett & Co. Ltd, 146p.

1676. UNIVERSITY OF DELHI (1970) Sociology of North Eastern Hill Area, Delhi, University of Delhi, Dept. of Sociology, 41p.

1677. UPADHYA, Baldev (1952) Assam ke adivasi (in Hindi).
Ajkal, June : 37.

1678. VADHERA, R.P. (1981) Adult education programme in Lohit District.
Aru. News, 10(6), Aug.: 19-20 and 10(7), Sept.-Oct.: 37-8,

1679. VAGHAIWALLA, R.B. (1954) Census of India, 1951, Vol. XII, Assam, Manipur and Tripura, part I-A, Report. Shillong, Printed at the Municipal Printing Press, Bombay. (NEFA: 6-8, 18-19, 23-24, 25, 58-59, 64, 108, 216, 246).

1680. VARMA, S.C. (1959) Problems of drinking in the primitive tribes.
Eastern Anthropologist (Lucknow), 12(4), June-Aug.: 252-56.

1681. VETCH, H. (1848) In a letter dated 3rd January, 1848. *India's North East Frontier in the Nineteenth Century.* Ed. by Verrier Elwin. Bombay, Oxford University Press (1959): 6-7.

1682. ———— (1873) Report on a visit by Capt. Vetch to the Singpho and Naga Frontier in 1842.

Selection of Papers regarding the Hill Tracts between Assam and Burmah and on the Upper Brahmaputra. Calcutta, Bengal Sect. Press.

1683. VIDYARTHI, L.P. (1973) Tribal researches in the Himalayan regions.
North Eastern Affairs (Shillong), Annual, 2(1), April-June: 75-86 (NEFA Region: 79-82).

1684. ———— (1978) Rise of Anthropology in India : A special Science Orientation (in two Vols.). Delhi, Concept Publishing Company.

1685. VIDYARTHI, L.P. *and* RAI, B.K. (1977) The Tribal Culture of India. Delhi, Concept Publishing Company 487p.

1686. VITTAL, S.P. (1977) The Culture of the Adis.
The North Eastern Spectrum, 1(7). Jan. 38-9.

1687. VIVEK Publishing Company (1978) (?) Hill Tracts between Assam and Burma : Selection of Papers. Delhi, Vivek Publishing Company, 342p. (Reprinted; 1st printed in 1873 at the Bengal Secretariat Press under the title "*Selection of Papers regarding the Hill Tracts between and Burmah and on the Upper Brahmaputra*").

1688. WADD, Francis Kingdom (1952) My Hill so strong. London.

1689. WADDELL, L.A. (1985) Note on the poisoned arrows of the Akas.
Jour. of the Anthropological Institute (Great Britain & Ireland, London), 24: 27.

1990. ———— (1900) The Tribes of the Brahmaputra Valley.
Jour. Asiatic Society of Bengal (Calcutta), LXIX (3); 1-127.

1691. ———— (1911) A note on the derivation of Miri.
Man (London), 11(56) : 86.

1692. WADE, J.P. (1805) Geographical sketch of Assam, 1800.
Asiatic Society of Bengal, (Annual Register).

1693. WARD, G.L.S. (1901) Military report on the Mishmi country.

Simla, Intelligence Branch, Quarter Master Generals" Dept.

1694. WANGNO, S. (1981) The Chief system in Nocte Society. *Aru. News*, 10(5), July: 14-5.

1695. WEBB, C.M. 1912) Census of India 1911, Vol. IX : Burma, pt. I Report. Rangoon, Govt. Press, 266p.

1696· WILCOX, R. (1832) Memoir of a survey of Assam and the neighbouring countries executed in 1825-6-7-8. *Asiatic Researches*, XVII: 314-469.

1997. ———— (1832) Memoir of a survey of Assam and the neighbouring countries executed in 1825-6-7-8. *India's North East Frontier in the Nineteenth Century*. Ed. by Verrier Elwin. Bombay, Oxford University Press (1959): 9-10, 133-35, 219-22, 302-11, 409.

1698. WILLIAM, Robinson (1841) A Descriptive Account of Assam, to which is added a short account of neighbouring tribes. London, Ostell & Lopage, 421p.

1699. ———— (1975) Descriptive Account of Assam. Delhi, Sanskaran Prakashak, 433p (Reprinted).

1700. WOOD, R. (1953) The Hill Tribes of Assam. *J.B.B. of R.A.S.*, 28 : 187-214.

1701. WOODTHORPE, R.G. (1878) Narrative report of the Naga Hills and Lakhimpur Expedition Survey Party. *General Report on the Topographical Survey of India*, 1876-7: 59.

1702. ———— (1878) Narrative Report of the Naga Hills and Lakhimpur Expedition Survey Party. *India's North East Frontier in the Nineteenth Century*. Ed. by Verrier Elwin. Bombay, Oxford University Press (1959) : 73-85, 411-14.

1703. YEME, Jama (1977) The Sarok Festival of Akhas. *Aru. News*, 6(3). June-July: 26.

1704. YOUNG, E.C. (1907) A Journey from Yunnan to Assam. *Geographical Journal* (London), 30: 152-80.

ADDENDA—I

1705. ADVISER to The Governor of Assam (1952) Dictionary of sentences : Apa Tani. Shillong, Adviser to the Governor of Assam, Assam Govt. Press, 137p.

1706. ———— (1952) Dictionary of sentences : Dafla. Shillong, Adviser to the Governor of Assam, Assam Govt. Press, 157p.

1707. ———— (1952) A Dictionary of sentences : Mishmi (Miju). Shillong, Adviser to the Governor of Assam, Assam Govt. Psess, 136p.

1708. ———— (1952) A Dictionary of sentences : Mishmi (Digaru). (Shillong, Adviser to the Governor of Assam, Assam Govt. Press, 137p.

1709. ———— (1953) Dictionary of sentences : Monpa (Dirang Area). Shillong, Adviser to the Governor of Assam, Assam Govt. Press, 136p.

1710. AITKEN, E.H. (1881 & 1892) Tribes on my frontier. Bombay.

1711. ALLEN, B.C. (1905) Assam District Gazetteer, vol. V : Darrang. Allahabad; 53-62.

1712. ———— (1906) Assam District Gazetteer, Vol. VII : Sibsagar. Allahabad : 58-62.

1713. AMRITA BAZAR PATRIKA (1985) Rise in tiger population in Arunachal.
Amrita Bazar Patrika (Calcutta), Feb. 26 : 3.

1714. ———— (1984) Orchid research centre in Arunachal.
Amrita Bazar Patrika, Feb. 26 : 3.

1715. ———— (1985) Exploration of oil, coal in Arunachal.
Amrita Bazar Patrika, Feb. 27 : 3.

1716. ———— (1985) Namchik Nampmuk coal field humming with activities.
Amrita Bazar Patrika, Feb. 37 : 3.

1717. ———— (1965) NEFA since Independence.
Amrita Bazar Patrika, Aug. 15.

1718. ANTHROPOLOGY Dept. (1969) Distribution of blood groups (ABO, MN and Rh) among the Adis of Pasighat, Arunachal Pradesh. Dibrugarh University, Anthropology Dept., M. Sc. Dissertation Unpublised).

1719. ———— (1969) Menarcheal age and body dimension of girls among Adis of Pasighat, Arunachal Pradesh. Dibrugarh University, Anthropology Dept., M. Sc. Dissertation (Unpublished).

1720. ———— (1969) Finger and Palm prints of the Adis of Pasighat, Arunachal Pradesh. Dibrugarh University, Anth. Dept., M. Sc. Dissertation (Unpublished).

1721. ———— (1970) Distribution of blood groups (ABO and MN) among the Nocte of Khonsa, Arunachal Prɑdesh. Dibrugarh University, Anth. Dept., M. Sc. Dissertation (Unpublished).

1722. ———— Finger and Palm prints among the Noctes of Khonsa, Arunachal Pradesh. Dibrugarh University. Anth. Dept., M. Sc. Dissertation (Unpublished).

1723. ———— (1970) Somatometric and Somatoscopic characteristics of Noctes of Khonsa, Arunachal Pradesh. Dibrugarh University, Anth. Dept., M. Sc. Dissertation (Unpublished).

1724, ———— (1971) Finger and Palm prints among the Mishmis of Tezu, Arunachal Pradesh. Dibrugarh University, Anth. Dept., M. Sc. Dissertation (Unpublished).

1725. ———— (1971) Distribution of blood groups among the Mishmis of Tezu, Arunachal Pradesh. Dibrugarh University, Anth. Dept., M. Sc. Dissertation (Unpublished).

1726. ———— (1973) Growth pattern in male and female children among the Singphos of Burdomsa, Arunachal Pradesh. Dibrugarh University, Ahth. Dept., M. Sc. Dissertation (Unpublished).

1727. ———— (1971) P.T.C. taste threshold distribution among the Mismis of Tezu, Arunachal Pradesh.

Dibrugarh University, Anth. Dept., M. Sc. Dissertation (Unpublished).

1728. ———— (1973) Finger and Palm prints (Male and Female) among the Singphos of Burdomsa, Arunachal Pradesh Dibrugarh University, Anth. Dept., M. Sc. Dissertation (Unpublished).

1729. ———— (1973) Somatometic and somatoscopic characteristics (male and female) of the Singphos of Burdomsa, Arunachal Pradesh.
Dibrugarh University, Anth. Dept., M. Sc. Dissertation (Unpublishaed).

1730. ———— (1973) Distribution of blood groups among the Singphos of Burdomsa, Arunachal Pradesh. Dibrugarh University, Anth. Dept , M. Sc. Dissertation (Unpublished).

1731. ARUNACHAL News (1975) Economic programmes. *Arunachal News*, 4(7), Oct. : 6-7

1732. ———— (1976) Botanical exploration in Tawang, Arunachal Pradesh.
Aru. News, 5(8), Nov-Dec. : 44-7.

1733. ———— (1980) Here and There : Mopin Festival.
Aru. News, 9(2), April-May : 38-9.

1734. ———— (1980) History of education in Arunachal Pradesh.
Aru. News, 9(4), Aug. : 12-7.

1735. ———— ARUNACHAL Newsletter (1914) Dree festival celebrated.
Arunachal Newsletter (Itanagar), IV(8), July 31.

1736. ———— (1985) Si-Donyi Festival observed.
Arunachal Newsletter, 5(3), Jan. 15.

1737. ———— (1985) Boori Boot Festival celebrated.
Arunachal Newsletter, 5(4). Feb. 15 : 1.

1738. ARUNACHAL Pradesh Forest (1983) The Arunachal Pradesh Forest Corporation Limited and its activities. *Arunachal News*, 12(4), June-July : 34-9.

1739. ASSAM Government (1914) Supplement to Assam District Gazetteers, Vol. VIII, Lakhimpur by R. Frier. (Chapter III). Shillong. Assam Govt. Press : 7-8, 72-4.

1740. ———— (1957) Dictionary of sentence in Abor. Shillong, Assam Govt. Press.

1741. ASSAM Tribune (1963) Statement by Prime Minister Nehru.
The Assam Tribune (Gauhati), Dec. 18.

1741A. ———— (1985) Tawang Buddhist Monastery May Be Renovated.
Assam Tribune, June 9 : 6.

1742. AVERY, J. (1985) The religion of the aboriginal tribes of India.
Indian Antiquary (Bombay), 1 : 125-34.

1743. BAGCHI, R.N. (1984) Bangnis of East Kameng.
Social Research : Jour. of Institute of Social Research (Shillong), 4(3-4), July- Dec. : 18-27.

1744. BAILEY, F.M. (1914) Report of an exploration on the North East Frontier, 1913. Simla.

1745. BAINES, Athelstane (1976) Ethnograohy. Delhi, Concept Publishing Company (Reprinted, 1st Published in 1912) : 135-36.

1746. BANERJEE, A.C. (1946) Eastern Frontier of British India, Calcutta.

1747. BARDOLOI, Muktinath (1965) Is their NEFA yati ?
Amrita Bazar Patrika, Dec. 12.

1748. BARPATRAGOHAIN, C.K. (1984) Arunachal Pradesh where hundred flowers bloom : A brief history of evolution of a State.
Arunachal Review (Itanagar), 1(2), July-Dec. : 1-10.

1749. BARTHAKUR, I. K. (1975) Problem of agricultural development in Arunachal Pradesh with special reference to Subansiri District. Gauhati University Ph. D Thesis (Unpublished).

1750. BARTHAKUR, J.K. (1978) Demography and socio-economic process in Arunachal Pradesh. Gauhati University, Ph. D. Thesis (Unpublished).

1751. BARUA, Arun (1977) Beginnings of freedom movement in Assam.
North Eastern Spectrum, 1(11-12), May-June: 48-53. (About Khamti, Singpho).

1752. BAYFIELD, G.T. (1873) Narrative of a Journey from Ava to the Frontiers of Assam and Back.
Selections of papers relating to Hill Traits between Assam and Burma and on the Upper Brahmaputra. Calcutta. (No. 5).

1753. BERTRAND, Gabrielle (1958) Secret lands where women reign. London, Robert Hale Ltd. (Chapter IV : Abor, Galong, Aka, Dafla, Apa Tani. Miri, Mishmi).

1754. BHATTACHARJEE, J. (1980) Rodent population and flowering.
Aru. News, 9(4), Au.: 35-7.

1755. BHATTACHARJEE, K.K. (1983) North East India : Political and Administrative History. New Delhi, Cosmo Publications.

1756. BHATTACHARJEE, P.N. (1959) The study of ABO, MN, blood groups and ABH secretion in saliva in the Nocte of NEFA.
Proceedings of Indian Science Congress, 46th Session (Abstract).

1757. ———— (1970) Secro anthropological studies of the Indian Mongoloids.
Proceedings of a Seminar of Physical Anthropology and Allied Disciplines. Calcutta, Anth. Survey of India (Cyclostyled).

1758. BIERWALTERS. W.H. *and* RAMAN, G. (1957) Endemic Goitre and cretinism in the Michigan and in the North Eastern Frontier Agency Area.
Current Medical Practice, 1(11): 613-18.

1759. BORAH, D.K. (1983) Missing thread of Ita Fort.
Aru. News, 12(3), April-May: 1-5.

1760. ———— (1983) Archaeological ruins of Naksaparvat.
Aru. News, 12(4), June-July: 1-7.

1161. ———— (1984) Archaeological heritage of Arunachal Pradesh.
Aru News, 1)2), July-Dec.: 10-6.

1762. BORGOHAIN, Hiren *and* BOMGIN, Ligin (1983) Tani and Taki: An Adi Myth.
Aru. News, 12(2), Feb.-March: 27-9.

1763. CENSUS (1872) Report of the Census of Bengal, 1872. by H. Beverley. Calcutta, Govt. Press, 200p.

1764. ———— (1883) Report of the Census of India, 1881, Assam, by F. Stock., Calcutta, Govt. Press: 86-90.

1765 ———— (1892) Census of India, 1891, vol. I, Assam, pt. I, Report by E. Gait. Shillong, Govt. Press, 2 2p.

1766. ———— (1902) Census of India, 1901, vol. IV, Assam, pt. I, Report Allen. Shillong, Govt. Press, 139p.

1767. ———— (1912) Census of India, 1911, vol. III, Assam, pt. I, Report by J. McSwiney. Shillong, Govt. Press, 134p.

1768. ———— (1923) Census of India, 1921, vol. III, Assam, pt. I, Report by G.T. Llyod. Shillong, Govt. Press, 150p.

1969. ———— (1923) Census of India, 1921, vol. III, Assam, pt. I, Report by G.C. Bardolai. Shillong, Govt. Press, (Appendix-B: XV-XVI).

1770. ———— (1923) Census of India, 1921, vol. III, Assam. pt. I, Report by G.A. Nevill et al. Shillong, Govt. Press: 10-6.

1771. ———— (1923) Census of India, 1921, vol. III, Assam, pt. I, Report by R.C.R. Cumming and edited by Llyod. Shillong, Govt. Press: App.-B, XVI.

1972. ———— (1923) Census of India, 1921, Vol III, Assam, pt. I, Report by R.C.R. Cumming. Shillong, Govt. Press.

1773. ———— (1923) Census of India, 1921, vol, III, Assam, pt. I, Report by C.S. Mullan. Shillong, Govt. Press, 22p.

1774. CHATTERJEE, S. ((1981) Archaeology in Arunachal Pradesh. Shillong, Research Dept., Govt. of Arunachal Arunachal Pradesh.

1775. DARIN, M. (1979) Law of the Pasi-Padam heirship. *Aru. News*, 8(8), Nov.D-ec.: 16-7.

1776. DAS. A.K. (1976) Techno-typological study of basketry of Arunachal Pradesh. Gauhati University, Ph. D. Thesis (Unpublished).

1777. DAS, B.M. (1967) Investigation on the palm prints of Khamyang. *Jour. of Gauhati University*, 15(2): 79-87.

1778. DAS, P.K. (1976) Natural resources of Arunachal Pradesh.
Aru. News, 5(5), Independence Day Number: 38.

1779. DAS, R. *and* DAS, B.M. (1973) A note on the ridge counts of finger patterns of the Khamyang: A Mongoloid population of Assam.
Proceedings of Indian Science Congress (Abstract).

1780. DAS GUPTA, K. (1976) A few features of the Tagin language.
Resarun '75, Cum. Vol.: 105-109.

1781. DATTA, Madhu S. (1984) Land and the Mishing economy: A study in change.
Agrarian Situation in India, vol. I. Edited by S.B. Chakrabarti, B R. Ghosh and Ajit K. Danda. Calcutta, Anth. Survey of India: 71-6.

1782. DIRECTORATE of Economics and Statistics (1974) Quick Issue of Statistical Handbook of Arunachal Pradesh, 1973-74.
Directorate of Economics & Statistics, Arunachal Pradesh.

1783. DIRECTORATE of Public Instruction (1982) National adult education programme in Arunachal Pradesh.
Aru. News, 10(2), Feb. 21-6.

1784. DONDRUP, R. (1985) Sherdukpen language guide. Shillong, Directorate of Research, Govt. of Arunachal Pradesh (In Press).

1785. DONG, Desmond: (1964) Journey to NEFA, pt. I & II.
The Statesman (Calcutta), April 1 and 5.

1786. DOUGAL, B.S. (1965) Practice of shifting cultivation (jhum) in tribal areas (NEFA).
Special Tribal Orient (Ranchi), June 57-62.

1787. DUNBAR, G.D.S. (1932) Frontiers. London: 245-67.

1788. DUPIT, Take (1983) Some aspects of marriage in Tagin society: A study.
Aru. News, 12(3), April-May: 35-8.

1789. DUTTA, D.K. (1981) The causes of the earthquake: A Nocte Myth.
Aru. News, 10(8), Nov.-Dec.: 6.

1790. DUTTA, Parul (?) A short note on the Wanchos of Tirap. Shillong, Research Dept., Arunachal Pradesh.

1791. DUTT, Shosee Chunder (1984) The wild tribes of India. New Delhi, Cosmo Publications (Reprinted, 1st Published in 1884): 131-46 (Akhas, Duflas, Meeris, Mishmis, Abors, Khamptis, Singphos).

1792. DUTTA, Sashi Dhar (1976) Hydro-Power Development in Arunachal.
North Eastern Spectrum, 1(6), Dec: 45-7.

1793. DUTTA, S.K. (1976) The Rascal in tribal folklore.
North Eastern Spectrum (Gauhati), 1(1), July: 23-6.

1794. DUTTA CHOWDHURY, S. (Ed) (1985) Arunachal Pradesh District Gazetteers: Siang Distrtct. Shillong, Govt. of Arunachal Pradesh.

1795. ECONOMICS and Statistics Branch (1983) Brochure on Tirap District (Tirap at a glance).
Khonsa, (A.P.) Economic & Statistics Branch, 10 p.+ IV. (Mimeographed).

1796. ELWIN, Verrier (1956) The Folklore of NEFA.
The Statesman, Oct. 17 (Assam Supplement).

1797. ———— (1957) Adventures in friendship.
The Statesman, Aug. 15 (Independence Day Supplement).

1798. ERING, Oshong (1974) Whither the traditional artistic culture of Arunachal,
Aru, News, 3(5) Aug. : 13-8.

1799. ———— (1983) Spiritual transcendency and the kingdom of Gods and Godesses: Adi belief and faith.
Aru. News, 12(3), April-May: 5-12.

1800. ———— (1984) Adis on dreams.
Arunachal Review (Itanagar), 1(1), March-June: 13-4.

1801. FURER-HAIMENDORF, C. von: (1948) The Tribes of of the Subansiri region.
Royal Central Asian Journal, 35, pt. III-IV, July-Oct.: 240-44.

1802. ———— (1950) Youth dormitories and community houses in India.

Anthropos, 45(1/2), Jan.-June.

1803. ———— (1983) Himalayan adventure: Early Travels in North East India. New Delhi, Sterling Publishers (P) Ltd., 243p. (Apatanis, Nishis).

1804. ———— (1938) The sources of the Subansiri and Siyem.
The Himalayan Journal, X.

1805. ———— (1941) Assam adventure.
London, 74p.

1806. GEOLOGICAL Survey Of India (n.d.) A note on the Geology and Economic Minerals of the NEFA. Shillong, Geological Survey of India, (Unpublished).

1807. ———— (1979) Know our district: Tirap.
Aru. News, 5(8), Nov.-Dec. 37-9.

1808. GHOSH, B.R. (1965) Women of NEFA have quality.
Amrita Bazar Patrika, April 25.

1809. GOHAIN, C. (1984) The Tai Fakes.
Aru. Review, 1(2), July-Dec.: 16-7 & 19.

1810. GOHAIN, U.N. (1950) A short note on the Tai.
Jorhat. (Khamti and other Shan clans of Asaam).

1811. ———— (1971) The Khamtis and other Buddhist tribes in Assam.
The Tai Khamtis. Compiled by Lila Gogoi.
Chowkham, (NEFA), Chowkhamoon Gohain (Namsoon): 67-73.

1812. ———— (1971) The Tai charaeteristics and their arts and culture.
The Tai Khamtis Comp. by Lila Gogoi.
Chowkham (NEFA), Chowkhamoon Gohain (Namsoo): 97-106.

1813. GOSWAMI, M.C. *and* DAS, P.B. (1985) Physical Anthropology of the people of Arunachal Pradesh.
Shillong, Directorate of the Research Dept., Govt. of Arunachal Pradesh (In (Press).

1814. GOVT. of India (1914) Gazetteer Notifications No. 977 EB to 979 EB dtd. 25th Sept., 194 on NEFA.

1815. GOYI, Taba Teni (1913) Marriage system in the Nishing society.

Aru. News. 12(4), June-July : 46-8.

1816. HAJRA, Durgadas (1959) The Annual Cycle of Agricultural activities in a Dafla village. *Proceedings of Indian Science Congress*.

1817. HALLET, S.H. (1890) Thousands of miles on an elephant in the Shan States. London : 85-6, 168-9 and 203 (Khampti).

1818. HAZARIKA, K.C. (1981) From the upper peaks of Dibang Valley. *Aru. News*, 10(7), Sept-Oct. : 26-32.

1819. ———— (1982) Communicational disability and social responsibility. *Aru. News*, 10(2), Feb. : 9-13.

1820. HAZARIKA, M.P. (1974) Tourism in Arunachal. *Aru. News*, 3(5), Aug. : 18-20.

1821. HAZARIKA, Munindra P. (1975) Tawang. *Aru. News*, 4(7), Oct. : 10.

1822. ———— (1976) Malinithan. *Aru. News*, 5(2), March : 32.

1823. ———— (1979) Horticulture no longer an idea. *Aru. News*, 8(1) : 14-8.

1824. HEGDE, S.N. (1985) Orchides of Arunachal Pradesh. Shillong, Directorate of Research Dept., Govt. of Arunachal Pradesh (In Press).

1825. HERMANNS, Matthias (1954) The Indo-Tibetans : The Indo-Tibetan and Mongoloid Problem in the Southern Himalayas and North and Noth-Eastern India. Bombay, K.K. Fernandes.

1826. HOLDICH, T. H. (1901) The Indian Borderland. London.

1827. ———— (1910) The Gates of India. London.

1828. HUNTER, W.W. (1868) A Camparative Dictionary of the languages of India and High Asia. London. (Contains Abor-Miri vocabulary).

1829. ———— (1879) A Statistical Account of Assam, vol. I. London, Trubner, (Now Reprinted by B.R. Publishing Corporation, Delhi : 332-42).

1830. INDIAN Folklore (1959) NEFA Highlanders. *Indian Folklore*, (Calcutta), 1(1) : 85-8.

1831. INTELLIGENCE Branch (1907) Frontier and Overseas Expeditions from India, vol. IV : North and North Eastern Frontier Tribes. Simla, Army Headquarters, Govt. Monotype Press : 162 67.

1832. JOSHI, M.C. (1980) Local Administration in Arunachal Pradesh. Gauhati University, Ph.D. Thesis (Unpublished).

1833. JOSHI, Seetharam (1962) Where India, China and Burma meet. Calcutta. (All about NEFA).

1834. KAR CHOUDHURY, Amalendu Bikash (1984) Tribal songs of North East India with special reference to Arunachal Pradesh. Calcutta, Firma KLM Pvt. Ltd. 98p.

1835. KARNICK, V.B. (*Ed.*) (1963) China Invades India. Bombay : 178-221.

1836. KAULBACK, Ronald (1934) Tibetan Trek. London (Abor and Mishmi).

1837. KINGDON-WARD, Jean (?) A plant hunter in Tibet. London : 284-95.

1838. ———— (1926) The Riddle of the Tsangpo Gorges. London.

1839. ———— (1946) What of the tribes (NEFA). *Man in India*, 26(2) : 110-19.

1840. KOHLI, Y.P. (1982) Our Scientific Heritage. *Aru. News*, 10(2), Feb. : 27-31.

1841. KOHLI, Yogendra Pal (1983) Our Scientific Heritage : Folk Medicines. *Aru. News*, 12(2), Feb.-March : 9-15 and June-July (1982).

1842. KOHLI, Yogendra (1984) Our glorious heritage. *Arunachal Review*, 1(1), March/June : 15-7.

1843. KOHLI, Y.P. *and* BAHADUR, K. (1983) Goitre in Arunachal Pradesh and its cure through folk medicines. *Aru. News*, 12(3), April-May : 29-31.

1844. KONDINYA, Bhikshu (1976) : Buddhism and society. *Aru. News*, 5(8), Nov.-Dec. : 55-61.

1845. ———— (1977) Influence of Buddhism and Pali on Tai Khamti and their literature. Delhi University Ph.D Thesis (Unpublished).

1846. KUMAR, B. (1982) Urbanisation in Arunachal Pradesh.
Aru, News, 10(2), Feb. : 1-8.

1847. ———— (1983) Agriculture in Arunachal Pradesh : Domographic aspects.
Aru. News, 12(4), June-July : 13-21.

1848. KUMAR, Krishan (1968) : Bori Society. Shillong.

1849. KUMAR, N. (1964) Taste, middle phalangeal hair and occipital hair whorls among Nocte Naga.
Bull. Dept. of Anth., (Anth. Survey of India), Calcutta, 4(2). July, (1955) : 61-8.

1850. KUNSTADTER, Peter (*Ed)* 1967) South East Asian Tribes, Minorities and Nations, vol. I.
Princeton (New Jersey), Princeton University Press: 215-29.

1851. LAHIRI, R.M. (1954) Annexation of Assam.
Calcutta, General Printers and Publishers, 250p. (Some account of the Singphos).

1852. LAL, P, (1967) Ecology and demography of NEFA.
Proceedings of a Seminar on Research Programmes in Cultural Anthropology and Related Disciplines.
Calcutta, Anth. Survey of India: 1-20 (Cyclostyled).

1853. LAMB, A. (1960) British and Chinese Central Asia. London.

1854. LOGAN, J.R. (?) The West Himalaic or Tibetan Tribes of Assam, Burma.
Jour. of the Indian Archipelage and East Asia, New series, II: 689.

1855. LOWANG. P. (1983) The Pang system of Noctes and its role.
Aru. News, 12(4), June-July: 32-3.

1856. LUDLOW, F. (1938) The sources of the Subansiri and Siyom.
The Himalayan Journal (Loddon), X.

1857. LUTHRA, P.N. (1968) Brochure on the Seminar of the Research Department, NEFA (1968). Shillong, T. P. Khaund, Director of Inf. & Pub. Relations, NEFA, 49 p.+ii+2 mps.

1858. MACLEISH, A. (1931) The Frontier Peoples of India. London.

1859. MACLEOD, D.A.(1837) A sketch of the Medical Topography of Bishnath and its immediate neighbourhood with an account of the diseases generally prevailing in Assam. Calcutta. (Some account of the Singhphos).

1860. MAHANTA, Bijan (1981) A century of administrative development of Arunachal Pradesh from 1875 to 1975. Gauhati University, Ph. D. Thesis (Unpublished).

1861. ———— (1984) (?) Administrative development of Arunachal Pradesh (1875-1975).

1862. MAHANTA, Dipjyoti *and* GOSWAMI, M.C. (1973) Ritual and secular role of a Duonia Monastery.
Bull. Dept. of Anth., Gauhati University, 2, December: 32-40.

1863. MAJUMDAR, Dhruv (1968) An innocent in NEFA.
Hindustan Standard, April 23 *and* 24.

1864. MANNON, C.I. (1983) Adult education programme and its feature in Lohit district.
Aru. News, 12(2), Feb. March: 21-4.

1865. M'COSH, John (1975) Topography of Assam.
Delhi, Sanskaran Prakashan (Reprinted).

1866. MEGU A. (1985) Bori language guide.
Shillong, Directorate of Research Dept. Govt. of Arunachal Pradesh (In Press).

1867. MEHTA, Gisela (1957) The colourful Apatanis of NEFA.
The Statesman, Feb. 24, Sunday.

1868. ———— (1957) Visit to the land of the Nokteys.
The Statesman, Dec. 15, Sunday.

1869. MEHTA. K.L. (1956) Administration in the NEFA. *The Statesman*, Oct. 17 (Assam Supplement).

1870. ———— (1958) NEFA in the second plan. *The Statesman*, July 31 (Supplement on Assam in the Second Plan).

1871. MEHTA, K.L. *and* VERMA, D.D. (1955) Health and Communication. *The Adivasis* (Delhi): 79-88.

1872. MIJI, Solung (1984) Dances of Mijis Akas. *Aru. Review*, 1(2), July-Dec. 22-3.

1873. MOSANG, Komoli (1983) Book Review: The Tangsas by Parul Dutta, Director of Research, Shillong. *Aru. News*, 12(3), April-May: 42-4.

1874. MURTY, T.S. (1971) The Eastern Himalayas in Sino-Indian Relations. *Jour. of the Institute for Defence Studies and Analysis.* III (4), April: 510-49.

1875. MURTI, V.S. (1984) Hydel potentials in Arunachal Pradesh. *Aru. Review* (Itanagar), 1(1), March-June: 1-8.

1876. NAG, Amit Kumar (1966) Apatanis live very much in yesterday. *Amrita Bazar Patrika*, Sept.

1877. NAGPAL, H.S, (1965) East Front Well Defended. *Amrita Bazar Patrika*, Aug. 15 (Supplement for defence of NEFA after the Chinese invasion).

1878. NAIR, P. Thankappan (1966) A short history of NEFA. *The Current Carreers* (Calcutta), June.

1879. ———— (1966) An Introduction to NEFA. *The Competitor* (Ambala), August.

1880. ———— Buddhist people of NEFA: The Khamptis. *Mahabodhi*, 74, Sept.-Oct.: 224-27.

1881. ———— (1966) The Buddhist people of NEFA: Monpas. *Mahabodhi*, 74, April.

1882. ———— (1966) The Buddhist People of NEFA: Sherdukpens. *Mahabodhi*, 74, July.-Sept.

1883. ——— (1966) The athletic Adis.
Mall (Madras), May 22.

1884. Buddhist people of NEFA: The Singphos.
Mahabodhi, 74, Jan.-Feb.

1885. ——— (1967) The hospitable Indus.
Enlite, Nov. 18.

1886. ——— (1967) Noctes in transition.
Enlite, Dec. 2.

1887. ——— (1967) The friendly Wanchos.
Enlite, Dec. 16

1888. ——— (1967) The barbarous Adis.
Enlite (Baroda), Sept. 9.

1889. ——— (1967) Enlightened tribe of Aka.
Enlite, Sept. 23.

1890. ——— (1967) The civilised Apatanis.
Enlite, Oct. 7.

1891. ——— (1967) The Martial Daflas.
Enlite, Oct. 21.

1892. ——— (1967) The knowledge thirsty Gallongs.
Enlite, November.

1893. ——— (1978) Weapons of NEFA Tribes.
The Assam Tribune (Gauhati), Nov. 17.

1894. ——— (1968) NEFA Tribes: Good Medium of Defence.
Bharat Jyoti, Dec. 1.

1895. ——— (1968) The dignified Monpas.
Enlite, Jan. 13 1968.

1896. ——— (1968) The Sherdukpens of NEFA.
Enlite, Feb. 10.

1897. ——— (1968) Primitive warfare in NEFA.
Modern Review, July, Aug. and Sept.

1898. ——— (1968) Power development in NEFA.
Capital, Oct 17.

1891. ——— (1968) The Indolent Khamptis.
Enlite, June 29.

1900. ——— (1968) The opium addicts near Burma Singphos.
Enlite, Aug. 31·

1901. ———— (1969) The All-Ladies Club of NEFA. *Amrita Bazar Patrika* (Calcutta), Feb. 11.

1902. ———— (1999) Marriage customs of NEFA tribals. *Hindustan Standard*, Sunday, Nov. 16.

1903. ———— (1972) Power development in Arunachal Pradesh. *Engineering Times*, Feb. 17.

1904. NEEDHAM, J.F (1984) Outline Grammar of the Khamti Language. *India's North East Frontier in Nineteenth Century. Edited* by Verrier Elwin. Bombay, Oxford University Press (1959): 382.

1905. NEFA Administration (1957) The Years of Progress in NEFA. Shillong, NEFA Administration.

1906. ———— (1964) NEFA on the March. Shillong, NEFA Administration.

1907. ———— (1971) Festival and Folk Dances of NEFA. Shillong, NEFA Administration.

1908. ———— (1972) Arunachal Pradesh on the March. Shillong, NEFA Administration.

1909. ———— Arunachal's rich heritage. Shillong, NEFA Administration.

1910. NEOG, Maheswar (1971) A Buddhist Tribe of Assam: The Khamti. *The Tai Khamtis*. Compiled by Lila Gogoi. Chowkham (NEFA) Chowkhamoon Gohain (Namsoon): XVII-XLIV.

1911. NEUFVILLE, John Bryan (1828) On the Geography and population of Assam. *Asiatick Researches*, XVI : 373 (contains some account about the Singphos).

1912. NORTH East Frontier Agency (1968) Brochure on the Seminar of the Research Department, NEFA (1968). Shillong, Director of Informations and Public Relations NEFA, 49p.

1913. NORTH Eastern Spectrum (1976) Arunachal Pradesh Newsletter (Itanagar).

North Eastern Spectrum (Gauhati), 1(2), Aug.: 69-70; 1(6), Dec. (1976): 76-7; (11-12), May-June: (1977): 58.

1914. ———— (1976) Book Review: Enchanted Frontiers by Nari Rustomji, Oxford University Press, Calcutta. *North Eastern Spectrum*, 1(2), Aug.: 83-4.

1915. OSIK. N.N.(1982) The real concept of Donyi-Poloism. *Aru. News*, 10(10), Jan.: 13-6.

1916. ———— (1982) How Mithun came to the world. *Aru. News*, 10(10), Jan.: 13-5.

1917. ———— (1983) The Genesis of Anglo-Adi Relation. *Aru. News*, 12(2), Feb.-March: 25-7.

1918. ———— (1983) Some Absurdities in the Historical Hypothesis on Arunachal Pradesh. *Aru. News*, 12(3), April-May: 20-2.

1919. ———— (1984) History of Adi : Bihia Sonwal Relation (1603-1912). *Aru. Review*, 1(2), July-Dec.: 24-5.

1920. PADMANABHAN, P.B.S.V. (1985) A demogenetic profile of Singphos. Proceedings of a Seminar on "*Small Populations*", organised by Anthropological Survey of India, Calcutta from 12.3.'85 to 14.3.'85, (Cyclostyled), 11p.

1921. PADU, Gamnyan (1984) The Adi belief in Yapom. *Aru. Review*, 1(1), March-June: 30.

1922. PAKYNTEIN, E. H. (1964) Census of India, 1961, Assam, District Census Handbook: Lakhimpur. Gauhati, Govt. of Assam (contains some account about NEFA).

1923. PARAMPANTHI, Swami Bangovinda (1971) Parasuram Kunda: A study in historical and geographical perspective. *Jour. of the Assam Research Society (Kamarupa Anusandhan Samiti)*, Gauhati, XVIII-XIX (1970): 76-89.

1924. PAREEK, R.N. (1983) Duwanias. *Aru. News*, 12(3), April-May: 39-41.

1925. PERTIN, Belatee (1983) Letters to the Editor: Adi Kebang (A tribal Institution, Par excellence). *Aru. News*, 12(3), April-May: 55.

1926. ———— (1983) Are we heading for a crisis of cultural identity ?
Aru. News, 12(4), June-July: 7-12.

1927. PRITCHARD, B.E.A. (1912) Report on a Journey from Myitkyina to Sadiya via the N'Mai Kha River and Khampti long. Simla, Govt. Press.

1928. PUGH, B.M. (1946) Agriculture in the Monpa country of the Balipara Frontier Tract, Assam.
Allahabad Farmer, 20(6), Oct.-Nov.

1929. RAIKAR, Y.A. (n.d,) Ita Fort.
Shillong, Directorate of Research Dept., Govt. of Arunachal Pradesh.

1930. ———— (n.d.) Khomong in the History of the Khamtis. Shillong, Research Dept., Govt. of Arunachal Pradesh.

1931. ———— (1974) The Twelve principles of Buddhism: An attempt at Buddhist unity.
Aru. News, 3(5), Aug.: 6-12.

1932. RAJKUMAR, Bowang (1983) The Wancho Pah : Youths' Dormitory.
Aru. News, (12)2, Feb.-March: 46-8.

1933. RANGAIYA, D. (1950-54) Pamphlet, No. 8.
Delhi, Bharatiya Adimjati Sevak Sangh (Contains some account about Abors, Mishmis).

1934. RAO, M.R.L. (1984) Clouds of memory do we come.
Aru News, 1(1), March-June. 20-1.

1935. RAY, P.C. (1955) The tensional feeling among the Abors and Gallongs as indicated by the Rorschach technique.
Indian Jour. of Psychology, XXX: 95-103.

1936. RECLUNG, W. (1935) Jogli language guide.
Shillong, Directorate of Research Dept., Govt. of Arunachal Pradesh (In Press).

1937. ———— (1985) Mingchang language guide.
Shillong, Research Dept., Govt. of Arunachal Pradesh (In Press).

1938. RESEARCH Dept. (1966) Resarun 1975.
Shillong, Research Dept. Govt. of Arunachal Pradesh, 133p.

1939. ———— (1977) Resarun 1976.
Shillong, Research Dept., Govt. of Arunachal Pradesh.

1940. ———— (1972) Arunachal Research Bulletin.
Shillong, Research Dept., Arunachal Pradesh Administration.

1941. ———— (1977) Research in Arunachal Pradesh.
Shillong, Research Dept., Govt. of Arunachal Pradesh.

1942. ———— (1978) Research in Arunachal Pradesh.
Shillong, Research Dept., Govt. of Arunachal Pradesh.

1943. RIBA, Dakkar (1983) Ritual Practice of the Adis after snake biting.
Aru. eNws, 12(4), June-July· 42-3.

1944 ROY, Nilima (1950) Abor house type.
Abstract of *Indian Science Congress.*

1945. ROY, Sachin (1950) Weapons of war and chase of the Abors.

1946. ROY. Shibani (et al) (1984) Major Ethnic Group of North Eastern India (Ethnographic Notes).
Shillong, Anthropological Survey of India, (Mimeogrophed).

1947. ROY BURMAN, B.K. (1968) Some dimension of transformation of tribal societies in India.
Jour. of Social Research (Ranchi), 11(1).

1948. RUKBO, Talom (1983) Identity of married and unmarried Adi women: A social crisis.
Aru. News, 12(4), June-July: 22-4.

1949. ———— (1984) Land of no begger.
Aru. Review, 1(1), March-June: 17-9.

1950. SASTRI, B. (1972) Legend of Ita.
Jour. of Assam Research Society. Gauhati, XX: 43.

1951. SECRETARIAT, N.E.C. (1980) Basic Statistics of North Eastern Council (*NEC Pub. No. 12*) 243p.

1952. SEN, A.K. (1982) Study to find out alternative approaches to reduce the malaria transmission in Miao proper.
Aru News, 10(1), Jan.: 16-21.

1953. SEN, A.K., KRISHNAN, John V.M. *and* RAJGOPAL, R. (1973) Studies on Malaria transmission in Tirap District, Arunachal Pradesh (NEFA).
Jour. Common Disease, 5(2): 98-100.

1954. SEN, A.K. *and* DUTTA SHARMA, A.B. (1980) Susceptibility of vector of Malaria: AB balabacensis to DDT in Miao.
Aru. News, 9(6), Oct.-Nov: 6-7.

1955. SEN, S.N. (1976) The Activities and achievements of Geological Survey of India in North Eastern Region.
Aru. News 5(8), Nov-Dec: 40-2.

1956. SHARMA, S.N. Ram (1984) Parasuram and Parasuram Kund.
Aru. Review, 1(1), March-June: 22-4.

1957. ———— (1984) Tamreswari temple and its historical background.
Aru. Review, 1(2), July-Dec.: 18-9.

1958. SHUKLA, B.K. (?) The Dafla of the Subansiri region.
Man (London), XI: 94.

1959. SHUKLA, S.P. (1983) Planning and the agricultural development in Arunachal Pradesh: The task ahead. Proceedings of a Seminar on "*Planning*" organised by NEICSSR, Shillong.

1960. SHYAM, H.N. (1983) Induced breeding of major corps and its prospect in Arunachal Pradesh.
Aru. News, 12(4), June-July: 25.

1961. SIKDAR, Sudatta (1981)Assam trade of the Arunachalis 1874-1905: A study of the British Policy.
North Eastern Hill Univ. (Shillong) M. Phil. Dissertation, 106p. (Unpublished).

1962. SINGH, D.R. (1984) Teaching of Hindi in Arunachal Pradesh.
Aru. Review, 1(2), July-Dec.: 25-9.

1963. SINGH, Ranjeet (1983) Role of small scale industries in Arunachal.
Aru. News, 12(2), Feb.-March: 1-8.

1964. SINGPHOW, G. (1982) The Tiger and the Cat: A Singphow Folk Tale.
Aru. News, 10(2), Feb.: 18.

1965. SPECIAL Correspondent (1967) Impressions of NEFA.
The Hindu, April, 21, 22 and 24.

1966. SRIVASTAVA, L.R.N. (1968) Habitation, origin and migration of a North Eastern Tribe.
Vanyajati, 16(5), Oct.: 123-32.

1967. STATISTICS Branch (1983) East Siang at a glance (Position as on 31-3-83 & 84).
Pasighat (A.P.), Statistics Branch, 6p. (Mimeographed).

1968. STATISTICS Dept. (1972) Statistical Handbook of Arunachal Pradesh, 1971-72. Shillong, Statistics Dept., Aru. Pradesh.

1969. STEPHENS, Michael D. (1966) North East Frontier and India and China.
Asian Review (London), 3(2), Aug. : 49-61.

1970. STONOR, C.R. (1972) The Sulung tribe of the Assam Himalaya.
Arunachal Pradesh Bulletin, August.

1971. SURVEY of India (1981) Map of North Eastern Region of India. Dehradun, Survey of India.

1972. TAMUT, Tago (1983) Concept of Donyi-Polo : Popular side must be accepted.
Aru. News, 12 (3), April-May : 31-5.

1973. TAYENG, A. (1985) Adi Proverbs and Sayings.
Shillong, Directorate of Research Dept., Govt. of Arunachal Pradesh (In Press).

1974. THANGAM, E.S. (1980) Cash crops cultivation in forest department.
Aru. News, 9(4), Aug. : 19-21.

1975. THOMAS, Menamparampil (1975) A Glossary of Tribal Group of North East India.
The Thinker, III (2-3), May-Aug.

1976. TOYSON, Geoffrey (1945) Forgotten Frontier.
Calcutta. (contains mention of the help rendered by the Mishmis, Singphos and Abors to the Indian Tea Association in assisting the escape into India of refugees from Upper Burma during the Second World War).

1977. VAIKAR, P.G. (1963) Welfare work in NEFA area. *Vanyajati*, 11(4), Oct. : 145-83.

1978. VIVEK Publishing Company (1978) Hill Tracts Between Assam and Burma. Delhi, Vivek Publishing Company.

1979. WADDELL, L.A. (1895) The Falls of the Tsangpo (San-Pu) and the identity of that River with Brahmaputra.
Geographical Journal (London). 5 : 258.

1980. WANGHAM, Bowang (1982) The Wangcho youth association and its background.
Aru. News, 10(1). Jan. : 46-7.

1981. WANGCHUK, Leiki (1984) Letters to the Editor : Kalaktang Monpa.
Aru. Review, 1(1), March-June. 31.

ADDENDA—II

1982. ACHARYYA, N.N. (1985) Modernisation of the Tagins of Arunachal Pradesh.
Jour. NEICSSR, 9(1), April : 26-30.

1983. ACRO Economic Research Centre (?) Socio-Economic Survey of Three Dafla villages in Assam. Jorhat, Agro Economic Research Centre for North East India (*Mimeo.*)

1984. ———— (?) Pakem : A village in Siang District in Arunachal Pradesh, Jorhat, Agro Economic Research Centre for North Eastern India (*Mimeo.*)

1985. ———— (1977) Apple cultivation in Arunachal Pradesh. Jorhat, Agro Economic Research Centre for North Eastern India (*Mimeo.*)

1986. ———— (1978) Bamin : A socio-economic survey of an Apatani village in Arunachal Pradesh. Jorhat, Agro Economic Research Centre for North Eastern India (*Mimeo.*)

1987. ———— (1982) Hatiduba : Socio-economic survey of a Miju Mishmi village in Lohit District of Arunachal Pradesh. Jorhat. Agro Economic Researsh Centre for North Eastern India (*Mimeo.*)

1987A. ANTHRGPOLOGY Dept. (1985) Anthropological Perspectives on North East India (Bulletin of the Department of Anthropology), volume X, 1981. Dibrugarh, Dept. of Anthropology, Dibrugarh University.

1988. AITCHISON, C.U. (1931) Treaties, Engagements and Sanads. vol. XII : 230-33.

1989. AMRITA Bazar Patrika (1985) Tawang comes under TV net work. *Amrita Bazar Patrika*, April 21-3.

1990, ———— (1985) Survey of Arunachal plant life urged. *Amrita Bazar Patrika*, May 14, Tuesday : 10.

1990A. AMRITA Bazar Patrika (1985) N. E. region needs more hydel Prcojects. *Amrita Bazar Patrika*, June 14 · 7.

1991. ASSAM Govt. (1959) Proceeding of the third meeting of Advisory Council for Scheduled Tribes in the Autonomous District between 28.5.1957 and 6.6.1959. Shillong, Govt. of Assam (*Mimeo.*)

1992, ———— (1968) Statistical Hand Book of Assam, 1967. Shillong, Deptt. of Economics & Statistics, Govt. of Assam.

1993. ASSAM Tribune (1985) NEC's Investigation Programmes. *Assam Tribune*, April 6 :4.

1994. BAREH, Hamlet (Ed) (1965-66) District Gazetteers, North East Frontier Agency.

1995. BARTHAKUR, I.K. (?) Census of India 1961. vol. III, Arunachal Pradesh · Socio-economic survey of Koreng (Pasighat Sub-division, Siang District, NEFA). (*Mimeo.*)

1996. ———— (1974) Statistical Hand Book of Arunachal Pradesh. Shillong, Directorate of Economics & Statistics, Arunachal Pradesh Administration, 162p.

1996A. BARUA, Saumitra (1984) A Study on indigenous heallth prcactices among the Kaman Mishmis of Lohit Distrcict of Arunachal Pradesh. *Human Science* (Calcutta), 33 (4), Dec. : 332-44.

1997. BORGOHAIN, B.K. (1975) Folk tales of Meghalaya and Arunachal Pradesh. New Delhi, Sterling Publishers Pvt. Ltd. 112p.

1998; BORGOHAIN, H. (1985) Why the Adi people do not kill tiger. *Folklore*, 26(3), March : 55-6.

1999. CHANDA, A.M. (?) Census of India 1661. vol. III, pt. VI, Arunachal Pradesh : Socio-economic survey of Momong (Lohit District of NEFA) (*Mimeo.*)

2000· ———— (1981) Statistical Hand Book of Arunachal Pradesh, 1978-79. Shillong, Directorate of Economics & Statistics, Arunachal Pradesh, 216p.

2001. CHATTERJEE, S.K. & NAULA, R.P. (?) Census of India 1961, vol· III, pt. VI, Arunachal Pradesh : Socio-economic survey of Jia (Lohit District) (*Mimeo.*)

2002· DAS, Jogesh (1972) Folklore of Assam.
New Delhi, National Book Trust, India (Mishmi:28,29, 73; Adi :22, 23, 38, 73, 84; Aka : 27,28,39; Dafla : 28, 78), 142p.

2003. DUTTA, P.C. (?) Sulong.
Shillong, Director, Information & Public Relations, Arunachal Pradesh.

2004. DUTTA BARUAH, Bichitra Narayan (1957) Asamor Parbat Bhoiyamor Bhaisakal (*In Assamese*).
Gauhati, Lawyers' Book Stall (2nd edition) : Abor, Mishmi, Dafla, Aka and Miri.

2005. GOVT. OF INDIA (1971-72) Industrial Potential Survey : Arunachal Pradeh.
Delhi, IDBI, Govt. of India.

2006. ———— (1984) Census of India, 1971 : Modernisation and Elites in Arunachal Pradesh.
Delhi, Manager of Publications.

2007· ———— (1984) Anusuchit jati tatha anusuchit janajati Ayog ki report, April 1980 to March 1983. (*In Hindi*).
Delhi, Manager of Publications.

2008. JHA, S.D. (1985) The wealth of Arunachal Pradesh.
Delhi, Manager of Publications (*In Press*).

2009. KULKARNI, M.G. (?) Problems of tribal developments : A case study.
Aurangabad, Dept. of Sociology, Marathawada University.

2010. KUMAR, D.P. (1985) Hydro-electric potential of Arunachal Pradesh.
The Statesman, April 22 : 9.

2011. ——— (1985) Kameng river valley project : Arunachal ready to discuss agreement with States.
The Statesman, April 23 : 9.

2012. MILLS, A.J. Moffatt (1980) Report on Assam, Chapter 13: Luckimpoor. Delhi, Gian Publications : 1-7 (*Reprinted*).

2013. NEFA Administration (1964) Statistical outline of NEFA. Shillong, Statistical Branch, NEFA Administration. (*Mimeo.*)

2014. ——— (1965) Report of the Committee appointed to consider expansion and development of local self Governmentin NEFA. Shillong, NEFA Administration.

2015. ——— (1968) Draft Fourth Five Year Plan.
Shillong, Planning & Development Dept., NEFA Administration (*Mimeo.*)

2016. RAO, V. Venkata (1976) A Century of Tribal politics in North East India, 1874-1974. New Delhi, S. Chand & Co. Ltd.

2017. SHAKESPEAR, L.W. (1914) History of Upper Assam, Upper Burmah and North Eastern Frontier.
London, Macmillan & Co. Ltd.

2218. SHARMA, H.C. *and* SEN, Chandra (?) Census of India 1961, North East Frontier Agency : Socio-economic survey of Ramsing (Daporijo Sub-Division). (*Mimeo*).

2019. SHILLONG Times (1985) Letter from Arunachal.
Shillong Times, April 20 : 3.

2020. SHRIKANT, L.M. (1962) Report of the Commissioner for Scheduled Castes and Scheduled Tribes for the year 1960-61, pt. II.Delhi, Manager of Publications, 392p.

ADDENDA III

2021. AHMAD, S.H. and CHAKRAVARTY, S.K. (1979) Cogenital deffects of the cultural nervous system associated with Hyperendemic Goitre among the Gallongs (Doke) in Siang District of Arunachal. Proceeding of a Seminar on *Bio-cultural Profile of North East India*, Anthropological Survey of India, Shillong, April 26, 1979.

2022. ADMINISTRATIVE Reforms Commission (1968) Report of the study team of the Administration of the Union Territories and NEFA, vol. 1. New Delhi, Ministry of Home Affairs, Govt. of India.

2023. AMRITA Bazar Patrika (1985) Dreb festival of Arunachal. *Amrita Bazar Patrika*, July 8 ; 5

2024. AMRITA Bazar Patrika (1985) Stone age tools discovered in Arunachal. *Amrita Bazar Patrika*, Oct. 17 : 7.

2025. ARUNACHAL NEWS LETTERS (1985) Nyokum festival celebrated. *Aru. News*, 5 (5), March 15 : 2.

2026. BAGCHI, R.N. (1953) Socio-Cultural profile of the Monpas of Kalaktang areas. *Resarun*, 9(1), Sp-Sum ; 12-22.

2027. BARUA, Saumitra (1985) Effect of urbanisation among the Monpas. Shillong, *Proceedings of Anthropologcal Svrvey of India's Seminar Forum* on 19.5.85.

2028. BOPARDIKAR, B.P. (1972) Prehistoric investigation : Dophabum scientific Survey Expidition (NEFA). *Archaeological Congress & Seminar Papers*, Nagpur University : 1-8.

2029. BORA, N. Zaman (1983) Museums of Arunachal with reference to District Museum. Bomdila. *Resarun*, 9(1), Sp-Sum : 41-5.

2030. BORAH, D.K. (1983) Archaeological ruins of Naksa Parbat. *Resarun*, 9(1), Sp-Sum ; 26-33.

2031. BORTHAKUR, D.N. *et al.* (1978) Shifting cultivation in the North Eastern Region.
Resources development and environment in the Himalayan Region, Dept. of Science & Technology, Govt. of India : 330·42.

2032. BHANDARI, J.S. (1984) Ethnohistory, ethnic identity and contemporary Mishing society.
Indian Anthropologist (Delhi), 14(2), Dec. : 1-79.

2033. BHATTACHARJEE, T.K. (1983) Tsangya Gyatso : the Dalai Lama and Urgeylling Gampa.
Resarun, 9(1), Sp-Sum : 1-11.

2034. CENSUS (1964) Census of India 1961, Vol. I, pt. II-C (ii) : Language tables. Delhi, Manager of Publication.

2035. CHAKMA, U. (1974) The religious beliefs of Munyongs.
North Eastern Affairs, 3(2-3), July-Dec. : 11-5.

2036. CHAKRAVORTY, S.K. (1977) Bolld group system in East India.
Paper read in *Seminar on Human variation* at Calcutta.

2037. CHIB, S.S. (1984) Caste, tribe and culture of India, vol. VIII : North Eastern India. New Delhi, Ess Ess Publications, 384 p.

2038. DALTON, E.T. (1973) Tribal History of Eastern India. New Delhi, Cosmo Publication (Reprinted, original name of the book is: Descriptive Enthology of Bengal).

2039. DAS, A.K. (1985) Book Review : A Phrase book in Singpho by K. Das Gupta, published by the Director of Information and Public Relations, Govt. of Arunachal Pradesh, Shillong.
Man ana life (Calcutta), 11 (1-2), Jan-June : 124.

2040. DAS GUPTA, Biman (1984) Minyong.
Tribal Education in India, Memoir no. 61. Edited by Biman K. Das & Ajit K. Danda. Calcutta, Anth. Sur. of India · 22-23.

2041. DAS GUPTA, K. (1983) A brief note on the Khowa language.
Resarun, 9(1), Sp-SuA : 23-26.

2042. DATTA, Birendranath (1985) Re-emergence of Folklore : the North East Indian Scene.

Man and life, 11 (1-2), Jan-June : 77-78.

2043. DEB BHARATI, Tarak (1973) Eastern Indian handicrafts : a preliminary survey.
Folklore, xiv (9), Sepi. : 354-59.

2044. DEURI, R.K· (1984) Customary land tenure system of the Khamtis of Lohit District.
Resarun, 10(1), Sp-Sum · 1-4.

2045. DHINGIA, Homeswar (1980) Assam's struggle against British rule. New Delhi, Asia Publication, 160p.

2046. DIBRUGARH University (1985) Anthopological perspective on North East India.
Bulletin of the Dept. of Anthropology vol. x, 1981. Dibrugarh, Dibrugarh University.

2047. DUARAH, Dwijendra Kumar & Das, Priya Bala (1984) A crors-sectional study of growth in four somatometic characters of the Khamti boys of Arunachal Pradesh.
Resarun, 10(1), SpSum, : 38-40.

2048. DUTTA, Dipak Kumar (1984) Dances of the Hrussos.
Resarun, 10(1), Sp-Sum : 38-40.

2049. ENCYLOPAEDIA (1973) Lisus.
Encylopaedia Britannica, vol. 14 (1968).

2050. FURER, HAIMENDORF, C. von (1983) Modern development and traditional ideology among tribal societies (4th D.N. Majumdar lecture) Lucknow, Ethnographic and Folk Culture Society : 1-26, 27-44.

2051. GOSWAMI, P.C. (1983) The Economic development of Assam, Bombay, Asia Publishing House ; 1, 15, 32, 32, 38, 207, 213.

2052. GOSWAMI, P. C. (*Ed.*) Socio-Economic research in tribal areas. Jorhat, Agro-Economic Research Centre for North Eastern India, 130 p.

2053. HIMALAYA (1985) Arunachal Pradesh : the land of no beggars.
Himalaya : Man and Nature, 9(3), Aug : 1-3.

2054. ICSSR (1972) A survey of research in sociology and social anthropology, vol. III. Bombay, Popular Prakashan : 11, 50, 52, 148 p.

2055. KAPFO, Weprenvi (1970) Chairman's address in the Sociology on NEFA, Kohima, April 7-14, 1970. *Sociology of North Eastern Hill Area* (proceedings of the 3rd Summer School, Dept. of Sociology and Culture, University of Delhi, Delhi).

2056. KHANDPUR, Swarn (1971) Our country series, India : the Land and its people, Bombay, Ratnabharati : 130-35.

2057. KUMAR, K. (1983) The traditional economic life of the Bokars. *Resarun*, 9(1), Sp-Sum : 34-40.

2058. KUMAR, Krishan (1984) The traditional economic life of the Bokars. *Resarun*, 9(2), 1983 ; 10(1), Sp-Sum : 5-15 and 10 2), Aut-Win.

2059. KUSUM, Nargolkar (1965) In the wake of the Chinese thrust. Bombay.

2060. MALHOTRA, R. (1985) Tribal groups in India : their problems and development. *Vanyajati*, 33 (2), April : 9-17.

2061. MEGU, Arak (1984) Sobo Panam : a feast of merit of the Pailibos. *Resarun*, 10 (1), Sp-Sum : 31-37.

2062. PADMANABHAN, P.B.S.V and JAISWAL, I.J.S. (1985) A demographic study of Apatanis. INEICSSR, 9(2), Oct. : 15-22.

2063. PAKYNTEN, E.H. (1965) Census of India 1961, vol. III, Assam, pt. I-A : Scheduled tribes and scheduled castes (Reprinted from Old Census Reports and Special Tables). Delhi, Manager of Publications, 428 p.

2064. PATASKAR Commission (1966) Report of the Commission on the Hill Areas of Assam, 1965-1966. New Delhi, Ministry of Home Affairs, Govt. of India.

2065. SACHCHIDANANDA (1985) Economic development, education and social change in Arunachal. *Man in India*, 65(1), March : 33-57.

2066. SARKAR, J.K. Ecological adjustments and identity formation among the people of Arunachal Pradesh (Misc. pub. no. 43). Shillong, Geological Survey of India.

2067. SARKAR, Jayanta (1984) Kaman Mishmi.
Tribal Education in India, Memoir No. 61. Edited by Biman K. Das Gupta & Ajit Kumar Danda. Calcutta, Anth. Sur. of India : 14-6.

2068. SEN GUPTA, P. (1970) Census of India, pt. IX, Census Atlas. Delhi, Manager of Publications.

2069. SENGUPTA, Sarthak (1984) Finger prints of the Bangnis of Arunachal Pradesh.
Resarun, 10(1), Sp-Sum : 25-30.

2070. SHARMA THAKUR, G.C. (1972) The plains tribes of Lakhimpur, Dibrugarh, Sibsagar and Nowgong. Shillong, Tribal Research Institute, Govt. of Assam.

2071. SHILLONG Times (1983) North Eastern affairs : focus on the small tribe (Lisu).
Shillong Times, Dec. 31 : 4.

2072. TALUKDAR, A.C. (1985) Electoral politics and political changes in Arunachal Pradesh.
INEICSSR, 9(2), Oct. : 1-8.

2073. TIMES OF INDIA (1974) The demand of a Miri land for the Miris, a large Mongolian tribe living in the plains (Lakhimpur) and the Abhor foot hills in Arunachal Pradesh (NFEA).
Times of India (Delhi), March 14, 1974.

APPENDIX–A

The following are the Scheduled tribes of Arunachal Pradesh according to the Census of India, 1981 :

1. Abor
2. Adi
3. Adi Gallong
4. Adi Minyong
5. Adi Padam
6. Adi Pasi
7. Aka
8. Apatani
9. Ashing
10. Bagi
11. Bangni
12. Bangro
13. Bogum
14. Bokar
15. Bolok Tangsa
16. Bomdo
17. Bori
18. But Monpa
19. Dafla
20. Darok Tangsa
21. Deori
22. Digaru/Taraon Mishmi
23. Dirang Monpa
24. Gallong
25. Haisa Tangsa
26. Havi Tangsa
27. Hill Miri
28. Hotang Tangsa
29. Idu/Chulikata Mishmi
30. Janbo
31. Kaman/Miju Mishmi
32. Karka
33. Katin Tangsa
34. Kemsing Tangsa
35. Khalim Tangsa
36. Khamba
37. Khamiyang
38. Khampti
39. Khowa
40. Khrodeng Bangni
41. Komkar
42. Kongbo
43. Korang Tangsa
44. Langkai Tangsa
45. Libo
46. Lichi Tangsa
47. Liju Nocte
48. Lish Monpa
49. Longchang Tangsa
50. Longin Tangsa
51. Longphi Tangsa
52. Longri Tangsa
53. Longsang Tangsa
54. Lowang Tangsa
55. Meyor
56. Miji
57. Mikir
58. Millang
59. Millang Abor
60. Minyong
61. Mishing/Miri
62. Mishmi
63. Moglum Tangsa
64. Momba
65. Monpa
66. Morang Tangsa

67. Mossang Tangsa
68. Muktum
69. Namsang Tangsa
70. Ngimong Tangsa
71. Nishang
72. Nissi
73. Nocte
74. Nonong
75. Padam
76. Pailibo
77. Panchen Monpa
78. Pangi
79. Pasi
80. Phong Tangsa
81. Pongkong
82. Ponthai Nocte
83. Ramo
84. Rangai Tangsa
85. Rongrang Tangsa
86. Sanke Tangsa
87. Sherdukpen
88. Simong
89. Simsa Tangsa
90. Singpho
91. Siram
92. Sulung
93. Sulung Bangni
94. Tagin
95. Tagin Bangni
96. Taisan Tangsa
97. Tangam
98. Tangsa
99. Taram
100. Tarang Monpa
101. Thai Khampti
102. Tikhak Tangsa
103. Takha Nocte
104. Namcho
105. Yanoo Bangni
106. Yatong
107. Yobin
108. Yongkuk Tangsa
109. Yougli Tangsa
110. Zakhrin

APPENDIX—B

PERIODICALS/NEWSPAPERS (used as source material) :

1. Acta Anthropogenetica, (Delhi).
2. The Adivasis, (Delhi).
3. Ajkal, (Allahabad).
4. Akashvani, (Shillong).
5. Allahabad Farmer, (Allahabad).
6. Amrita Bazar Patrika, (Calcutta).
7. Anthropos, (West Germany).
8. (The) Anthropologist, (Delhi).
9. Anthropological Linguistics, (Chicago, U.S.A.).
10. Army Review.
11. Arunachal News, (Shillong).
12. Arunachal News, (Itanagar).
13. Arunachal Newsletter, (Itanagar).
14. Arunachal Review, (Itanagar).
15. Asian Affairs : Journal of the Royal Central Asian Society.
16. Asian Review, (London).
17. Asiatic Researches, (London).
18. Assam Bani, (Gauhati, Assamese Daily).
19. Assam Tribune (Gauhati, English Daily).
20. Assam Quarterly, (Gauhati).
21. Babylonian and Oriental Record.
22. Bharat Jyoti.
23. Bulletin : Archaeological Survey of India, (Delhi).
24. Bulletin of the Bihar Tribal Research Institute, (Ranchi).
25. Bulletin : Botanical Society of Bengal.
26. Bulletin : Botanical Survey of India, (Calcutta).
27. Bulletin : Cultural Research Institute, (Calcutta).
28. Bulletin of the Department of Anthropology, Anthropological Survey of India, (Calcutta).
29. Bulletin : Department of Anthropological Survey of India (Calcutta).

30. Bulletin : Department of Anthropology, Dibrugarh University, (Dibrugarh).
31. Bulletin: Department of Anthropology, Gauhati University (Gauhati).
32. Bulletin of the Department of Tribal Culture and Folklore Research, Gauhati University, (Gauhati).
33. Bulletin of International Committee on Urgent Anthropological and Ethnological Research, (Vienna).
34. Bulletin of the Research Department, NEFA, (Shillong).
35. Bulletin of the Tribal Research and Training Institute, (Chhindwara).
36. Bulletin of Tribetology, (Gangtok).
37. Calcutta Review, (Calcutta).
38. Capital.
39. Careers and Courses.
40. Central Asiatic Journal.
41. Commerce.
42. (The) Competitor, (Ambala).
43. Constituent Assembly Debate.
44. (The) Current Careers, (Calcutta).
45. Current Medical Practice.
46. Current Science.
47. Eastern Anthropologist, (Lucknow).
48. Economic and Political Weekly, (Bombay).
49. Economic Review, All India Congress Committee.
50. Economic Times, (Bombay).
51. Economic Weekly.
52. Engineering Times.
53. Enlite, (Baroda).
54. Ethnology of India : The Quarterly Journal of the Mythic Soeiety, (Bangalore).
55. Ethnos, (Stockholm).
56 Folklore, (Calcutta).
57. Fortnightly Review.
58. Frontier.
59. Geographical Journal, (London).
60. (The) Geographical Magazine, (London).

61. Hill Geographer : The Geographical Society of the North Eastern Region,'(Shillong).
62. (The) Himalayan Journal, (London).
63. Himalaya : Man and Nature, (New Delhi).
64. Hindusthan Standard.
65. (The) Hindusthan Times, (New Delhi).
66. (The) Hindu, (Madrans).
67. (The) Hornbill, (Shillong).
68. Human Science [Anthropological Survey of India],. (Calcutta).
69. Illustrated Weekly of India, (Bombay).
70. Indian Affairs Record.
71. Indian Antiquary, (Bombay).
72. India Cronicle.
73. Indian Folklore, (Calcutta).
74. Indian Farming.
75. (The) Indian Forester, (Dahredun).
76. Indian and Foreign Review.
77. Indian Geographical Journal, (Madras).
78. Indian Journal of Agricultural Economics.
79. Indian Journal of Local Self Government.
80. Indian Journal of Medical Research, (New Delhi).
81. Indian Journal of Physical Anthropology and Human Genetics, (Lucknow).
82. Indian Journal of Psychology, (New Delhi).
83. Indian Journal of Social Work, (Bombay).
84. Indian Quarterly, (New Delhi).
85. Indian Vetenary Journal.
86. International Journal of Comparative Sociology.
87. Journal of the Anthropological Institute, Great Britain and Ireland, (London).
88. Journal of Asiatic Society of Bengal, (Calcutta).
89. Journal of the Asiatic Society of Bengal, Science,. (Calcutta).
90. Journal of the Asiatic Society of Bengal, New Series,. (Calcutta).
91. Journal of the Assam Research Society (The Kamarupa Anusandhan Samiti), (Gauhati)

92. Journal : Assam Science Society, (Gauhati).
93. J.A.I.
94. J.B.B. of R.A.S.
95. Journal : Bombay Natural Historical Society, (Bombay)
96. Journal Clinical Endoerinology and Metabolism.
97. Journal : Common Disease.
98. Journal : Indiau Anthropological Society, (Calcutta).
99. Journal : Indian Anthropological Institute.
100. Journal of the Indian Archipelago and East Asia, new series.
101. Journal of the Indian Botanical Society.
102. Journal of the Institute for Defence Studies and Analysis
103. Journal : Natural Historical Society, (Bombay).
104. Journal of the North Eastern Couacil, (N.E.C., Shillong)
105. Journal of the North East Indian Council for Social Science Resenarch, (Jour. NEICSSR, Shillong).
106. Journal of the Royal Asiatic Society, (Calcutta).
107. Journal of the Royal Asiatic Society of Bengal. (Calcutta)
108. Journal of Gauhati University, (Gauhati) [Arts & Science]
109. Journal of the Royal Anthropological Institute, Great Britain and Ireland, (London).
110. J.R.G.S.
111. Journal of Social Research, (Ranchi).
112. J.R. Soc., Arts, (London).
113. Kew Bulletin.
114. Mahabodhi.
115. (The) Mail.
116. Mainstream.
117. Mall, (Madras).
118. Man, (London).
119. Manav, (in Hindi, Lucknow).
120. Man in India, (Ranchi).
121. Man and Life, (Calcutta).
122. March of India, (Delhi).
123. Meghdoot, (Biweekly, Shillong).
124. Memoir of the Asiatic Society of Bengal, (Calcutta).
125. Modern Review.
126. Na Lekhani, (Assam).

127. National Geographical Journal of India, (Varanasi).
128. Natun Asamiya, (daily, Gauhati).
129. Natural History.
130. Newsletter : Anthropolo gical Survey of India, (Calcutta).
131. Newsletter : Indian Council of Agricultural Research, (ICAR, Shillong).
132. North Eastern Affairs, (Shillong).
133. Notth Eastern Economic Review, (Gauhati).
134. NEFA Information, (Shillong).
135. North Eastern Research Bulletin, (Dibrugarh Uuiversity, Dibrugarh).
136. North Eastern Spectrum, (Gauhati).
137. North Eastern Review
138. North East Times, (Gauhati).
139. Oriental Insects.
140. Pakistan J. Sci. and Ind. Research, (Dacca).
141. Patriot, (Shillong).
142. Pines, (Shillong).
143. Principle.
144. Proceedings of Indian Science Congress.
145. Proceedings of National Institute of Science of India (B), (Calcutta).
146. Quarterly Journal of the Mythic Society.
147. R.G.S. Suppl. Papers.
148. Record Geological Survey of India.
149. Royal Central Asian Journal, (R. Cent. Asian Journal).
150. Resarun, (Shillong).
151. Resarun, (Itanagar).
152. Resarun Cumulative Volume, (Shillong).
153. Research in Arunachal, Arunachal Govt.. (Shillong).
154. R.B.S.I.
155. Royal Engineers' Journal.
156. Royal Society of Edinburg.
157. Science and Culture, Calture, (Calcutta).
158. Social Research : Journal of Institute of Social Research, (Shillong).
159. Sociological Bulletin, University of Delhi, (Delhi).
160. Sociologus.

161. Social Welfare.
162. Special Tribal Orient, (Ranchi).
163. States.
164. (The) Statesman, (Calcutta).
165. (The) Thinker.
166. (The) Times of India, (New Delhi).
167. Tribe, (Udaipur, Rajasthan).
168. Tribal Welfare, West Bengal Weekly, (Calcutta)
169. United Asia.
170. United Empire.
171. Vanyajati, (Delhi).
172. Vivekananda Kendra Patrika.
173. Yojana, (Delhi).

INDEX

(References are to the serial number of entries in the Bibliography)

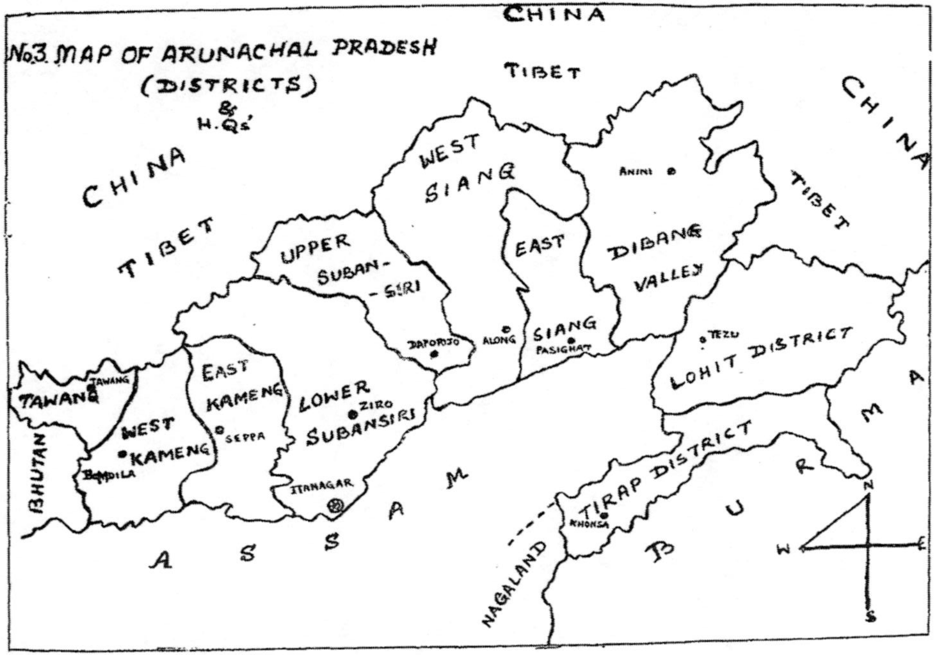

No.3. MAP OF ARUNACHAL PRADESH (DISTRICTS) & H.Qs'

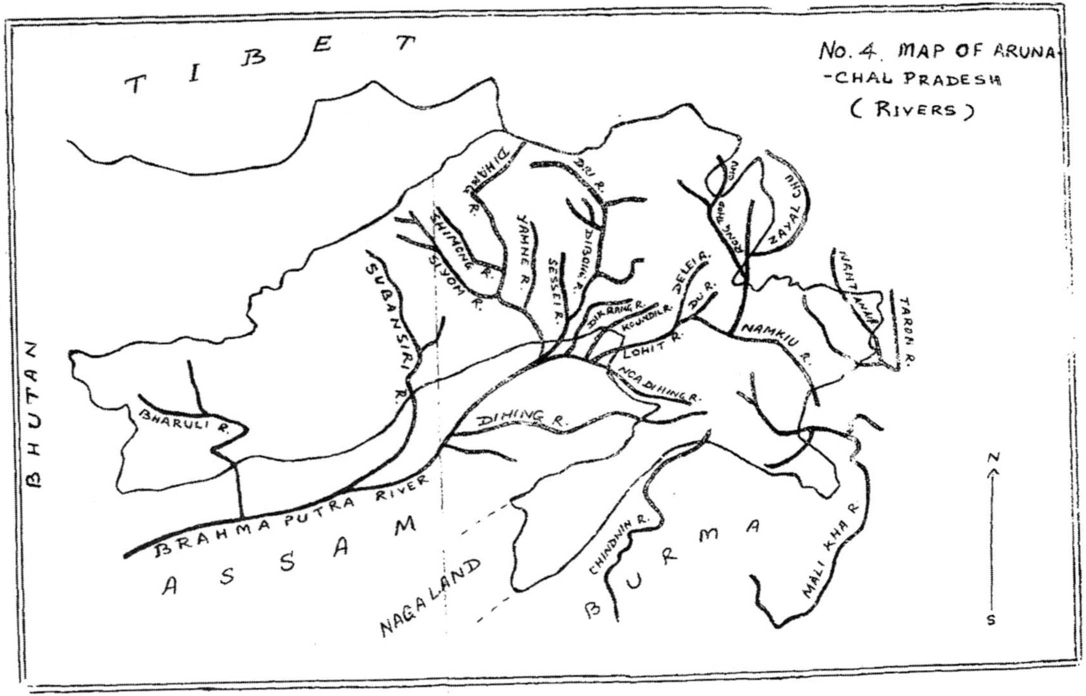
No. 4. MAP OF ARUNA-
-CHAL PRADESH
(RIVERS)
TIBET
BHUTAN
ASSAM
NAGALAND
BURMA
BRAHMA PUTRA RIVER
BHARULI R.
SUBANSIRI R.
SIYOM R.
SHIMONG R.
DIHANG R.
YAMNE R.
SESSEI R.
DIBONG R.
DRI R.
DIK RANG R.
KOUNDIL R.
DELEI R.
DU R.
LOHIT R.
NOA DIHING R.
DIHING R.
NAMKIU R.
ZAYAL CHU
RONG THOD CHU
TARON R.
CHINDWIN R.
MALI KHA R.
N
S

NO. 5. MAP OF ARUNACHAL PRADESH
(TRIBES & DIST. HQ.s' ETC)

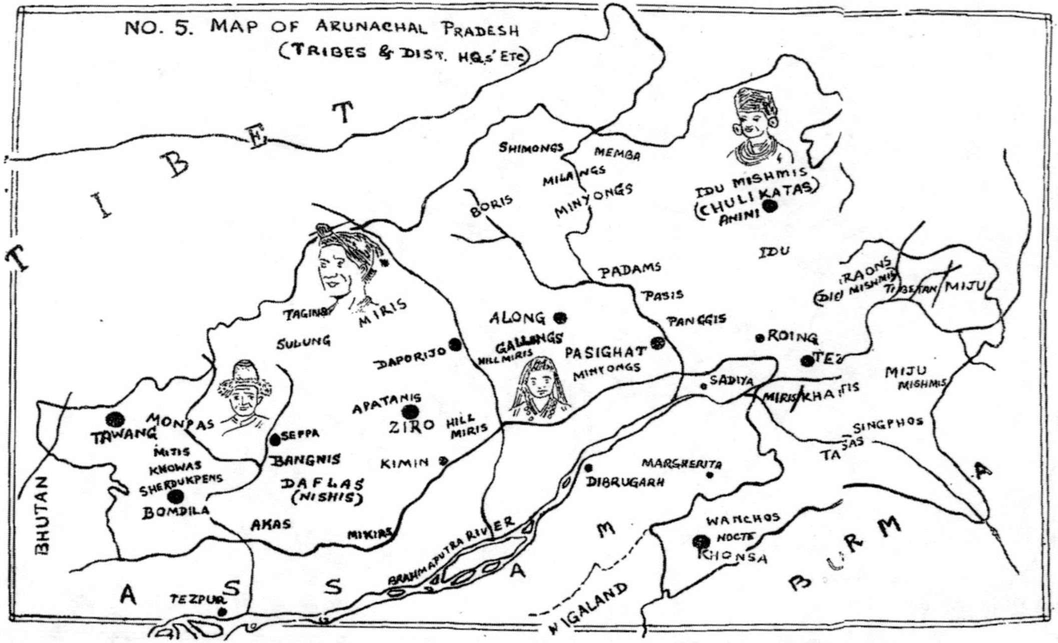